GARY-1

SILENT CITIES, SACRED STONES

endpapers Pottery vessels
and oil lamps being
carefully freed from debris
in the excavations of the
Jewish Quarter, Jerusalem
frontispiece A corner of
the 'archaeological garden'
behind the home of Israeli
Defence Minister Moshe
Dayan near Tel Aviv (see
page 29)

SILENT CITIES, SACRED STONES

Archaeological discovery in Israel

Jerry M. Landay

McCall Books

For Donna
'. . . more than wine,
. . . more than any song.'

Published in the United States by
The McCall Publishing Company, New York

Designed by Alex Berlyne for Weidenfeld and Nicolson Jerusalem
Picture research and selection by Irène Lewitt

Library of Congress Catalog Card Number: 74–154249

ISBN 0–8415–0112–2

Composed by Keter, Inc., Jerusalem, printed by Japhet Press,
Tel Aviv, 1971

Contents

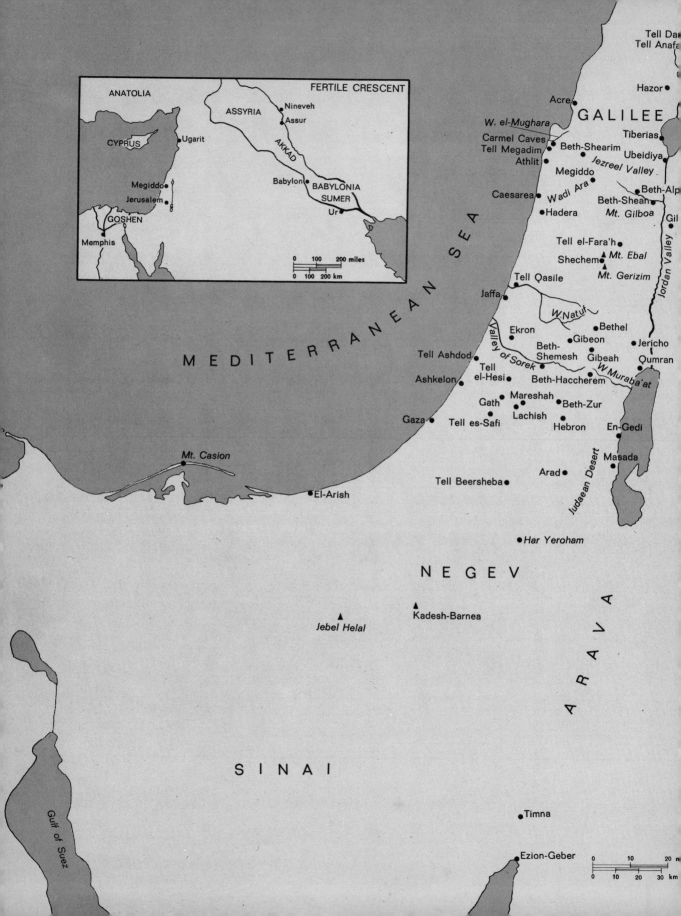

Inset map (Fertile Crescent):

ANATOLIA

ASSYRIA

Nineveh
Assur

CYPRUS

Ugarit

AKKAD

Babylon BABYLONIA
SUMER

Megiddo

Jerusalem

GOSHEN

Ur

Memphis

0   100   200 miles

0   100   200 km

Main map:

MEDITERRANEAN SEA

Tell Dan
Tell Anafa

Hazor

Acre

GALILEE

W. el-Mughara
Carmel Caves
Tell Megadim
Athlit

Tiberias

Ubeidiya

Beth-Shearim

Jezreel Valley

Megiddo

Beth-Alp

Caesarea

Wadi Ara

Beth-Shean

Hadera

Mt. Gilboa

Gil

Tell el-Fara'h

Jordan Valley

Shechem

Mt. Ebal

Mt. Gerizim

Tell Qasile

Jaffa

W. Natuf

Ekron

Bethel

Gibeon

Jericho

Valley of Sorek

Beth-Shemesh

Gibeah

Qumran

Tell Ashdod

Beth-Haccherem

W. Muraba'at

Ashkelon

Tell el-Hesi

Mareshah

Beth-Zur

Gath

Lachish

Hebron

En-Gedi

Gaza

Tell es-Safi

Masada

Arad

Judaean Desert

Tell Beersheba

Har Yeroham

NEGEV

ARAVA

Jebel Helal

Kadesh-Barnea

Mt. Casion

El-Arish

SINAI

Timna

Gulf of Suez

Ezion-Geber

0   10   20 m

0   10   20   30 km

Preface

To the many who have given so generously of their time, counsel, wisdom and inspiration go my deepest thanks for calling this book into being. Professor Yigael Yadin, Director of the Institute of Archaeology, Hebrew University, Dr Ofer Bar-Yosef, Professor of Prehistory and Miss Renate Rosenthal at the same institution, were kind enough to read and offer their suggestions on several portions of the manuscript. I naturally accept full responsibility for any errors which may nevertheless have crept in.

Other scholars also supplemented my research with invaluable information and suggestions of their own: Professor Yohanan Aharoni; Mrs Ruth Amiran; Professor Nachman Avigad; Dr Yosef Aviram; Professor Michael Avi-Yonah; Pesach Bar-Adon; Dr Richard Barnett; Meir Ben-Dov; Dr Avraham Biran; Magen Broshi; Père Roland de Vaux; Dr Moshe and Professor Trude Dothan; Professor David Flusser; Professor David Noel Freedman; Colonel Mordecai Gihon; Dr Nicu Haas; Baruch Hofri; Miss Kathleen Kenyon; Dr Moshe Kochavi; Professor Abraham Malamat; Professor Benjamin Mazar; Dr Ya'akov Meshorer; Dr Joseph Naveh; Dr Avraham Negev; Peter Parr; Professor Hans Polotsky; L.Y. Rahmani; Dr Benno Rothenberg; Dr Joseph Seger; Dr Solomon Steckoll; Dr Geza Vermes; Professor Saul Weinberg; Professor Schmuel Yeivin.

Thanks are also due to those organizations and individuals who generously assisted in planning my research schedule and supplied helpful complementary material: Mrs Gillian Webster of the Palestine Exploration Fund, London; Mrs Ina Pomerantz of the Israel Department of Antiquities and Museums; Mrs Hilary Grainger of the Anglo-Israeli Archaeological Society, London; Mrs Aviva Rosen and Richard Oesterman of the Hebrew University, Jerusalem; Colonel Yosef Carmel of Tel Aviv University; officials of the Israel and Rockefeller Museums, Jerusalem; Mrs Moshe Dayan; Mayor Teddy Kollek of Jerusalem; and Mrs Ilana de Perelstein, Gershon Achituv, Aharon Megged, Raanan Sivan and Dr Meron Medzini of the Israeli Government.

I should like also to mention the wise counsel and patience of my publishers in converting raw manuscript into a finished book: in particular, John Curtis in London and Asher Weill and his editorial staff in Jerusalem, Mrs. Irène Lewitt for the choice of illustrations and Alex Berlyne for his beautiful design and layout.

Finally I must thank my friends and associates, whose warm interest and encouragement kept author and typewriter functioning through difficult moments: Madame Rose Vernier de Meissner, Susan and Rege Hicklin, Jay Bushinsky, Peter Allen-Frost, Sylvie Nesbitt and my research assistant, Gabriel Barkai.

To Benjamin Jaffe of the Jewish Agency, Jerusalem, and his wife Malka, who offered friendship and support through a number of vicissitudes, my deep admiration and respect. And to Aubrey Wolston, who insisted that the book not only could be done but should be done, more appreciation than words can possibly express.

Jerry M. Landay
Southwold, Suffolk
June, 1971

Chronological Table

BC

c. 5,000,000	*Homo erectus* settles in the Upper Jordan Valley
c. 50,000–40,000	Palestine Man in Galilee
c. 10,000–8,000	The Natufians become food producers
c. 9,000	The Natufians found their settlement on bedrock at Jericho, the oldest known city
c. 8,000	The round defence tower is built at Jericho
c. 5,500	The art of pottery making reaches Palestine
c. 4,000	Ghassulian culture and the early population of the Negev, with the knowledge of working in copper
c. 3,200	The early Negev peoples vanish. The rise of the civilization of Sumer-Akkad
c. 3,100	Narmer (Menes) unites Egypt and founds the First Dynasty
c. 2,000–1,800	The Amorite invasion of Mesopotamia, Syria and Canaan. The age of the Patriarchs
c. 1,750	The *Hyksos* invade Canaan and Egypt. The patriarchal clans may have moved to Egypt with them
c. 1,290	Moses and the Israelites begin the Exodus from Egypt
c. 1,250	Joshua and the Israelites enter Canaan, the Promised Land
c. 1,230	Joshua conquers Canaanite Hazor
c. 1,200–1,020	The tribes of Israel are ruled by the Judges
c. 1,190	The Philistines settle on the coast of Palestine
c. 1,020–1,000	The reign of King Saul
c. 1,000–960	King David reigns over Israel, and defeats the Philistines
c. 996	David captures Jerusalem from the Jebusites and founds his capital
c. 960–930	The golden age of Israel under Solomon. The Gezer Stone is dated to this period
c. 950	Solomon begins to erect the First Temple
c. 922	King Rehoboam, Solomon's son and successor, seeks the loyalty of the northern tribes and is rejected; the Israelite kingdom is split in two, with Israel in the north and Judah in the south
c. 922–907	The reign of King Jeroboam I of Israel, and the golden calves at Dan and Bethel
885–874	The reign of King Omri of Israel, who establishes his capital at Samaria
874–853	The reign of King Ahab of Israel, the great builder of the northern kingdom
c. 830	King Mesha of Moab erects a stele commemorating his victory over Israel
841–814	The reign of the regicide Jehu, who is forced to pay tribute to Shalmaneser III of Assyria

Foreword

Every tablet, every little scarab, is a portion of life solidified . . . When we look closely into the work we seem almost to watch the hand that did it; this stone is a day, a week of the life of some living man. I know his mind, his feeling, by what he has thought and done on this stone. I live with him in looking into his work, and admiring and valuing it.

Sir W.M. Flinders Petrie (1853–1942)

Archaeological interest in the tiny land-bridge known variously as the Holy Land, Palestine and Israel is of relatively recent origin, compared to the fervent pursuit of the past that led an army of scholars and treasure-hunters to the ruins of ancient Greece, Rome, Asia Minor, Mesopotamia and Egypt. The civilizations of ancient Canaan and Israel were poor and backward compared with the great empires of their day. The humble material remains of Israel could not lure zealous antiquarians with the hope of either riches or aesthetic treasures. Her legacy to posterity is of a far different order, though certainly no less central to our heritage, than Knossos, Thebes, Athens or Rome. Until the nineteenth century the land which nurtured Judaism and Christianity was a twilight zone, isolated from scientific and scholarly enquiry by the *cordon sanitaire* of 'sacredness'. Even though monotheism, the Old Testament and the central figures of the early days of Christianity were accepted by the enlightened as common property, the story of the Hebrew nation itself was seen as separate from the mainstream of Western culture and tradition.

Intellectual curiosity, scientific detachment, the modern hunger for the roots of faith, popular interest in such exceptional finds as the Dead Sea Scrolls, the rebirth of Israel after two thousand years and the zeal of her people to rediscover their ancient past have ended the quarantine of centuries. The union of archaeological, historical and biblical research has brought a sense of wonder and adventure to the exploration of Palestine's past.

So much of the recent work of Palestinian archaeologists, together with that of scientists and scholars in allied fields, has been buried in learned journals, so much fragmented among specialized texts, and so much neglected by current popular works on archaeology that I felt that a survey for the general public might be of

opposite The pioneer British archaeologist, Sir W. M. Flinders Petrie, whose 6-week campaign at Tell-el-Hesi in 1890 opened the age of scientific 'prospecting' for the lost cities of the Bible. Petrie died in Jerusalem in 1942

some value. Because I am neither a biblical scholar nor a trained scientist, I believe that the adventure of research and excavation which so totally engaged me might interest others like me, simply told and shred of the technical complexities which have deprived so many of its fruits.

Some excavations have had to be given preference over others. Scientific terminology has been kept to an absolute minimum, particularly 'shorthand' labels which have little meaning for the general reader (in certain cases scholars themselves continue to argue over terminology, particularly that dealing with archaeological periods).

I have chosen to begin this book in prehistoric times, with the earliest evidence of man's lowly ancestors in the Holy Land. Discoveries in the field of prehistory provide a unique perspective on the role of this land as a crucible of human beginnings thousands of centuries before the Israelites. Beyond that the wealth of contributions that Palestine has made to prehistoric research is not generally appreciated. It seemed logical to bring this volume to a close with the collapse of the second Jewish revolt against the rule of Rome in AD 135—to all intents and purposes the end of ancient Judaea as a Jewish territorial entity.

I can only remind my audience that this book is written for the layman rather than the scholar. While I have had to choose representative material from a wealth of excavations, I have tried never to compromise on either objectivity or accuracy. The book has been woven round three major aims: to tell the story of important discoveries, to describe how they were made and by whom, and to provide some historical background against which the significance of the finds can be understood. In addition, particularly in the first section, I have tried to capture some of the history and flavour of archaeological discovery in the Holy Land. Few endeavours have added so much to our store of knowledge in so short a time.

I offer this volume in the same spirit which prompted a Jerusalem craftsman 1,600 years ago to chisel into a Herodian stone in the Western Wall of the Temple Mount part of a verse from the Book of Isaiah; it was uncovered by excavators in May 1969:

And when ye see this, your heart
    shall rejoice;
and your bones shall flourish like an herb.

(Isaiah 66: 14)

1 The Curious Pilgrims

In the middle of April 1890, a thirty-seven-year-old British Egyptologist named William Matthew Flinders Petrie dismounted at a lofty mound of earth and rubble, known to archaeologists as a tell, about sixteen miles east of Gaza. The local Arabs called the hill Tell el-Hesi. 'A striking place', Petrie later recorded in his journal.

The tell rose sixty feet above the gently rolling countryside between the plain of Philistia and the foothills of the Judaean Hills. There was not a building to be seen from its summit, only straggling groups of low brown tents which marked the settlements of the Bedouin. Nominally, the land belonged to the Turks. In practice, however, it was the preserve of the local Arabs, who did not pay a lira of tax to the local officials simply because no Turkish governor was strong enough to dare to collect it. Some days earlier, an important Turkish official and his escort had been accosted by Arabs a few miles outside Gaza and literally stripped of everything.

With the country in such a turbulent state, Petrie accepted that his scholarship was being pursued at considerable risk. Only a few nights before his arrival at Tell el-Hesi he was awakened by the noise of a thief crawling through a gap in the tent. He recorded with aplomb: 'I challenged, he ran, and four bullets went over his head to improve his pace.'

From his exploration of the tell Petrie concluded that it was the necropolis of 'a great city and early'. He reported with some excitement in a letter to the Palestine Exploration Fund, his sponsors in London: 'There was so much pottery about, but none of it Roman—all earlier.' This is certainly what the society wanted to hear, for they had dispatched this highly experienced excavator to the Holy Land with the meagre sum of £1,110 and the specific task of 'prospecting' scientifically into an ancient tell to recover one of the lost cities of the Bible. This was the first time such a task

An Egyptian stone sculpture of a seated man discovered during the 1902 excavations of R. A. S. Macalister in the Canaanite fortress-city of Gezer

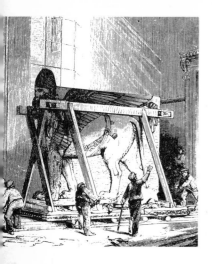

A winged lion discovered
by the British archaeologist
Sir Austen Layard at
Nineveh was brought to
England and installed in the
British Museum in 1858

had been undertaken. The arrival of Flinders Petrie opened the modern era of exploration beneath the surface of ancient Israel.

Considering the profound reverence which the Holy Land has commanded in the hearts, minds and prayers of Christians and Jews over so many centuries, Petrie's austere one-man expedition came rather late in the chronology of Western archaeological discovery. Over a century and a half before, marble sculptures at Herculaneum and the amphitheatre at Pompeii had been prised from the hardened lava and ash of Vesuvius. Nearly a century earlier, Napoleon's scholars launched their explorations amid the tombs and pyramids of ancient Egypt—where Petrie later established his considerable reputation. Enormous wonders from the palaces of the Assyrian kings had by this time been safely ensconced in the museums of London and Paris by Botta and Layard. Schliemann's 'golden hoard of Troy' was an archaeological legend over a decade old. The fabled sites of ancient empires had kindled the imagination and, in some cases, the avarice of adventuring antiquarians with the promise of glory and riches. In many cases, the promise had paid off.

Ancient Israel had never, however, been one of the great imperial powers, but a corridor of trade, political expansion and conquest. There was very little profitable spoil hidden under the dust and ruin of this naked land, and the booty once stored in its Holy Temple and royal treasuries had been carried off by the mighty invaders and occupiers of ages past.

It was as a treasure house of religious, ethical and historical beginnings that the soil of ancient Israel beckoned men like Petrie in the nineteenth century. Many dug for personal trophies or museum objects. They destroyed or failed to record the exact places where the relics were found, or seemingly insignificant objects associated with them, losing invaluable scientific information in the process. Petrie, on the other hand, excavated in order to glean the knowledge of ancient times which the objects contained. 'Spoiling the past', he was to write, 'has an acute moral wrong in it. . .'

Petrie's undisputed genius lay in an exacting mind and a passion for detail. He had been an avid student of the mathematics of measurement. In 1880, when only twenty-seven, he produced the first precise measurements of the Great Pyramid at Gizeh. He was equally exacting in his disbursement of limited funds. On first climbing to the rounded summit of Tell el-Hesi, he saw that it was a motley quilt of wheat, barley and beans grown by the Bedouin. He would have to buy the crops outright if he wanted to excavate

there. So the archaeologist dutifully reported to London that he had decided to restrict his digging to the sides, because the Arabs insisted the crops were worth £4 ('which is rather much for it')!

Many years earlier, a noted American biblical scholar, Edward Robinson, had taken a look at the same spot and then written: 'We could discover nothing whatever to mark the existence of any former town or structure at Tell el-Hesi.' In his brief six-week season at the same mound, Petrie showed it to be the accumulated ruin of eight superimposed cities, subsequently identified as biblical Eglon. One of the levels, a so-called 'destruction layer' separating the third from the fourth, was a three-foot bed composed of black charcoal dust and white ash which subsequent scholars have attributed to the conquest of Joshua and the Israelites.

In Petrie's day, giving absolute dates to biblical events was a haphazard process at best. His major scientific task was first to note and record systematically the objects he recovered from the tell, no matter how insignificant, and the strata from which they came; then to suggest the ages of the eight towns that lay exposed in the cuttings before him. From the Canaanite, Phoenician and Greek pottery which Petrie found distributed among the various levels, he concluded in a report to the Fund that 'the place is as old or older than the Judges, and was destroyed at Nebuchadnezzar's invasion', which culminated in the Hebrew exile in Babylon. Here at Tell el-Hesi, history was unlocked from an ancient mound in Palestine for the first time by a skilled scientist, and could be seen in the frozen physical profile of a many-tiered city long dead and forgotten.

More important from a long-term scientific standpoint was that Petrie established in the Holy Land a reliable technique for unlocking historical secrets—dating by pottery. Earthenware

Tell el-Hesi, the first of Palestine's biblical mounds which was excavated scientifically. Standing 60 feet high, it was formed of the accumulated rubble of eight cities, each built atop the ruins of its predecessor. Petrie, one of the first to use photography in archaeological research, also took this picture

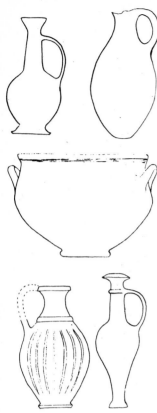

Detailed drawings by
Petrie of the pottery types
found at Tell el-Hesi

opposite Ancient Beth-shean,
perhaps the most striking
of the many tells in Israel.
On its towering wall, the
naked headless corpse of
King Saul was hung. The
tell was excavated in ten
seasons between the years
1921 and 1933 by a team of
excavators of the University
of Pennsylvania. In the
foreground is a Roman
amphitheatre built long
after the city atop the
mound had ceased to exist

jugs, vases, oil cruses, pots and dishes are the identifying fingerprints
of the times in which they were made, and of the cultures which
made them. They carry their 'styles' in their varying designs,
shapes, decorative markings and colours, and in their methods of
manufacture. Pottery objects are fragile but, like human bones,
the broken pieces seem to last as long as time itself. Petrie believed
that if the pottery fragments in the strata of the tell could be dated,
so could the ruins in the levels which contained the fragments.

By relating the litter of pottery at Tell el-Hesi with similar
styles he had examined in Egyptian tombs and to objects in the
tell whose dates were known, Petrie developed the scientific cri-
teria for dating and systematically recording the complex records
of people, trade and conquest buried in the tells of the Holy Land.
During his short reconnaissance at Tell el-Hesi, Petrie estimated
that he painstakingly examined up to a thousand pieces of shattered
pottery each day, and predicted that 'in future all the tells and ruins
of the country will at once reveal their age by the potsherds which
cover them'. The findings of others proved the theory to be sound.
They refined Petrie's technique. The principle that pottery is the
essential alphabet of archaeological exploration is Petrie's unique
contribution to the science (and art) of digging in biblical soil.

Petrie's achievements as the father of Palestinian archaeology
must be shared with a veritable army of nineteenth-century explorers, biblical scholars, geographers, surveyors and map-makers,
who catapulted the Holy Land out of the isolation of centuries.
Before them, the gap between what men thought and what they
actually knew about a land so central to their heritage was nothing
less than appalling. Most early travellers had put faith ahead of
fact and credulity before curiosity in the accounts they offered to
an avid readership. To these pilgrims or Crusaders each step on the
perilous road to Palestine was entered in the heavenly annals as a
credit toward the expiation of past sins, and each triumph over
the infidels who lay along the way was an added guarantee of
radiant glory in the afterlife.

Most pilgrims required no direction to the well-known centres
of their faith such as Jerusalem, Bethlehem and Hebron. But what
had become of such places as Lachish, and Ai, and Hazor, those
great cities of the Canaanites which Joshua had taken for the Israelites; and Gibeon, where it was written that he commanded the sun
to stand still? What had become of Mizpah, where Samuel proclaimed Saul as king before the tribes of Israel? Where were Bethel
and Dan, where King Jeroboam set his high places and calves of
gold to rival the Holy Temple in Jerusalem?

More than six hundred place-names figure in the prolific history of our biblical sources in ancient Israel. Yet most of these remained hidden to the pilgrims and map-makers whose imaginations had been fired by this tiny plot of ground for the better part of two thousand years. They were places which had been buried, literally or metaphorically; or whose names had been changed or corrupted from the ancient Hebrew, most often into Arabic. It might be said that to a large extent the Old Testament had become an atlas to a lost land.

Three dedicated scholars had foreseen both the problem and the need. In the fourth century, Bishop Eusebius of Caesarea, one of the first historians of the Christian Church, compiled a geographical dictionary of biblical place-names called the *Onomasticon*. The work was then enlarged by St Jerome, one of the Church Fathers, who also translated it from Greek into Latin. The *Onomasticon* listed a thousand place-names in alphabetical order, along with the historical events which had made them important. In about three hundred cases Eusebius and Jerome connected the names with actual sites.

Nine hundred years later a Jewish scholar named Esthori ha-Parhi, who lived in Beth-shean, spent seven years 'spying out the land' in order to recover the sites of biblical history for future generations. He compiled a fourteenth-century work called *Kafthor Wapherah*. His explanation of the work is dominated both by a deep sense of historical duty and by a profound sense of loss:

> I will make known what has disappeared to this generation since it does not know about the land of Israel, the boundaries of the tribes or their towns, as the good hand of God is upon me . . . I come poor and humble, to tell my brothers and my people what I have found of that which has been sought.

Relatively little attention was paid to the work of these early scholars, and much of the information they gave had to be redis-covered by the geographers of far more recent times. It was an ambitious young French general and an American Bible scholar who paved the way for the belated end of the dark ages in the Holy Land.

The general, twenty-eight-year-old Napoleon Bonaparte, still basking in the popular glory of his Italian Campaign, landed in Egypt in 1798 with forty thousand men and his dream of a French empire in the East. With the expedition he brought a corps of 176 intellectual luminaries, from geographers to artists. They were to

opposite The magnificent Canaanite 'high place' of Gezer, its towering stelae first uncovered by R. A. S. Macalister in 1902, and then re-interred 'so that it would be preserved *in situ* until the remote time when a national pride in monuments of antiquity. . . shall have been developed locally.' The standing stelae were re-excavated by an expedition of the Hebrew Union College some 60 years later

Dr Edward Robinson, the American divinity scholar, who in 1838 made an arduous exploration of Palestine to identify the sites of 'lost' biblical cities.

below The Baroness Burdett-Coutts, whose donation of £500 towards a modern water and sanitation system for Jerusalem in 1864 launched the Palestine Exploration Fund

obtain knowledge of the ancient land claimed forcibly by Napoleon for France. To protect his eastern flank against an attack from Turkish forces in Syria, he dispatched an army of thirteen thousand men to Palestine with orders to seize the port of Acre. With the expedition went a geographer named Pierre Jacotin and a team of military surveyors. The walls of Acre, however, were stoutly defended. The British harried Napoleon at sea. His campaign faltered, and he was forced to withdraw. But in the arduous four-month advance and retreat, Jacotin and his surveyors made the first serious attempt to produce an accurate map of Palestine. It was printed in five beautifully engraved sheets in 1808, but it was kept under lock and key as a state secret until 1817. Although the map was later classed as nothing more than 'a magnificent military sketch', Napoleon's ill-fated Eastern Campaign inspired the systematic modern study of Egypt and renewed interest in the area as a whole.

The historical geography of Palestine became a sound science with Edward Robinson, an American scholar in biblical literature at the Union Theological Seminary in New York. In 1838, with an American companion who spoke Arabic and a team of camels and drivers, Robinson travelled through Sinai and Palestine, uncovering more topographical information in two and a half months than scholars had unearthed since the times of Eusebius, Jerome and ha-Parhi. In his attempts to identify ancient biblical sites, Robinson used the same technique as ha-Parhi: he assumed that many of the Arabic place-names were derived or corrupted from the original Hebrew. Therefore, he reasoned, the best sources of geographical information were not the resident clerics and guides to the well-trodden pilgrim paths but the Arab population itself. His method was successful. In only two days, for example, he identified eight places north of Jerusalem with important cities or towns referred to in the Old Testament. For example, El-Jib was identified as the biblical Gibeon, at whose pool the men of David strove with the servants of Saul. Beitin became Bethel, where Jacob erected a pillar to God, and Jeroboam later set up his golden calf.

On 10 May 1838 Robinson climbed to the top of a hill in the rugged wilderness of the southern Hebron mountains. 'The sun rose in his strength, and poured a flood of golden light upon the plain and the hills beyond, so that every object was distinctly seen', he later wrote. 'We were here in the midst of scenes memorable of old for the adventures of David, during his wanderings in order to escape from the jealousy of Saul.' On that day Robinson identified eight more biblical towns. Many of his identifications have been confirmed by later archaeological evidence.

The pace of exploration and discovery accelerated quickly after Robinson. One of the biggest single spurs to the systematic investigation of biblical history came from a source outside the Holy Land, the recovery of ancient Assyria from the barren mounds of Mesopotamia. This vaunted empire which lay between the Tigris and the Euphrates had been the scourge of the Hebrew nation.

Over a period of only a bare twenty-one years, roughly from 1849 to 1870, excavators unearthed the magnificent royal monuments of Nineveh, Nimrud and Khorsabad. Dedicated palaeographers also succeeded in deciphering and translating the language of its kings—the early wedge-shaped writing called cuneiform—in which were recorded the triumphs and accomplishments of such conquerors as Shalmaneser III, Tiglath-pileser III, Sargon II and Sennacherib. In these annals Israelite kings such as Ahab, Menahem, Hezekiah and Jehu were mentioned by name. With only thirty years of work, excavators and scholars had broken the silence of over twenty-five centuries. If so much had been learned from the soil of ancient Assyria, what more might be uncovered systematically in the Holy Land itself?

Quite apart from the historico-religious implications of Palestinian exploration, a number of other more wordly considerations quickened the pace of interest in the land itself. Napoleon had underscored for Europe's imperial powers the strategic importance of this land bridge between Asia and Africa. The Ottoman Empire began to totter, and with it Constantinople's control over its possessions. The leaders of such aspiring successor states as Great Britain realized how little intelligence they had about the area. Beyond this, there was the phenomenon of national rivalry. Archaeological discoveries, as well as the acquisition of important objects of antiquity by the great museums of London, Paris, Berlin and Vienna, were as much a matter of national pride as of cultural achievement.

The British were to establish their proprietary interest in the Holy Land in a most unusual way. A wealthy British peeress, Baroness Burdett-Coutts, wanted to supply a modern water and sewage system for Jerusalem. British authorities advised her that an accurate ordnance survey of the city was the necessary first step. She donated £500 to the project, the Turkish authorities gave their permission, and Captain C.W. Wilson of the Royal Engineers was sent to carry out the work in June 1864. By the following May he had finished an accurate city-plan and a map of the environs.

The Jacotin Map was the first serious attempt to produce an accurate map of Palestine. The data were hastily gathered by Napoleon's geographers and surveyors during the abortive 4-month French campaign against Acre in 1799, and remained a state secret until 1817

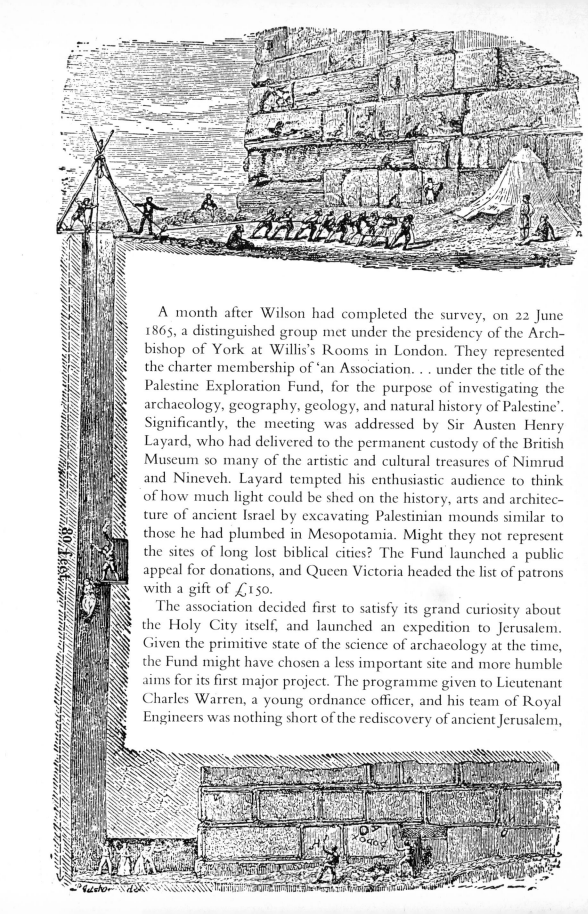

A month after Wilson had completed the survey, on 22 June 1865, a distinguished group met under the presidency of the Archbishop of York at Willis's Rooms in London. They represented the charter membership of 'an Association. . . under the title of the Palestine Exploration Fund, for the purpose of investigating the archaeology, geography, geology, and natural history of Palestine'. Significantly, the meeting was addressed by Sir Austen Henry Layard, who had delivered to the permanent custody of the British Museum so many of the artistic and cultural treasures of Nimrud and Nineveh. Layard tempted his enthusiastic audience to think of how much light could be shed on the history, arts and architecture of ancient Israel by excavating Palestinian mounds similar to those he had plumbed in Mesopotamia. Might they not represent the sites of long lost biblical cities? The Fund launched a public appeal for donations, and Queen Victoria headed the list of patrons with a gift of £150.

The association decided first to satisfy its grand curiosity about the Holy City itself, and launched an expedition to Jerusalem. Given the primitive state of the science of archaeology at the time, the Fund might have chosen a less important site and more humble aims for its first major project. The programme given to Lieutenant Charles Warren, a young ordnance officer, and his team of Royal Engineers was nothing short of the rediscovery of ancient Jerusalem, a city destroyed and restored so often that its early features lay buried in ruin, rubbish and fill up to a hundred feet deep, not to mention the obscurity of centuries of scholarly neglect. Did the Moslem Dome of the Rock indeed stand on the ruins of the Jewish Temple? What were the actual lines of the three walls of Jerusalem through which the Romans broke to destroy the city in AD 70? Where were the ancient gates? What were the sites of the original City of David and the Palace of Herod?

For so grand a project, the Fund should have engaged an army of prophets, not a military engineer. Warren lacked archaeological experience. He was hampered by Moslem strictures against ex-

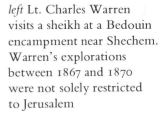

opposite The dangerous 'mining' technique used by Lt. Charles Warren of the Royal Engineers between 1867 and 1870 to investigate the lower courses of the retaining walls constructed by Herod the Great in the 1st century BC, enclosing the Temple Compound

left Lt. Charles Warren visits a sheikh at a Bedouin encampment near Shechem. Warren's explorations between 1867 and 1870 were not solely restricted to Jerusalem

One of a series of watercolours painted by the British artist William Simpson following a visit through the deep shafts and galleries sunk by Warren to the lowest courses of the Temple Mount's massive retaining walls

In another Simpson sketch, Warren himself examines a Herodian water conduit beneath Robinson's Arch, named for the American scholar who identified it as a remnant of the massive royal bridge connecting the Temple with King Herod's palace

cavating within the sacred 120,000 square feet of the Temple Enclosure. He was limited to investigating the outside perimeter of its massive retaining walls. Warren hired workmen and began mining into the roots of ancient Jerusalem with a series of vertical shafts, some 125 feet deep. From their bottoms, Warren ran long galleries up to and along the walls. The work was dangerous, because the fill and debris through which he tunnelled was formed by stone chips which had no cohesion and rubbish compressed into loose shingles which had a tendency to shift and run like water. There were frequent cave-ins. The rubbish contained sewage that caused hands to fester. The areas Warren could 'open' were limited by the tunneling technique, and, as a result, so were his findings. He dated the outer walls of the great compound to the time of Solomon, instead of to the reign of Herod the Great. However, by digging to bedrock, Warren was able to describe the form of the original valleys which surrounded the sacred area, ending all disputes as to the location of the First and Second Temples.

The dawn of scientific excavation at Tell el-Hesi was to await one more piece of pioneer field work. The Holy Land still lacked a completely reliable map. The Palestine Exploration Fund decided that scientific exploration of the country below ground could not proceed without a complete and thorough mapping of its surface, showing all geographical and topographical features, including ancient ruins and tells. Because of the military intelligence that it would provide, the British Government was equally anxious that the project should be carried out. The scale of the effort was prodigious for those days. The mapping party was to survey six thousand square miles from the Mediterranean to the River Jordan, from Tyre and Banias in the north to Beersheba in the south. The Fund raised £18,000 through public subscription. The survey party, under a royal engineer named Captain R.W. Stewart, succeeded in mapping five hundred square miles between January and July 1872. But Stewart succumbed to fever early in the campaign, and a replacement was dispatched. Lieutenant Claude Reignier Conder, a product of the Royal Military Academy at Woolwich, and the Royal Engineers' establishment at Chatham, was brought ashore from his steamer at Jaffa on a pitching flat-bottomed rowing-boat and the broad shoulders of a Nubian. Conder took charge of the party of sixteen men and sixteen horses and mules in Samaria. By the time he returned to England a little over three years later, the victim of such afflictions as malaria, opthalmia, skin ulcers, rheumatism and dysentery, over two-thirds of the work had been completed.

Conder's basic tools were a hundred-foot chain, the magnified equivalent of a tape measure, to establish base lines of a fixed length on the ground, and a theodolite to determine precise angles to fixed points. The theodolite was also used with a chronometer for celestial sightings to determine exact locations on the earth's surface. Starting from either end of the base line, usually about four miles long, Conder could triangulate on prominent features, such as a mosque tower or a mountain,.and determine distances.

Conder's adventures and difficulties read like a compendium of all the perils ever encountered by the legion of Western travellers who had preceded him through the centuries. The party was beset by illness, by insect bites, by the climatic rigours of desert and mountain, and by marauding Bedouin. The team archaeologist, C.F. Tyrwhitt Drake, contracted an inflammation of the liver from which he died.

In 1874 Conder was joined by Lieutenant (ultimately Field Marshal) Horatio H. Kitchener, who was to gain fame a decade later as the leader of the expedition which tried to relieve the besieged forces of General C.G. Gordon at Khartoum. The next year, Conder and Kitchener were nearly killed in an attack against the survey team at Safed by three hundred Bedouin, wielding stones, battle axes, scimitars, clubs and guns. Brought to trial at Acre, the Bedouin sheikh, Aly Agha, was sentenced to nine. months in jail, and ordered to pay a fine of £270 to the Palestine Exploration Fund. Conder recorded, with characteristic Victorian hauteur: 'The affair in the end proved a salutary lesson and has shown the natives of Palestine that English subjects cannot be insolently treated with impunity.' The mapwork clearly represented the most thorough single effort of exploration in the history of western Palestine; it remained the definitive cartographic reference to the country for over half a century.

It took a decade for the Palestine Exploration Fund to liquidate the equally monumental cost of producing the map. Only then, in 1890, was the society financially able to launch its long-awaited campaign of exploration beneath the ground into the tells of the Holy Land. It was thus that Petrie came to Tell el-Hesi, opening one of the unique chapters in the annals of modern archaeology. In the same decade, a revival of anti-Semitism in Europe and the publication of a book called *The Jewish State* by Theodor Herzl gave urgent meaning to the idea of *Aliyah*, or 'return'. These two streams, one scientific and the other political, would ultimately merge in the modern campaign of rediscovery in ancient Zion.

Lt. Horatio H. Kitchener

Theodolite, sidearms, rifle, notebook, umbrella and Bedouin *kefiyeh* (headdress) —basic equipment for a Palestine mapping party

2 The Passionate Reacquaintance

When your children ask their fathers in time to come, 'What mean these stones?' then you shall let your children know, 'Israel passed over this Jordan on dry ground.'

(Joshua 4 : 21)

In 1970 there were some twenty-five official large-scale excavations throughout the 7,990 square miles of tiny Israel proper, making it easily the most dynamic archaeological setting in the world. About half the digs were being carried out by foreign expeditions— museums, scientific institutions, divinity schools, church missions. The remaining half were Israeli, representing an unparalleled campaign of concerted archaeological research by a native body into its own soil. And this figure does not include the more than thirty so-called 'rescue operations' undertaken in that year alone by the Israeli Deparment of Antiquities and Museums to salvage the fruits of ancient sites exhumed accidentally by bulldozers, shovels and picks on building sites throughout the land.

What were the excavators digging for? Not treasure, at least not as we are conditioned to define the word. Modern archaeologists pose scientific problems about the nature of the site or questions of history and then set out to solve them. These determine the ancient tell or ruin to be excavated, the scope of the dig and the specific areas of the site to be opened. The choice of sites in Israel is wide. The official register of the Department of Antiquities lists over 2,750 known tells or *khirbet* (ruins) within the pre-1967 borders, from the haunts of prehistoric hominids half a million years ago to the material vestiges of the Crusades.

The activities of Israel's professional archaeological community are only one facet of a popular fervour to recover, understand and preserve the past that is unique in the world. In Israel archaeology is not merely a national pastime, it is more a national passion, part of the Israeli's passionate reacquaintance with his land. He has walked it, camped upon it, slept in its embrace, dug in it, felt the rough edges of its ancient stones in communion with his fingertips, and rushed pieces of it to his museums.

opposite A group of Israeli amateur archaeologists on a survey of the slopes above the Dead Sea oasis of En-gedi. Hikes such as these are usually led by professional archaeologists

A girl volunteer engrossed in cleaning the dust of ages from a newly discovered skeleton in a recent excavation

He has lingered for hours on the edges of major excavations, gone off on unofficial expeditions of his own to hunt for Roman coins or glass in the sands at Caesarea or into the small nearby *khirbet* to enlarge the holdings of the kibbutz museum (over ninety such collections are registered with the Department of Antiquities by Israeli settlements). He has prowled the antique shops of Jerusalem, Haifa and the Arab west bank—for a rare coin, a piece of Israelite pottery, a Canaanite bronze dagger, an Egyptian scarab. His newspapers assign regular correspondents to front-page coverage of archaeological news. His children have volunteered for pick-and-shovel brigades at professional excavations, marched on desert pilgrimages up the tortuous nine-hundred-foot Snake Path to the top of Masada before sunrise, received lectures on their land by professional archaeologists as part of basic Army training (the Army printing house is the largest publisher of popular historical and archaeological material in the country).

It was a half-educated Moroccan immigrant, one of a team of soldiers sweeping the caves of the Dead Sea cliffs for scroll documents, who walked up to Israel's most renowned archaeologist, Professor Yigael Yadin, with a piece of shrivelled leather in his hand and proudly announced, without the help of a biblical concordance, 'We have Psalm 15'.

L.Y. Rahmani, the national Curator of Museums, recalls the exhausted group of soldiers who were relieved from their posts at the height of the bloody fighting at the walls of Jerusalem's Old City during the Six-Day War. The air thick with bullets, they crossed to the imposing Palestine Archaeological Museum across the street and knocked at the door. Rahmani thought they wanted a safe place to rest. What they really wanted was a tour of the museum.

The lure of antiquity is part of a military tradition that began with the unconventional British officer Orde Wingate. This brilliant tactician established the night squad defence units among Jewish settlers during the Arab troubles of 1936, setting an example for his young Jewish commanders by stalking the land with a Bible in his hand identifying the sites and reconstructing the events of epic battles recounted in the Old Testament. The chief of operations in the 1948 War of Independence was a student of archaeology named Yigael Yadin, and the study of antiquity was to have a profound effect on the course of that war. Reference to a map of ancient Roman roads led to the discovery by military scouts of a cobbled highway two thousand years old buried and forgotten under the desert between Gaza and Beersheba. Engineers

below Two professionals, a statesman and an archaeologist: the link has always been strong in Israel. Former Premier David Ben-Gurion is shown one of the remarkable finds from the 'Copper Treasure' of Nahal Mishmar by archaeologist Pesach Bar-Adon

hastily cleared it for use by a makeshift armoured brigade which stabbed deep into the Egyptian rear at Ouja in a lightning surprise attack, breaking the enemy hold on the Negev.

The almost mystical attachment of the fighting man to his ancient sources goes a long way towards explaining the phenomenon of Israel's Defence Minister Moshe Dayan, whose house appears to be not so much a home as an archaeological museum—bookshelves lined with ancient ceramic vessels, walls covered with display boards of bronze spearheads, axes and daggers, cases of anthropomorphic and zoomorphic figures and vessels, imported Cypriot flasks, Philistine 'beer mugs'. Dayan owns one of the finest sets of Egyptian scarabs in the world. His terraced archaeological garden is a cluttered catch-all of standing columns, ancient capitals, huge storage jars, lintels and vases. In his jumbled workshop adjacent to the garden are heaped boxes of ancient jar fragments which he reassembles ('It helps me to think'). Most of this Dayan has excavated himself, to the distress of Israel's professional archaeological fraternity; the rest he has haggled over personally with Arab and Jewish dealers in tiny out-of-the-way shops. The Israel Museum has catalogued this priceless collection, and Dayan has handed over some of it for public display. He personally discovered one of the richest pre-Israelite tomb sites in the country,

A corner of the 'archaeological garden' of Moshe Dayan at his home near Tel Aviv

at Azor, near Tel Aviv. It was here that he nearly lost his life in March 1968, when an excavation trench collapsed, burying him under four tons of earth. With seven broken ribs, crushed vertebrae and internal haemorrhages, he required months to recover.

Dayan is by no means alone in his enthusiasm, merely the most prominent member of a legion of dedicated amateurs, many of whom can identify an Upper Acheulian handaxe or Nabataean potsherd just as readily as a graduate of Israel's two major archaeological institutions. It was a young kibbutz worker, for instance, who first led professional excavators to an important prehistoric site near Beersheba; a businessman whose fast action spared the Maccabean burial site called Jason's Tomb in Jerusalem from blasting by a contractor. A group of Haifa fishermen who are continually finding submerged relics tangled in their nets boasts one of the finest collections of ancient amphorae in the country. Similarly, David Amir, a shepherd at Kibbutz Dan, began his formal archaeological studies at fifty-four, after publishing definitive studies on ancient cuneiform texts (his ability to translate them was self-taught), the territory of the Tribe of Dan, and the geographical history of upper eastern Galilee.

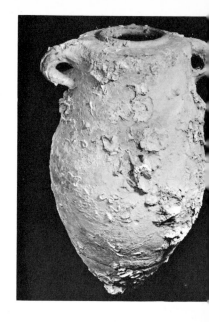

Barnacle-encrusted from its long submergence at the bottom of the Mediterranean, this Greek amphora is one of many collected by avid amateurs in the course of their work as fishermen in Haifa

The preservation and study of ancient sources is innate. It began with the Books of the Bible, and continued with sages who completed the compilation of the Jewish Law in the tragic days after the Roman destruction of Judaea. The tradition was also taken up in Rome by Flavius Josephus, a Jewish general in Galilee who deserted to the forces of Vespasian. Josephus became a favourite of the Roman imperial court. Under his royal patron he turned historian and wrote three major works, *The Jewish War*, *Antiquities of the Jews* and *Against Apion*. Superficially, they are a blatant effort to justify his own treacherous act. But underneath they are a compendium of the historical, geographical and architectural knowledge of his time—a memoir for posterity of the Jewish nation which Rome had destroyed. The excavation of a number of sites which Josephus graphically described, including the Masada fortress, confirms the meticulous accuracy with which he set down architectural details, despite his tendency to exaggerate on other matters.

Like the tells of Palestine, the Israelis' ardour for their past cuts through many layers of a complex national psyche. What the archaeologist Pesach Bar-Adon calls 'this clasping of hands across the centuries' has been explained as a search for identity, an attempt to span the frightful centuries-long gap when their nation no longer existed, a quest for roots, a manifestation of nationalism, an attempt to justify political claims to a land claimed by many through the ages. All of these reasons are part of the truth.

But essentially archaeology is a new outlet for an ancient tradition—the study of the Jewish heritage. In the centuries of wandering, Israel learned about its sources only in the abstract, maintained its ties with the land through the Bible and the Talmud—a storehouse of history, ethics, law, religion, philosophical speculation, science and folklore. With the long-promised return, which began in earnest at the turn of the twentieth century, this democratic tradition of scholarship—never the proprietary interest of a small intellectual élite as in the modern West—could in part be transferred to the soil. The land itself became a source of prime knowledge, the layers of its tells and ruins, the pages of yet another book begging to be read.

As we saw in the last chapter, Christian scholars and scientists, propelled by the traumatic erosion of faith by science in the nineteenth century, began the first serious Palestinian research. The exploration of the tells by foreign expeditions had gained tremendous momentum by the time Jewish settlers began to arrive in significant numbers. One of them, Dr Abraham J. Brawer, spoke to me of those days. At the age of eighty-seven he was still writing weekly articles on archaeological and geographical subjects for the Tel Aviv newspaper *Ha'aretz*. In Europe, he recalled, the Bible was a spiritual statement, a document of theological study. To the settlers in Palestine, it acquired a quality of living history with its reflections in the very soil on which they had begun to fashion a new life. Brawer, a geographer, established the basis for the teaching of geographical studies in the new Jewish schools. Its most essential element was a series of walking tours of the country. Israel's Director of Antiquities, Abraham Biran, recalls these tours as the high point of his educational experience: 'In no other way could I have captured the feel and spirit of the land, the sense of present in communion with past.' It was not unusual for student groups to hike the fifty miles from Haifa to Samaria, or the thirty miles from Hebron to Beersheba on study projects.

It was in 1913 that Brawer and a number of other scholars and pioneers founded the Jewish Palestine Exploration Society (JPES) (now called the Israel Exploration Society): 'We decided to formalize a program of geographical exploration and archaeological research on matters of Jewish interest. There were American societies, German societies, English societies, French societies. While we walked the country, foreigners were busy digging it up. . .'

Another keen archaeological amateur, Jerusalem's Mayor Teddy Kollek, 'guards' a unique ancient treasure being flown to the Holy City aboard a military helicopter: a woven basket and belongings found by Prof. Yigael Yadin in a Judaean Desert cave in which fighters of the Second Jewish Revolt (132–135 AD) under Bar-Kokhba took refuge

The popularization of archaeological discovery must really be linked with the arrival in Palestine of a bushy-haired Jewish youth from Russia named Eleazar Lipa Sukenik. Denied the right to attend the Institute of Oriental Studies in St Petersburg on religious grounds, he emigrated in 1911 to take up a teaching job in a Palestinian settlement.

Eleazar Sukenik wrote the first Hebrew guide book to Jerusalem. When he was thirty-three, and the father of two young sons (one of them Yigael Yadin), he began to study classical archaeology and Semitic languages in Berlin and Philadelphia; he founded a Department of Archaeology at the Hebrew University of Jerusalem, which had been opened in 1925. The basis for a modern Jewish archaeological tradition indigenous to its own soil had now been established.

In the next few years Sukenik undertook two projects which were to mark the turning-point in popular awareness of archaeological exploration. With Professor Leo A. Mayer, Sukenik began excavating the remains of the so-called 'third wall' of Jerusalem, which Herod Agrippa began to build in about AD 42 to protect the northern suburb of Bezetha and which the Jews of Jerusalem completed during the revolt against the Romans in AD 66–70. The stones which emerged were the living evidence of an event referred to briefly by Josephus from the final years of ancient Judaea. Jewish Jerusalem flocked to see them.

Then, in 1928, the members of a newly-founded farming settlement called Beth Alpha in the shadow of Mount Gilboa came upon the remains of an ancient building while digging an irrigation channel. Scraping away the earth cover, they also disclosed a portion of what appeared to be a mosaic floor. Word was rushed to Jerusalem, and Sukenik hurried to the site. He excavated for four months, hampered by tremendous rains. The ruined building was that of a Byzantine synagogue of the sixth century AD, the floor of which was composed of a striking mosaic in virtually perfect condition. The great central panel in the centre of the pavement depicts the Cycle of the Zodiac, while a panel near the entrance portrays the Sacrifice of Isaac. Another panel contains ritual objects of the Jewish service. There is also an Ark of the Law. Surrounding the entire work is a marginal mosaic of animals found in Palestine enclosed by intertwined vine leaves. Crowning the discovery, sensational for its time, was a mosaic inscription in Aramaic and Greek: 'This mosaic was laid down in the year (*obscured*) of the reign of Justin the King. May the craftsmen who engaged in this work, Marianos and his son Hanina, be held in remembrance.'

opposite In an excavation hut at Afula in 1938, the first Palestinian archaeologist to achieve international eminence, Prof. Eleazar Sukenik, discusses a technical point with his assistants and students; on his left, his son Yigael (Yadin), and to his right, Ruth Amiran and Nachman Avigad. All three are today top-ranking archaeologists and scholars

Prof. Sukenik's renowned son, Yigael Yadin, carefully cleans a partially damaged vessel discovered in a late Canaanite tomb at Hazor

An old-fashioned studio bellows camera is mounted on crude scaffolding to photograph the Beth Alpha mosaic discovered by chance during the excavations of 1928

opposite A reconstructed Natufian necklace of bone pendants and beads found in a tomb at el-Wad Cave in the Carmel range, excavated by Dorothy Garrod. The ability to see symmetry and beauty in nature was a Natufian attribute. The object is dated to 10,000–8,000 BC

From the archaeological point of view, the inscription permitted the exact dating of the structure, most probably to the reign of Justin I (AD 518–27). But what electrified the popular imagination was something which went beyond mere data. Under the soil of the new Jewish settlement lay a dramatic remnant of a Jewish community of 1,400 years ago. The sense of continuity, the link with the craftsmen who had laid down this classic example of primitive Jewish art ('Greeting from our ancestors', one has observed) had an effect which could only be described as overpowering.

Others had been engaged in research into synagogue remains since the great French scholar Ernest Renan undertook an initial study in 1861. But now there was a sizable Jewish population in modern Palestine with emotions and imaginations to be kindled. And kindled they were—by the remains of Beth Alpha, by a virtually unspoiled example of Jewish popular art in the first few centuries after the destruction of the Second Temple, and by the fact that here were 'graven' images of biblical subjects on holy ground in seeming defiance of the sacred injunction against them in the Second Commandment.

The controversy which swirled around the Beth Alpha mosaic was to be resolved in 1931 with the discovery that such synagogue art had at one time received Rabbinical sanction. A scholar named I.N. Epstein found the lost passage in a copy of the Jerusalem Talmud owned by the State Library in Leningrad. The passage read: 'In the days of Rabbi Abun they began to depict designs on mosaics, and he did not hinder them.' Rabbi Abun lived in the first half of the fourth century.

At any rate, the Hebrew University was deluged with so many inquiries about the Beth Alpha excavations that it was forced to issue periodic reports on its progress to the local press. A steady wave of visitors clogged the flooded roads to Beth Alpha. The chancellor of the university, Dr J.L. Magnes, could reach the site only on horseback. A people so fundamentally bound to its sources suddenly became the heirs of a material past.

The emotional impact of Beth Alpha was repeated in 1936, with the excavation of the magnificent second-to-fourth century AD necropolis of Beth-shearim by Professors Benjamin Mazar and Nachman Avigad. Since then the popular ardour of modern Israel to discover itself in the soil of ancient Israel has never abated. Rather the interest has widened to encompass the entire spectrum of history and culture locked in the land, Jewish and non-Jewish, biblical and extra-biblical.

3   In the Beginning

Today we can view with amusement the intellectual struggles of earlier scholars who tried to use Genesis as the literal yardstick by which to reconstruct the history of the world. There was, for instance, the devoted and pious Archbishop of Armagh, James Ussher, who in 1650 could proclaim from the evidence of the Bible that the Creation began precisely at 9 AM on 23 October 4,004 BC. Until the nineteenth century his hypothesis was widely accepted. However, having adjusted to their first harrowing encounters with the disquieting discoveries of science, man came to view with equanimity the fact that the creation of life required more than three billion years, rather than three days; and that he emerged from the crucible of evolution over four billion years after the formation of the earth, rather than having been spontaneously formed on the sixth day.

Nonetheless, archaeology, anthropology and palaeontology have since established that many great episodes in man's earliest development did indeed take place in the very region from which the Bible itself sprang. In the land later to be variously known as Canaan, Palestine and Israel, mankind devised tools and weapons which helped give him 'dominion over the fish of the sea, and over the birds of the air. . . and over all the earth'. The great Fertile Crescent of the Near East, of which Palestine forms a part, has provided the earliest evidence of animal domestication, recalling God's gift to man in Genesis of dominion 'over the cattle. . . and over every creeping thing that creeps upon the earth'. Here man took his earliest steps from predator to civilized food cultivator. He launched his monumental experiment in cultivation, became an agriculturalist, created the first farm economy and erected in Palestine the world's earliest known city. Here he devised the first stone fortifications to protect his surplus stores of goods and crops,

One of prehistoric man's first tools, this bi-facial flint hand axe was discovered at Maayan Barukh

opposite This example of a magnificently carved Natufian sickle handle in the shape of a fawn is surely one of the finest objects of prehistoric art known

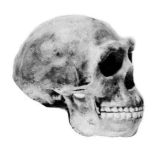

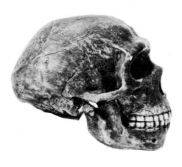

Three stages in the physical evolution of man: top: *Australopithecus africanus,* centre: *Homo erectus,* bottom: Neanderthal

opposite The late Prof. Moshe Stekelis commences excavation operations within the Kebarah Cave in the Carmel Range, a dwelling for prehistoric man 50,000 years ago

his fertile land and water supply from acquisitive enemies less well-endowed than he, and sought to deal with those fundamental questions about the mysteries of life and death from which religion would spring.

It is thought that the earliest precursor of *Homo sapiens* in Israel arrived from Africa about five hundred thousand years ago, during the cool wet period of the Grand Pluvial, which roughly coincides with the first two stages of the Ice Age in Europe. He and his small migratory band roamed slowly northwards through the swamp and savannah country of the Jordan Valley, its waters swollen into a vast lake or series of lakes by the rains which moved ahead of the spreading ice mass in Europe. *Homo erectus* was half-man, half-simian: his forehead sloping steeply to a small flat cranium, ridges overhanging his eye sockets like a shelf, the vestiges of a snout still visible in his broad nose, massive palate and large chin-less jaw, offering to the mind's eye an appearance somewhat like that of a large gibbon. He shared not only some of the ape's facial characteristics but a limited brain capacity of somewhere around sixty cubic inches (twenty-one less than the average modern man). But with his well-developed thighs he stood about 5 feet 7 inches tall and his posture and gait were akin to *Homo sapiens.* His game migrated northwards as well. Elephant fed in the shoreward margin of low vegetation and bush or in the higher woodland of the sloping Jordan Valley. Rhinoceros and hippo wallowed in the marshes on the rim of the still and steamy lake. All came to drink from its brackish waters. On a strip of sand, clay and shingle very close to the lake's edge *Homo erectus,* who was less than a savage, laid a bed of branches and pebbles for his living floor and waited for his quarry.

The green fields and fish ponds of Kibbutz Afiqim lie on gently rising and rolling ground two miles below the southern tip of the Sea of Galilee near the confluence of the Jordan and Yarmuk Rivers. Just above it rears a terraced hillock of some twenty acres called Ubeidiya. This, too, is kibbutz land. Early in 1958 driving winter rains washed a deep gully into the tomato field on the Ubeidiya slope. A bulldozer was brought to scrape fill into the gully. Afterwards, a *kibbutznik* in charge of tending the tomato field noticed a litter of animal bones in scarred earth exposed by the machine. Amateur archaeologists of Kibbutz Afiqim were consulted. At a glance it was obvious that the bone fragments were not of recent origin. They dispatched the bones to the Hebrew University for study and notified Professor Moshe Stekelis.

Stekelis was Israel's senior authority in prehistory, and since 1932 had directed many of the important prehistoric excavations in the land. At the Hebrew University, where he became a research fellow in 1935, the Russian *émigré* was a colourful and flamboyant teacher. His promising student and successor Ofer Bar-Yosef recalls Stekelis sawing through classroom furniture with replicas of ancient flint tools which he had learnt to make himself, in order to demonstrate to his classes how effectively they worked. In his time Stekelis lectured extensively to amateur archaeological groups, particularly in the *kibbutzim* of the Jordan Valley, rich with the deposits of the peoples for whom it served as a highway of migration in prehistoric times. On the basis of a survey of the Jordan—Yarmuk—Sea of Galilee triangle in 1943, Stekelis had alerted his amateur teams to evidence that the site of a very early culture, perhaps the earliest in Palestine, lay buried somewhere beneath the surface of the area—awaiting only a bit of luck and a good pair of eyes. Stekelis had noticed some pebbles about the size of potatoes lying on the ground. These were common enough in themselves, but at one end they had been chipped or flaked by two opposing blows to form a crude cutting or chopping edge. The primitive pebble tool is perhaps man's earliest invention. Somewhere near at hand, in incomprehensibly distant times, a people of this 'pebble culture' had made these tools, and laid down strata of debris and refuse that were later sealed beneath 'sterile' layers of alluvium. The run off of recent rains, eroding deeply through these layers, had washed the pebble tools free. But from where? The mysteries of this culture could be unlocked only if the source of these tools were discovered.

So fifteen years later, the *kibbutzniks* of Afiqim contacted Stekelis with news of their find in the tomato field. Zoologist Georg Haas of the Hebrew University informed him that the animal bones were perhaps the oldest ever found in the land of Israel. In the spring of 1959 Stekelis and several of his colleagues went to Afiqim to survey the site, keen with the anticipation of potential discovery which is one of archaeology's greatest thrills. On the littered surface where the bones had been discovered Stekelis found some of the same pebble tools that he had first encountered on the Jordan Valley exploration fifteen years earlier. The hoard from which they came obviously lay buried beneath the tomato vines of Ubeidiya.

The first official excavation season was launched in the spring of 1960. Stekelis and a group of students, including Bar-Yosef, began a series of soundings. Hardly had they started digging the

This pottery figurine of a neolithic fertility goddess (rear view) was discovered in the prehistoric settlement of Horvat Minha in the Jordan Valley near the Sea of Galilee

pits when two fragments of human skull were spotted on the surface. Two teeth, one an incisor, were found in a clay layer deposited by the waters of the Grand Pluvial perhaps half a million years ago. The bits of skull, too fragmentary for detailed analysis, were four times thicker than that of modern man. Together with the large teeth, they pointed to *Homo erectus*.

But how had he lived? The pits suggested an answer, which just as quickly posed a new problem. The students' spades encountered what at first glance appeared to be ramparts or walls made of large pebbles, inclined about seventy degrees from the horizontal. But stone construction at such an early date was clearly impossible. Then what were they? Geology soon produced the answer. The Great Rift Valley is one of the vast wonders of terrestrial mechanics —a gash or fault in the earth's surface, forming a network of narrow steep-sided valleys, sheer escarpments, and deep lakes which span 3,500 miles from Lake Nyasa in East Africa to the Jordan Valley in the north. The primal volcanic eruptions and tectonic spasms which created the Jordan Valley began some two million years ago, but profound settling movements continued long after man reached Palestine, grinding and warping the crust on either side of the fault, scoring the valley floor into the deepest trough on earth—1,200 feet below sea level. What Stekelis and his team had found were Ubeidiya Man's crude open-air living platforms, each up to a hundred feet long. Together they comprised a multilayered mosaic of pebbled 'flooring' packed thickly with dis-

Diggers at Ubeidiya use whiskbrooms, toothbrushes and step ladders to uncover the midden of *Homo erectus* on the shores of the Jordan. Clusters of pebble tools and the bones of prehistoric animals thrust by geological forces to their present inclination emerge from the alluvium of countless centuries

A collection of the bolas shaped and used by Ubeidiya Man. The small spheroids and the Ubeidiya 'football'

carded stone tools and the bony remains of his meals. Most probably, given the absence of any sign of fire, the meat was eaten raw. These platforms had been bonded by an alluvial coating of silt and clay deposited during cyclical encroachments of the lake, and then tilted almost upright in the final throes of the valley's spasms. Thus these haphazard collages of stone and bone, laid down perhaps five hundred thousand years ago, represented an act of self-commemoration by the earliest known species of man in Palestine.

Working with infinite care and patience, exposing perhaps no more than three hundred square feet of surface a year, clearing away the soil covering with small hand-picks and whisk brooms, first on hands and knees and then, as the trenches deepened, leaning from tall ladders propped against the sides of the living floors, individually numbering, recording and examining each of the thousands of objects forming each platform, straining and washing the earth for the smallest particles of debris, Stekelis' team began to piece together a profile of the first of countless waves of migration to Palestine.

With the pebble chopping tool Ubeidiya Man tore his meat and probably shaped his wooden lances. By edging two sides of an elongated flint core, he fashioned a bi-facial handaxe to cut wood, dig through hard-packed soil and skin his game. *Homo erectus* shared his living floor with the debris of his 'kitchen'. Bones, yellow-brown with the mineralized patina of millennia, litter the margins of the living floors where they were thrown. They reveal that the valley was a zoological melting-pot in early Stone Age times. Animals from ice-bound Europe shared the land with species from equatorial Africa and Asia. The mandible and tusks of a young hippopotamus, the skull of a giraffe and the ribs of a rhinoceros are contemporary with the skeletal remains of boar, wild bears and fallow deer. From the distribution of bones it appears that Ubeidiya Man's favourite meal was young hippo, whose relative inexperience made him no match for a small band of hunters. His ample meat supply (his total weight was about a ton) made the long labour of the messy kill worth the effort. He was most probably stunned by bolas—small boulders of limestone chipped by *Homo erectus* into spheroids weighing perhaps a pound. Two mammoth bolas, called 'Ubeidiya footballs' by Bar-Yosef, weighed seventeen and thirty-three pounds respectively. The stone spheroids might have been thrown, dropped or hurled from crude leather slings. In all likelihood the quarry was finished off with wooden lances. Unlike the bolas, wooden implements, assuming that they existed, have not survived.

That Ubeidiya Man was low on the scale of human development is clear. He displayed rudimentary signs of human choice and understanding of materials in selecting flint for his choppers, basalt for his handaxes and limestone for his bolas. But his talents, his imagination and initiative were limited. He found most of his raw material, and even his game, very close to home. Originality and enterprise were traits reserved for his descendants. But he did at least develop a mode of existence which supplied his simple needs and permitted him to survive in a basically hostile environment for quite a long time. There are about a dozen layers of living platforms stacked like rows of leaning dominoes beneath the terrace of Ubeidiya. Only seven complete floors have been excavated in eleven summer digging seasons. Ofer Bar-Yosef, who inherited the mantle of his teacher upon Professor Stekelis' death in 1967, suggests that the richness of the site offers enough material for 'several lifetimes of digging'. For him the fascination of prehistory is easy to explain. 'The origins of civilization can be traced to the very dawn of man', he has said. 'Long before historic times, man came to possess all the basic knowledge, skills, and intellectual promise he was ever to have. And Ubeidiya Man is part of the common pool of what we were to become and what we are.'

Two openings dominate the wall of dolomitic limestone which marks the southern boundary of the Wadi el-Mughara (Valley of the Caves). It is a small hillocked and rock-strewn plain cutting across the Carmel range, which bulks steeply above the Mediterranean along twelve miles of the north Palestine coast. The Mugharet el-Wad (Cave of the Valley) and the Mugharet e-Jamal (Cave of the Camel) were visible for miles, like the gaping eyes of a nameless behemoth. A third cavern, et-Tabun (The Oven)

The imposing bulk of the Valley of the Caves. El-Wad lies slightly to the left of the tents, Jamal looms above them, and Tabun can be seen above the huge mound of talus to the right. The tents formed the camp of Dorothy Garrod's famous and successful expedition

Reconstruction of a prehistoric sickle, clearly showing flint blades, or teeth. The configuration of the jaw bone may well have inspired this revolutionary device

lay hidden behind a screen of carob trees. A fourth cave, es-Skhul, was concealed behind a spur of hill nearby. The only visitors to the caves were Arab goatherds, who penned their flocks on the terrace of el-Wad. In 1928 the peace of the herdsmen was disturbed by the demands of an awakening Palestine. Engineers had selected the wadi as a quarry to produce stone for the building of the harbour at Haifa, eighteen miles to the north. Blasting operations had already begun in the vicinity of Skhul cave, when a concerned Department of Antiquities of the British Mandate Government sent an inspector on a routine visit to 'test the value' of the caves as an archaeological site.

He sank sounding pits into the mound of talus which encircles the opening of el-Wad to a radius of 180 feet, and found it rich with flint tools. More importantly, he returned to Jerusalem with an amazing discovery—the head of a fawn carved on a long polished piece of bone. The workmanship was breathtaking. The fawn was rendered partly in the round and partly in relief. Its head is tilted backwards, as though startled by a sudden sound. Its eyes are opened wide in alarm. Its mouth, and the legs which flank the sides of the slender shaft of bone in relief, have been rendered by a deft hand. If preliminary judgments were correct, the investigator had found the oldest example of art known in the Near East. But that was not the only surprise. Found with the carved fawn was a large number of flint sickle blades for reaping grain.

At some point, man had embarked on a revolutionary experiment —his first attempt to harness nature. Rather than remaining totally dependent on the kill of the hunt or seasonal forages for wild fruit, he began to tame wild grain-bearing grasses and produce his own food on a systematic basis. As we have already seen, some scientists had long believed that this epoch-making step toward civilization could have taken place in the Near East. Given

left 'Mount Carmel' Man, found by Dorothy Garrod in es-Skhul Cave, represented an ancient species combining both the characteristics of Neanderthal and modern *Homo sapiens*. He is roughly contemporaneous with 'Galilee Man'

The front of the skull of Turville-Petre's 'Galilee Man', whom scientists later judged to be a young woman

the unique assemblage of finely shaped sickle blades found at Mount Carmel, together with a sculptured shaft of bone which might have served as the handle of a sickle, would the primitive men who produced them have been the first to master the secret of acquiring power over nature? Needless to say, the quarrying operation was transferred elsewhere.

To appreciate fully the excitement of the find at the Mount Carmel caves, it should be recalled that Palestine was virtually *terra incognita* for prehistorians in the early 1920s. They had been concentrating their prospecting efforts elsewhere, notably in Europe, leaving Palestine as a scientific backwater. Then, within only a few decades, discovery followed so rapidly upon discovery that a former director of the American Schools of Oriental Research in Jerusalem, C.C. McCown, could state in 1943 in his excellent book *The Ladder of Progress in Palestine:* 'Palestine now offers the most complete and continuous picture of prehistoric human evolution that is at present available in any part of the world.' Even today Israel remains one of the major areas for prehistoric research. From one end to another, the country has yielded the mineralized skeletons of literally hundreds of specimens of early men together with their artifacts, from the arrival of Ubeidiya Man to the advent of *Homo sapiens*.

The first man to tap the archaeological riches lying below the layers of recorded history was a young British scholar called Francis Turville-Petre. In 1925, three years before the dramatic 'rescue' of the Mount Carmel caves, prehistorians were electrified by Turville-Petre's discovery of four large fragments comprising a nearly complete Neanderthaloid skull at a place called by the Arabs the 'Cave of the Gypsy Woman' (Mughâret ez-Zuttîyeh) near Tiberias.

Buried beneath the large boulder Turville-Petre found the shattered skull of 'Galilee Man', as he was labelled, who had roamed the shores of the Sea of Galilee perhaps forty to fifty thousand years ago. Never before had human remains quite so old been found in Palestine, though many examples of classic Neanderthals had previously turned up throughout Europe. Under a prominent eight-column headline which proclaimed the find—'PREHISTORIC MAN IN PALESTINE: THE GALILEE SKULL'—the London *Times* of 14 August 1925 featured nearly a full page of photographs from ez-Zuttiyeh. One showed the exultant Turville-Petre in an outfit more befitting a guest at a country house party than a scientific explorer within the forbidding chamber of a vast cave: the decorous young archaeologist is labelling a specimen box attired in broad-brimmed felt hat, Edwardian jacket and perfectly creased trousers, a cane nattily hooked over a well-tailored right sleeve.

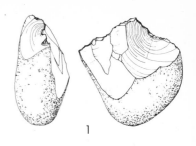

The skull of 'Galilee Man' was long and narrow, which is typical of a classic Neanderthal. But it also displayed certain characteristics of modern man. Its forehead was far less sloping than that of the Neanderthal, while the vault of the skull was as high as that of *Homo sapiens*. Here was a vital link in the evolutionary chain. Palestine Man, as later examples of this intermediate species were to be called, represented a transitional stage between the pure Neanderthal of Europe and ourselves. And Palestine had been a breeding ground for this development. A number of preachers were quick to take up the comparative theme of Galilee Man and the Man from Galilee.

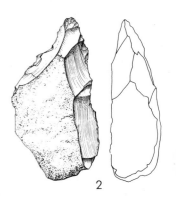

In the years which followed, scientists not only discovered more examples of this advanced hominid, but found that in some cases he had actually lived side by side with some of the earliest specimens of *Homo sapiens* himself. The interplay of evolutionary relationships between the two is still a matter of scholarly discussion. At any rate, it was probably from here that *Homo sapiens* made his way into Europe. Because of its geographical position at the cross-roads of the continents, Palestine was destined to be the melting-pot for the meeting and interbreeding of the species—and from this clash modern man would emerge paramount.

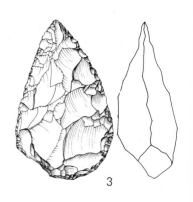

One of the many prehistorians attacted to Palestine by Turville-Petre's discovery was an extraordinary British woman called Dorothy A.E. Garrod, who had won a diploma in anthropology from Oxford 'with distinction', an exceptional feat for a woman in those days. In 1928, as the authorities responsible for antiquities were trying to rescue the Mount Carmel caves from the engineers of Haifa harbour, Miss Garrod led a small expedition to Shuqba Cave in the Wadi Natuf, seventeen miles north-west of Jerusalem. This conjuction of events marked the beginning of one of the most

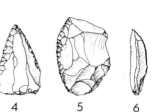

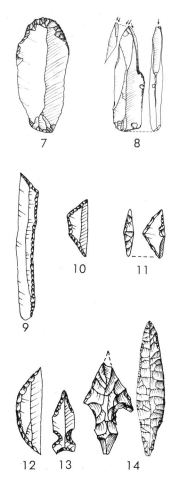

The evolution of flint tools:
1. chopping tool; 2. crude handaxe, 500,000 BC; 3. developed handaxe, 100,000 BC; 4. Mousterian point; 5. side scraper, 70–35,000 BC; 6. backed blade; 7. end scraper and 8. burin, 35–15,000 BC; 9. obliquely-truncated, backed bladelet, 15–10,000 BC; 10. geometric microlith-trapeze, 10,000 BC; 11. geometric microlith-triangle, 10,000 BC; 12. lunate, 10–8,000 BC; 13. primitive arrowhead and 14. developed arrowheads, 8–6,000 BC

important breakthroughs in man's understanding of his origins. The early people of Wadi Natuf could be called technological revolutionaries. Compared, for instance, to Ubeidiya Man, they possessed an astounding range of flint tools, cutting blades of all types, barbs and bone points. The flint implements were also very small, usually no more than half an inch to an inch and a half long and under a quarter of an inch wide. Instead of having irregular forms they had been retouched into regular geometric shapes: rectangles, trapezoids, triangles and delicately curved crescents with straight cutting edges called lunates. With the Natufians, for this was the name Miss Garrod gave to this new culture (after Wadi Natuf) lunates abounded. In the many years since Ubeidiya, the technical skills of man had slowly become more sophisticated and diversified.

In 1929, having been elected to a research fellowship at Newnham College, Cambridge, Miss Garrod prepared to resume her excavations at Wadi Natuf. But the discovery in the caves near Haifa changed her plans, for the preliminary survey there had produced a sampling of flint microliths which included a surprising number of lunates. Had the caves of Mugharet el-Wad to the north also sheltered bands of the same advanced culture which had settled in the Wadi Natuf? The British School of Archaeology in Jerusalem and the American School of Prehistoric Research invited Miss Garrod to delay her work at Wadi Natuf and tackle the Mount Carmel sites instead.

She never regretted her change of plan. She set up camp in Wadi el-Mugharet in April 1929 for a dig that was to stretch over six successive seasons. In those days expedition facilities were anything but luxurious. Miss Garrod and her staff of three were forced during the first season to establish expedition headquarters and their own accomodation within the caves themselves. Her associates, including palaeontologist and camp doctor, were all women, as were, with a single exception, the pool of labourers recruited from the nearby village of Jebah. The exception was a man hired to handle the heavy work of chipping and loading the cave deposits into baskets, which he carried to the women workers for sifting and sorting.

In fifty weeks of actual excavating time Miss Garrod uncovered a wealth of evidence which still represents one of the richest single contributions to the study of primitive man ever made by a single excavator at a single site. Cambridge University marked her achievements by making her the first lady professor in its history. One can get an idea of the extent of her work from the excavations

The skull of a Natufian skeleton discovered at el-Wad Cave in the Carmel Range was decorated with a headdress made of dentalium shells reminiscent of a modern Arab *kefiyeh*

at Tabun cave alone. The Garrod team penetrated through nearly eighty feet of debris deposited by wind, water and human habitation over a period of up to a hundred thousand years. The thick deposits of the Mount Carmel caves produced a virtually continuous record of human development which began with the closing phases of the early Stone Age. It ended with the epoch of the Natufian cultural revolution, which took place between 10,000 and 8,000 BC.

What distinguishes the Natufian culture from contemporary cultures in other parts of the world is the rich store of evidence which indicates that it was the first to make the transition from food collecting to food producing. Miss Garrod and her team prised hundreds of serrated flint sickle blades up to three quarters of an inch long from both the terrace and the concrete-hard conglomerate of stone and clay called breccia within the mouth of the lofty cavern. The teeth were abraded and worn to a polished sheen with use. The carved fawn had undoubtedly served as a sickle handle. Other similarly carved handles were found, along with sections of sickle-shafts made of long animal bones, often ribs, into which the flint teeth had been embedded. The final evidence for the beginnings of agriculture lay beneath the red earth and breccia of the terrace—two complete limestone mortars and fragments of basalt pestles for grinding grain into flour.

The Natufians, after centuries of trial and error, were granted a tentative insight into the mechanics of nature and a step towards controlling the environment. Many scientists are convinced that the Natufians were not only among the first people to engage in the systematic reaping of grain, but were probably the first to engage in systematic planting of domestic crops. By learning how to cultivate and store rather than merely collect his food, man took his first great stride towards relative security, the ability to settle down, towards surplus and trade, and the audacious concept of a living city.

Maturing with the seeds of the field were the seeds of religious thought. Having embarked on a quest for power and knowledge, Natufian Man's material successes must have made him aware at the same time of his own frailty. Having grasped some slight insight into the phenomenon of life, he became aware of the mystery of death. The forces which granted him his grain could as readily and capriciously deny it. Great as he was, there were things greater than he before which he cowered, and yet to which he also aspired. In that very same land, hundreds of thousands of generations hence, the authors of Genesis would attempt to enunciate the preoccupation which could haunt men like the Natufians

left A quern with grinding stone, and a mortar with pestle, telltale signs of early agriculture. Their basic shapes have remained unchanged since prehistoric times

below A 'self-portrait' of Natufian man. A man's head incised on a small pebble

—the price of having eaten from the Tree of Knowledge.

The Natufians attempted to devise a set of answers to these abstract and apparently unfathomable mysteries. The skilled aboriginal artist sought to impart some magical efficacy to the sickle to assure a plentiful yield by carving in its handle a symbol of one of nature's gifts, the fawn. He sought to immortalize himself as well. With a group of burials inside the cave complex Miss Garrod found a calcite pebble roughly incised with a Natufian image—a face with prominent eyebrows, large nose and ample skull—remarkably similar to anthropological reconstructions of Natufian Man himself.

The incised calcite pebble found with one group of Mount Carmel burials is one of the earliest examples of the cult tradition of graven images against which the prophets of ancient Israel would ultimately direct their wrath and monotheistic zeal.

The main living area of a Natufian cave complex was an outdoor terrace immediately before the vaulted opening. At el-Wad Miss Garrod found buried the skeletal remains of at least fifty-nine Natufians. The burials are remarkable. Many of the skeletons were found flexed in a foetal position, knees drawn towards chin. In some cases, limestone 'pillows' were placed under their heads and chert axes or other votive objects at their feet. One communal group of burials lay in a semi-circle round a limestone mortar. One couple was buried in a permanent embrace. Many had been

buried wearing strangely pleasing adornments, including headdresses, necklaces, pendants and circlets—made of cylindrical
dentalium shells and the small bones of birds and gazelles. The
burial form was deliberate. A precise ritual attitude had developed
towards the corpse and this apparently envisaged some form of
life in or after death. The bodies were given a permanent place
beneath the feet of the living, remaining a part of the communal
group which had sustained them, and which they had helped to
sustain. The Natufians were not the first of the early peoples to
ponder the essential contradictions between life and death, or to
surround their corpses with a ritual of awe. But they were possessed
of an awareness of themselves and their surroundings that preceding
cultures lacked. Their successful experiments with farming, the
sculptured sickle handles and small stone figurines of copulating
couples and phallic pestles found at other Natufian sites indicate
that they were probably the first people to develop an insight into
nature—especially into the phenomenon of cause and effect.
Natufian man came to relate copulation to pregnancy and
birth, and linked the abstract concepts of fertility and growth to
their harvests and to the living world round them. This giant
intellectual step from the particular to the abstract, and from
mystery to a system of ritual belief, was made at a very early date,
and the Natufians seem to be one of the more important links
in the chain.

They still, of course, remained largely dependent on the food they
gathered. They were hunters. Some scholars believe that their
arsenal included rudimentary bows, and that some of their small
fashioned flints were used as arrowheads. A study of bone deposits
reveals the fleet-footed gazelle as their favourite prey—an animal
of open grassland and drier climate. The cool and damp climate
of the pluvial rains had ended in Palestine. In the north, the glaciers
were retreating. In the south, stands of woodland in the higher
altitudes were retreating and thinning out. Along with gazelle,
deer, wild oxen and goats were in plentiful supply. But here, too,
there is evidence that the Natufians played an important transitional
role in the domestication of animals. In an intermediate level of
el-Wad Cave, Miss Garrod found the skull of a jackal-like animal,
an ancestor of the dog. Some experts think that the find represents
an early stage in the civilizing partnership of man and beast. If
Natufian Man spearheaded farming, he also had a hand in the
very early stages of animal husbandry. There is some evidence
at several Natufian sites that wild goats, pigs and oxen had either
been penned in captivity or tamed.

above On the floor of a
Natufian hut two pestles
and five pebbles were
found in this arrangement.
Whether there was any
significance in the
arrangement or the number
of 7 is not known
below A 'self-portrait'
of Natufian Man. A man's
head incised on a small
pebble

Subsequent excavations have turned up a dozen Natufian
sites—from the fertile coastal plain and the central mountain
ridge to the Jordan Valley and the far more hostile environment
of the Judaean Desert. The Natufians adapted their settled ways
not only to caves but to hamlet life as well. For instance, on the
terrace of Eynan on what had been the shore of ancient Lake Hula,
the French archaeologist Jean Perrot excavated a Natufian 'open
air' hamlet of circular huts with bases of stone. The settlement
consisted of perhaps fifty huts, each twenty-three feet in diameter,
and covered about 22,000 square feet. Along with mortars and
pestles, some of the huts were equipped with mud-plastered
storage bins in which cereal surpluses may well have been stored.

It has been estimated that the Natufian settlements were able
to support up to three hundred people, implying an orderly mixed
economy of hunting, gathering, and crop cultivation which
supplied more than normal daily food needs. The surplus could,
at least in part, be stored. It is hard to imagine that these settlements
could have existed for any length of time without some notion
of the concept of private property, a rudimentary form of collective
organization, and a social code defining in the most basic terms
the individual's obligations with regard to the welfare of his
hamlet society as well as its obligations to him as a productive member of the body politic.

Agriculture was the seedbed in which men first learned to work,
live and share the hazards of survival together. Everything that
men would eventually create under the general heading of 'civilization'—city-states, nation-states, empires, laws, specialization
among artists, artisans and scribes, formalized religion—was
implicit in the primitive Natufian villages. Many of these institutions would ultimately come to full flower at either end of the
Palestinian bridgehead—Egypt to the south and Mesopotamia to
the east.

Even Dorothy Garrod did not at first foresee the full implications of her discovery. In 1957 she told the British Academy:
'There is no trace of Natufian occupation at the base of any of the
Palestinian tells.' At the very time that this statement was being
made, another British woman archaeologist was encountering
dramatic evidence to the contrary. She picked up the archaeological
trail of the Natufians, who had apparently been caught up in a vast
revolutionary impulse of their own creation. Their momentum
led them, in a huge leap forward, to found Jericho, the oldest
known city in the world—a city some five thousand years ahead
of its time.

4 Prelude to History

It is easier to explain why the phenomenon called Earliest Jericho should not exist, than why it should. It is a reality which challenges our comprehension. To ancient man, Jericho must have seemed a miracle. Perhaps that is why Joshua was told when he first arrived before the city: 'Put off your shoes from your feet; for the place where you stand is holy.'

Jericho is a place of superlatives and extremes. The oldest known city in the world lies in one of the lowest, most desolate, hottest and driest places on earth. Slightly north-west of the point where the waters of the Jordan are lost in the fetor of the Dead Sea, Jericho's lush oasis—gardens, tropical bushes, banana groves and date palms—stands bold and green in the harsh sunlight against the bleached whites and pale yellows of the desert sea round it. Jericho has defied its surroundings for at least eleven thousand years, though there was no suspicion of its age when the British archaeologist John Garstang arrived to excavate the tell west of the oasis in 1930.(A joint German-Austrian expedition had previously carried out some excavations at the site) The object of Garstang's search was the remains of the wall which the Bible tells us was knocked flat by the trumpets of Joshua's Israelites. Garstang reported to the newspapers of the time that he had found the very wall (a claim which was to be disproved two decades later) and this predictably made headlines. The papers devoted little space, however, to his discoveries at the bottom of a deep, narrow pit in the north-east quadrant of the tell. In these low-lying levels Garstang found the remains of a building which appeared to be a temple. He also recovered a large number of shattered fragments which once constituted a large piece of sculpture made of sun-dried clay. The only intact fragment that was immediately recognizable was a large life-size representation of a male head. The sculptured face

A fragment of an idol from the late Stone Age. The eyes are inlaid with shells and the hair is indicated by brown stripes. It was discovered by British archaeologist John Garstang at Jericho in 1930

opposite The lush oasis town of Jericho in the Dead Sea Rift—the oldest known inhabited city on earth

was stylized—a small upturned slit for a mouth, embedded sea-shells for eyes, with thin lines of brown paint representing the hairline and a small beard. A striking achievement, for even before these people had learned to mould clay into pottery they were attempting to shape a plastic representation of the entire human figure.

The attempt was primitive: the head was moulded on one side of a thin two-dimensional disc, to be viewed from the front only. A study of the fragments revealed not one but three such life-sized figures, probably a man, woman and child. It seemed clear that near bedrock at the core of the seventy-foot-high tell there had been settled life at a very early date. The settlers had been a people far advanced for their time who had worshipped before this sculptured family of a god, mother goddess and divine offspring. A pantheon of personified deities had never been encountered before in this form, and would not reappear in the same land until much later, as the Canaanite trinity of El, Asherah and Baal. How ironic that this pagan concept appears so early in the very city which the Israelites would first claim from the Canaanites as their own in the name of the One God!

Garstang knew that this evidence came from the remote time which archaeologists call the Late Stone Age. But he lacked the scientific dating tools to extract precise information from his evidence. What seemed certain to archaeologists after Garstang had announced his findings and wound up his excavations in 1936 was that the lower strata of the old tell of Jericho had a more important story to tell.

Its secrets were not to be revealed until some time after the Second World War. On 1 July 1952 the London *Times* offered its readers: 'EARLIEST TOWN IN THE WORLD—DISCOVERIES AT JERICHO.' Early that year, and for the next six years to come, one of Britain's most eminent Palestinian archaeologists, Kathleen M. Kenyon, realized a long-standing dream: to apply modern excavation techniques to Garstang's findings on both the Joshuitic destruction of Jericho and the strata which lay on bedrock beneath seventy feet of Jericho's later history. Over the seven seasons of work she pooled the financial resources of more than forty societies, museums, universities, foundations and trusts. She recruited over eighty experts representing nine countries, from field supervisors and photographers to camp organizers. They oversaw a local Arab labour force which averaged about two hundred people per season. Each season lasted from early January to early April to avoid the worst of the heat. The total cost of the seven-year project was

The noted British archaeologist Kathleen M. Kenyon uncovered the earliest settlements of ancient Jericho during seven seasons of extensive excavation. She led another famous expedition which has added immeasurably to our knowledge of ancient Jerusalem

$85,000—a bargain, in the light of the vast amount of information it produced.

The tell, a man-made record of habitation, abandonment and destruction covers ten acres. The mound is small both by Near Eastern and by Palestinian standards. Four expeditions, beginning as early as 1879 and ending with the Kenyon project, have probed, gashed and shaved the artificial hill of packed clay and stone until under the slanting rays of the afternoon sun which hangs above the nearby Judaean Hills, its tortured humps and hollows resemble the melted remains of a megalithic sandcastle. The spring of Ain es-Sultan surfaces at the foot of the tell. It is fed from a rocky underground basin that funnels, filters and traps the winter rains of the Judaean highlands. It is the life force of Jericho's green oasis. It is the secret which has sustained settled life here for countless millennia—has raised Jericho above the wasteland around it and made it a 'holy place'.

Miss Kenyon drove three deep, narrow, wedge-like trenches into the northern, western and southern flanks of the tell to get a vertical cross-section of its history from the earliest periods of habitation to the latest. Her teams also excavated specific areas on the mound itself to obtain wider horizontal pictures of the ruined

An aerial view of the tell of ancient Jericho, clearly showing one of Miss Kenyon's major cuttings and a secondary trench leading to the famed round tower

cities which comprise its layers. In the final season at Jericho, towards the northern rim of the tell, Miss Kenyon's excavators uncovered on bedrock a clay platform 19 feet 10 inches long and 10 feet wide supported by a wall of stone and wooden posts. To Miss Kenyon, it appeared to be a place of worship, a cultic high place. In the debris that was associated with it she was surprised to find an assortment of the very same highly developed geometric flint tools that had connected the people of Wadi Natuf with those in the Mount Carmel caves of the Mediterranean coast. Moreover, in the centre of the bedrock at the very bottom of the tell lay the remains of the pioneer settlement of Jericho—a series of earthen humps which had served as the floors of flimsy rounded nomad huts. They were somewhat reminiscent of the remains that Jean Perrot had found at the terrace site of Eynan eighty-four miles to to the north, and these had also been identified as Natufian. The trail of the people first identified by Miss Garrod led clearly to Kathleen Kenyon's excavations in the desert oasis—a remarkable continuum of human development from the caves of Mount Carmel to the first settlement at Jericho. The settlement of humped floors lasted long enough to produce a mound of debris thirteen feet thick.

Thus Miss Kenyon was able to write, with understandable excitement: 'Jericho has provided evidence of the process for which archaeologists have long been looking, of the transition from man as a hunter to man as a member of a settled community.' This earliest Jericho was the Natufians' greatest achievement. Would it now be possible to obtain some idea of when they founded the urban settlement of Jericho?

Until the advent of the nuclear age, the best that archaeologists could do to fit their finds into a time scheme for the period before the invention of writing and pottery was to make enlightened guesses. In 1949 Dr Willard Libby, a member of the Manhattan Project team which produced the atomic bomb, developed a revolutionary dating tool for the archaeological researcher—an achievement which was to win him the Nobel Prize for Chemistry. Every living thing absorbs radioactive carbon, or Carbon 14 (that is, carbon with an atomic weight of 14), which is produced by the interaction of cosmic rays with the nitrogen of the earth's atmosphere. Dr Libby established that every organism, be it human, mollusc or tree, begins discharging Carbon 14 upon death. The rate of this discharge or decay is known. Radiocarbon has a half-life of about 5,700 years—constantly disintegrating by half its remaining amount during each 5,700-year period. This amount

is measurable, given a degree of error which naturally increases with the age of the organic material being measured. Peat, wood, charcoal or bones can thus be fixed relatively accurately in time. Their age in turn dates everything found in the same stratum with them. At some point the cultic high place of the Natufians was swept by fire, and its wooden posts were preserved as charcoal: ideal material for the Carbon 14 dating process. The material was sent to several laboratories, and when the findings were returned to Miss Kenyon she could confidently date the birth of Jericho under the Natufians to about 9,000 BC.

Whereas the first Natufian settlement is restricted in size, what follows—man's first known city—explodes to cover at least ten acres, the entire area of the present tell. The people of Jericho II had now translated the flimsy rounded tents or huts of the Natufian tradition into permanent houses of hand-moulded, sun-dried mudbrick, reinforced with wooden posts and wattling. The walls leaned slightly inwards and may have supported a domed roof. To their originators, inspired by the Natufians, goes the distinction of having built the earliest known permanent houses.

But there was more to come. The innovators who had constructed the world's first city had also devised for its defence the first known system of fortifications. In the third season of the dig, in 1954, the team assigned to Trench I on the tell's western flank encountered the remains of a series of impressive defence walls, some of its stones weighing several tons. Assuming that they had encircled the entire city, the walls must have been up to half a mile long. The defence complex also included a massive round tower, preserved to a height of thirty feet, standing just inside the walls and a moat cut into solid rock which was twenty-seven feet wide and nine feet deep. It represents the first known monumental building in stone. It was probably Jericho's early warning system to spot the advance of raiding bands across the Jericho plain and to alert the men in the fields.

Man's great successes have given rise to his greatest problems. His control of the environment produced the spiritual doubts from which the stirrings of religious belief sprang. His first city, its water source and its wealth aroused not only the wonder but also the avarice of others less well-endowed than himself. For Jericho had its enemies. Against them, Jerichoans responded with man's earliest known organized programme of public works—an awesome complex of fortifications. From the very start urban society was forced to offer defiance to the countryside, ratifying in its massive stoneworks the fundamental theme of conflict

The pictures on this and the preceding page show four stages in the Carbon 14 process developed by Dr. Willard Libby to date ancient objects and remains

between the 'haves' and 'have-nots'. The art of organized warfare seems to have begun at Jericho, nearly seven thousand years before the Bible relates that its walls 'fell down flat' before Joshua.

The round tower—thirty feet in diameter—is a pioneering technological effort in architecture and masonry. It contains a precipitous shaft with twenty-two well-shaped, hammer-dressed steps. It is the work of a genius. Had it been built by the Israelites thousands of years later, or even by the Byzantines three centuries after the birth of Christ, the round tower of Jericho would have been considered a superb piece of masonry. Yet carbon dating places it in the vicinity of 8,000 BC: over five thousand years before the first pyramid at Sakkara. It took nearly half a million years far ahead of its time? 'Jericho cannot have been unique', says Miss to the small highly specialized flint tool kit of the Natufians. The period from Jericho's frail huts to its great round tower spanned barely ten centuries.

Was Jericho the bizarre accident of a singularly gifted society far ahead of its time? 'Jericho cannot have been unique,' says Miss Kenyon. It must have shared its time and place with other great cities which await the excavators' spades. The fate of early Jericho points to this possibility. At some point in time, fire races through its houses. The entrance passage of the round tower is selected as a convenient place for a mass burial and twelve bodies are rudely jammed inside. The fortification wall collapses, the dwellings fall into rubble, their debris filling the large moat. The town lies silent.

Then a surprising thing happens. In about 7,000 BC a new culture constructs another city on top of the ruins of the old, a city far larger than the Bronze Age Jericho which would fall before Joshua and the Israelites. The newcomers represent a total break with Natufian tradition. Materially, everything about them is different —their tools, their construction methods, even their querns and grinding stones. Large, solidly built houses are constructed with mudbricks of a different design, pressed on top with the maker's thumb as keying for mortar. The rooms are rectangular, and arranged round a central court, and there is evidence that some of the openings were equipped with doors. The rooms have clay floors. Their walls too have been given several coats of plaster, usually painted red or cream-coloured and burnished to a high lustre.

The new arrivals were in every way as advanced as the Jerichoans whom they displaced or replaced, with a culture which surely matured in a settled environment elsewhere before their migration to the mound at Jericho. Therefore, at some point in its early

opposite The round tower of Jericho dates to about 8,000 BC. It is one of the earliest monumental constructions of man, an engineering achievement far ahead of its time. Its exact purpose is still a mystery. The opening (covered by a grille) leads to a precipitous staircase descending to the base of tower

development Jericho must have had contemporary parallels. But where? The British archaeologist James Mellaart discovered two very ancient towns in the uplands of Anatolia, Hacilar and Catal Huyuk, the latter giving a carbon dating of about 6,500 BC. There, too, walls and floors are coated with decorated and burnished plaster. Miss Kenyon believes that the people of Catal Huyuk and the new arrivals at Jericho may have had a common origin in an as yet undiscovered early settlement somewhere in northern Syria.

One singular aspect of the new Jericho culture deserves mention. For the greater portion of the digging season of 1953, part of a human skull protruded temptingly from the edge of one of the earthen walls called baulks which divide excavated areas into grid squares, usually five metres each side. These baulks also afford an excavator a clear standing record of the strata of the tell against which to relate the finds within the digging area.

Miss Kenyon scrupulously insists that nothing must be permitted to break the smooth vertical face of an earth baulk. At the very end of the season, however, the lure of the skull was irresistible: Miss Kenyon ordered that it should be carefully removed. When it was brought to her by the site supervisor for examination, she wrote that words could not 'convey any comprehension of our astonishment'.

All that had been visible in the side of the cutting was the top of the cranium. Now, however, it was obvious that this was no ordinary skull. Set into it with great artistry was a remarkable three-dimensional sculpture of a human face. It had been precisely rendered, even to the aquiline nose and the eye sockets. Carefully selected seashells had been set into the sockets to represent the eyes, as with the two-dimensional sculpture found by Garstang years earlier. Over a period of five days a total of seven moulded plaster skulls was removed from the niche in the earth trench—each, it would seem, a realistic portrait from memory of the face which graced the skull in life. It seems, then, that ancestor worship has a most ancient basis—though in the form of a cult of skulls, for which there are no contemporary parallels.

What called into being the phenomenon of Early Jericho? Miss Kenyon estimates that in its prime the early city supported a population of two thousand people. The recovery of querns, flint sickle blades, the remains of digging sticks and specimens of early forms of grain suggests that the foundation of an economy which could support a settlement of such a size was agriculture, supported by the dependable water supply of Ain es-Sultan. Miss Kenyon goes on to suggest that the first communal codes of

opposite A painted and burnished layer of plaster covered this skull of 7,000 BC Jericho (the skull has been partly restored)

The Dead Sea is totally unable to support animal life because of its uniquely high concentration of mineral salts. This salt-encrusted dead tree trunk is graphic testimony to the sea's salinity. Nevertheless, the minerals provided a major means of livlihood for early man and may have been a source of Jericho's great wealth

law enforcement must have sprung from the need to regulate the available water supply for irrigation—the lifeblood of the oasis of Jericho. Some experts do not agree that agriculture alone can explain the wealth which permitted Jericho to exist, to flourish so well so early. The Israeli archaeologist Emmanuel Anati suggests that Jericho lived in part from trading in the resources of the Dead Sea—salt for flavouring, religious ritual and medicinal purposes; bitumen as bonding material for composite tools of flint and wood, and perhaps for caulking the bottoms of primitive boats; and sulphur for lighting fires and for medicinal and ritualistic purposes. That Jericho could have monopolized the source of these materials and created a pool of great wealth behind its walls from commerce in them is quite conceivable. Anati cites, for instance, the discovery of lumps of sulphur in prehistoric levels at Jericho. Obsidian from Anatolia, turquoise matrix from Sinai and shells from the Red Sea were also found.

The city must, at any rate, have been the wonder of its times, sustained by its dependable 'magic' spring, and by a social and political structure which could mobilize a labour pool led by specialists in public works and defence. No other known settlements could rival Jericho in the eighth millennium. When the Commander of the Armies of the Lord tells Joshua that he stands before a holy place, the biblical author is drawing upon an almost mystical reputation and a legend that is surely one of the oldest on earth.

Anyone seeking the roots of ancient Israel must look to the desert.

Never is a sense of the beginning of things more palpable, or the tenacity of life itself more real than to one who has travelled along the parched yellow fringes of the Fertile Crescent—Sinai, the Negev, the Arava, or the empty reaches of the Syrian or Saudi-Arabian deserts. In these places existence in ancient times was the gift of an hour or a day, while salvation was the trickle of subsurface water beneath a layer of loess, or the certain knowledge of an oasis beyond the horizon or the farther reaches of a wadi. Little wonder that even the semi-arid fringes of Palestine seemed 'a land of milk and honey' to migrants from north, south and east who passed through the desert and came to its outer reaches. The ceaseless—often violent—interaction between those who have crossed or are forced to dwell in the yellow land and those who possess the green land is the recurring theme of the history of the Holy Land.

From perhaps the sixth or fifth millennium BC Palestine's destiny is shaped by the interplay of these elements. Settled towns, including Jericho, are overwhelmed or appropriated by intruders far more backward than those they dispossessed. The uprooted are forced to settle in the cruelly demanding environment of the fringe land. The camp-sites and hamlets of new settlers suddenly appear on ground that was formerly untenanted. Archaeologists find that some sort of cultural transmission is taking place. As groups brush against one another in their wanderings, or choose to coalesce and settle together, technological skills, techniques and customs are slowly interchanged and borrowed. A migration of three hundred miles might well encompass two or three generations. Within this slowly-moving vortex the arts of pottery and metalmaking are brought to Palestine.

There were, for instance, the exceptionally talented people who came to live on the rich broad table of black alluvium near the spot just below the southern end of the Sea of Galilee where the River Yarmuk flows out of the mountains of Gilead and joins the Jordan.

Their skilled potters brought a long-established craft to the northern Jordan Valley, and offered a surprising variety of wares. There were jars and vases with rounded necks for carrying water, wine or possibly olive oil, bowls in several sizes for cooking or serving, and larger vessels without rims or necks (called hole-mouth jars), perhaps for storing grain. Yarmukian artistry is also evident here. After shaping his clay, but before baking (or firing), the potter used a sharp point to incise a series of bands, usually round both the neck and waist of the vessel. The bands took the form of zigzags or chevrons. The space within the bands was grooved with

This sherd of Yarmukian pottery, dating from about the fifth millenium BC, was found in the foothills of the mountains of Gilead. It shows the incised zig-zag design used by the Yarmuk people to decorate their pottery

Yarmukian pottery: *left* hole-mouth jars, and *right* two bowls. They are from Sha'ar Hagolan. Some of these examples of Neolithic pottery were decorated with red slip as well as incised patterns

herringbones or parallel notches. With Yarmukian pottery the principle of the wheel may well have come to Palestine, since there is evidence that some of the ceramic ware was shaped on a primitive turntable.

Pottery is man's first pure invention. Clay is the first raw material which he learned to convert into a totally different and useful form through a technological process which he himself devised. The intellectual jump from a cheap, abundant material made plastic by water to a highly durable and useful vessel produced by a controlled amount of heat is vast. Undoubtedly, time and chance were involved. We have seen that men first learned to work clay into mudbrick and coats of painted and finely burnished plaster. It is not difficult to imagine that they also learned to mould rough coatings of hardened mud on the inside of baskets to make them waterproof or to protect the contents from rodents. Chance could have swept such a basket into a fire or onto very hot coals. The baked mud liner opened the door to pottery. A lot of early ceramic ware does, in fact, carry the imprint of woven baskets, and much early pottery decoration is a stylized imitation of basket-weave. But the intellect also had a part to play. Clay shrinks when fired, and if it heats or cools unevenly it may crack. Different types of clay have different characteristics. The choice of shapes and decoration also raised a large number of problems in technique that had to be overcome. The potter had to understand his material, acquire total control of the manufacturing process, and design the wheels and kilns that would make production more efficient. Pottery not only solved a whole range of domestic problems—how to carry liquid, store grain, cook, wash, serve food and transport goods. It also served as an aesthetic vehicle that projects to posterity an image of the temperament and quality of life of the culture which produced it.

Potsherds are one of the primary tools which an archaeologist uses to make patterns out of otherwise unrelated discoveries. His finds have a limited value unless they can tell a story. No matter how irrelevant or insignificant they may seem, clues uncovered by one excavator may suddenly illuminate the dim outlines of a historical enigma when placed alongside pieces of evidence from other sources.

Let us observe the process in operation. Our archaeological clues along the way include an odd assortment of objects: pots, butter churns, burial urns—and noses! The road littered with these bits of evidence carries Palestine into the metal age and the dawn of recorded history. It begins at a group of three low scrub-covered humps of chalky marl on the eastern side of the River Jordan opposite Jericho. The Bedouin call the place Teleilat el-Ghassul, or 'Little Mounds of the Washing Plant'—for they came there to make a coarse type of soap by boiling goat tallow with the caustic ashes of desert sage. In 1929 Father Alexis Mallon, SJ, of the Pontifical Biblical Institute of Jerusalem, who was leading a student field trip through the Ghor, decided to stop there for lunch. His trained eye spotted fragments of shaped flint and pottery round the mounds. Could people have managed to survive and settle in such a wasteland in ancient times?

The next year, Fathers Mallon and Robert Koeppel led an expedition to Ghassul, and in over eight arduous seasons under the searing sun they opened a new era in our understanding of man's progress from the cave to the beginnings of settled life. The humps proved to be the remains of three small hamlets. Together they comprised a village scattered over some eighty acres. At first the Jesuit fathers took the ruins to be the vestiges of the devastation of Sodom and Gomorrah, but later researches have dated the origins of Ghassul to perhaps 3,500 BC, far earlier than the legendary cities of sin could have existed.

There was a number of singular aspects in Ghassulian culture. Firstly, among the varied remains of stone implements were two copper axes. Clearly a new technological revolution was in the making. Secondly, there were artists among these people who specialized in decorating the plaster walls of some Ghassulian buildings with polychrome frescoes of exceptional artistry. Their remains were found on stumps of walls, and on plaster fragments

above The base of this vase from Teleilat el-Ghassul shows the imprint of basketwork
below The 'cornets' from Ghassul were possibly used as drinking cups

round them. Father Koeppel spent many painstaking hours cleaning them. Their only known parallels were found in houses of the even earlier Catal Huyuk, which, as we have seen, were discovered and excavated some years ago on the Anatolian plateau by the British archaeologist James Mellaart. Perhaps this offers a clue to the origins of the Ghassulians. Across the stump of one wall stretched the remnant of a mural that had been over thirteen feet long and was painted in red, yellow, white and black. In it we can identify the rays of the sun and seven pairs of feet, diminishing in size from left to right—perhaps representing a religious rite.

Another distinctive feature of these people is their pottery, one of the most elaborate and varied repertories in Palestinian history. One of the more interesting vessels was not made of earthenware but of hard basalt. Those familiar with the ceremonial vessels of later Israelite sanctuaries will instantly recognize it as a shallow bowl which is attached to a pedestal or stand. The stand has been fenestrated: that is, hollowed out, with sections of the sides removed to form a series of 'windows', an ingenious and attractive way of reducing the weight of the vessel. It was an incense burner and its basic design, translated into pottery, would persist in the Near East for many thousands of years.

Far more puzzling is a pottery object with a hollow barrel-shaped body tapering to small loop handles at either end. The excavators were baffled. A round neck rises from the top of this enigmatic object, reminding one of a conning tower. Other versions of the same object, found at a number of sites on our path, are reminiscent of a stylized submarine, or a representation of a boat or bird. The object became known as a 'bird vessel'. What was it? Some years

above A drawing made after the renowned fresco found on fragments of plaster from the wall of a Ghassulian building. The star is over six and a half feet in diameter

right The strange pottery vessel known as a 'bird vessel'. The restoration is based on a complete one now in an Amman museum

A drawing made by Prof. Nachman Avigad of a house-shaped ossuary found near Hadera. This was one of the first found. Ossuaries were used for reburial of human bones after the flesh had decayed

were to pass before an imaginative Israeli archaeologist offered a simple answer to what had become a major archaeological mystery. We will be coming to it later.

At first Ghassul stood in cultural isolation, but in the ensuing years links in ceramic techniques have been established with the early pottery people of Jericho, Syria and Asia Minor, pointing to the migration of an 'intrusive' culture from the north—that is, an advanced culture which, like the Yarmukian, obviously originated elsewhere. At the time of Mallon's and Koeppel's work virtually nothing was known about the period of the Ghassulians. But in 1934, while excavations were under way at the mounds, a discovery was made to the north-west which further illuminated the times and cultural connections of the Ghassul people within Palestine. In a hill of kurkhar rock which runs parallel to the Plain

Ossuary from Azor in the shape of a house built on stilts, with windows and a projecting 'nose', which may have symbolized the breath of life

opposite A part of the enormous treasure of copper objects found in a Judaean hill cave in Nahal Mishmar, now known as the 'Cave of the Treasure'. It was explored by one of the four expeditions which set out in 1960 and 1961 in order to find evidence of Bar-Kokhba. Volunteers in Pesach Bar-Adon's team hit upon this treasure trove belonging to a period 4,000 years earlier!

of Sharon at Hadera, a cave was found which contained a number of painted ceramic chests or ossuaries. They were about two feet long, nearly two feet high, and one foot wide. Eleazar L. Sukenik, the only lecturer in archaeology at Hebrew University, was told of the find and spent five days in October of that year excavating the cave. He was astonished to discover that these hollow chests, modelled to represent houses, contained human bones. In addition, they were found in association with pottery remains which strongly resembled the earthenware vessels uncovered by the Jesuit fathers at Ghassul. The cave had apparently been dug by hand for the sole purpose of storing these miniature houses of the dead. This burial custom would be revived in Israel in the time of King Herod.

These ossuary 'houses' of Hadera are unique. They are long enough to hold the longest bone in the human body, the thigh bone. And the aperture in one of the ends is just large enough to receive the skull. No remains have ever been found of the houses on which these ossuaries were modelled, but the architectural style and decorative elements indicate that they were made of wood, and enclosed on top with straw or palm leaves. They stood on legs or stilts, and had gabled roofs, which has led some scholars to suggest that their builders originally came from colder, wetter areas far to the north. The stilts are reminiscent of Bronze Age villages found on the marshy fringes of European lakes. The stilts could also have solved the problem of structural support for houses built on the marshlands of the coastal plain of Sharon in the fourth millennium. Sukenik saw these chests as illustrating a belief that the afterlife was an idealized extension of earthly existence. Thus the dead were given permanent dwellings resembling those that they had inhabited in life.

The spiritual beliefs of the Sharon people embodied a rich variety of symbols. The façade of the model house extends above the body of the urn. Its crown is usually decorated with prominently projecting noses, singly or in pairs. Large glaring eyes are often painted on either side of the nose. Frequently pairs of large knobs like beam ends or nail heads also project from the façade. Since 1934 many more of these ossuaries have been found at sites on the coastal plain. For instance, in 1957 fifty were discovered at Azor, three miles south-east of Tel Aviv on the road to Jerusalem. The ossuary caves are restricted to the coastal plain between Hadera and Yavneh. Nonetheless, the area still falls partly within the cultural orbit of Ghassul. For the mysterious 'bird-vases' and the pedestalled incense burners (in pottery rather than basalt) have been found with the ossuaries.

The path from Ghassul to the coastal plain now turns south again, to Beersheba and the Negev. There, fifteen hundred years before the Patriarchs arrived with their families and their flocks, an earlier wave of immigrants tried desperately to construct a permanent way of life in the hostile desert.

In the spring of 1951 a young amateur archaeologist from Kibbutz Mishmar Hanegev named David Alon led a group of professionals to the banks of the Wadi Sab' on the south-western outskirts of modern Beersheba. On a series of low hills that rim the wadi, Alon had found a surface collection of flints and coarse buff postherds. 'It was evident', wrote Jean Perrot, 'that they were the remains of a settlement going back to the fourth millennium BC —a period of which nothing had been known in southern Palestine.'

A housing project was being planned for the site, so archaeologists were pressed to begin work as soon as possible. Perrot started digging at one of the hillocks near a well called Abu Matar, and extended his excavations to the area of a second well, Bir es-Safadi. Six weeks into the excavation, Perrot's workforce was clearing a series of stone foundations on the surface of Abu Matar when a deep trench collapsed, revealing the drama of a desperate struggle for survival dating back some six thousand years. Beneath the trench lay an entire underground village—a network of galleries and rectangular chambers dug twenty feet deep into the loess— burrowed by an immigrant people who literally went underground to escape the heat of the day, the cold of the night and the cruel, wind-lashed sand of the desert.

These were anything but primitive troglodytes. They were a resourceful agricultural people equipped with a full complement of tools who farmed the surface and lived beneath it. Crops were grown on the moisture trapped in the loess from the winter rains. They were exceptional craftsmen, producing elegant work in flint, stone, pottery and ivory. When the soft soil crumbled and their subterranean chambers began to collapse, they replaced them with a series of egg-shaped units for added strength. Later, when these in turn collapsed, they abandoned their experiment in underground living and erected stone or mudbrick dwellings in the pits created by the cave-ins. In the final stages of the settlement's history they moved into mudbrick houses on the surface. Forced to leave their settled and highly developed way of life elsewhere, they had attempted to adapt their previous experience to the Negev. Each failure led them to devise new methods of adjustment. Their experiment in survival lasted about three hundred years before it was finally abandoned. The Beersheba people were swallowed up

An ivory head discovered near Beersheba in 1951 by the Perrot expedition.

opposite A vase in the shape of a man's head found during Garstang's excavations in Jericho and ascribed to a people called the *Hyksos*, which conquered Palestine and Egypt in the 18th century BC (see Chapter 6)

A small stylized ivory statuette of a nude from about 3,500–3,000 BC

opposite A view through Nahal Mishmar showing the 'Treasure Cave' excavated by Pesach Bar-Adon which yielded the rich hoard of copper objects dating from some six thousand years

by oblivion and the Negev again became the outpost of the solitary nomads.

The Beersheba people left something far more substantial behind them than the crumbling shells of their underground houses. When Perrot entered the chamber beneath the collapsed trench he found amid the litter of stone implements and pottery vessels on the floor a collection of copper tools, far more impressive than those of Ghassul. In addition to chisels, points and adzes of pure copper there were metal axes, rings, ornaments and mace heads. But this was a culture of producers as well as users. Large quantities of ore and slag were discovered. The Beersheba people had brought a metal-making industry to Palestine. The age of copper afforded man his first practical alternative to brittle flint and cumbersome stone. In the years ahead primitive metallurgists learned to convert copper into the far more durable bronze, giving farmers and artisans more effective tools, and warriors far deadlier weapons.

Three other points about the Beersheba people need to be emphasized. Among their material remains was a highly refined version of the basalt incense burner with the fenestrated pedestal found at Ghassul. In addition, Dr Moshe Dothan of the Israel Department of Antiquities uncovered the largest example of the puzzling ceramic bird-vessel yet found. There was also a group of artistically impressive cult statuettes and figurines in ivory. Recalling the ossuaries found in Azor and Hadera, which have been dated to the same period, we should take particular note of the faces on the ivory statuettes of the Beersheba people. Extending in an unbroken arc from the forehead to the chin and dwarfing the other features of the ivory figurines is a most prominent nose.

Before the discoveries of Father Mallon, Jean Perrot, Moshe Dothan, Nelson Glueck, Yohanan Aharoni, Emmanuel Anati, Benno Rothenberg and others, it had been thought that the Negev was an all but empty stage until biblical times. Wide-ranging scientific explorations of the desert now point to a density of population in the Copper Age which would not be equalled again until the advent of the Nabataeans, Romans and Byzantines some four millennia later. Evidence of literally hundreds of sites and stations has been recovered from this earlier period—places where men camped in their wandering, or tried to plant the roots of settlement in order to hunt, to farm, to feed their flocks, to mine and smelt their copper.

And there were some places where they sought refuge from great dangers at which we can only guess. Such a place is 'Scout's

Cave,' an almost inaccessible eyrie in the cliffs high above the marbled face of the Judaean Desert. There, in 1961, the archaeologist Pesach Bar-Adon, his small staff and a crew of forty volunteers came upon a breathtaking archaeological treasure. 'What we found', Bar-Adon recalled, 'was enough for twenty archaeologists.' His team, Expedition C, was one of four combing the caves of the Judaean Hills for ancient writings. After a week's reconnaissance of his assigned area, Bar-Adon decided to concentrate on Scout's Cave, which is gouged deeply into the angry rock high on the south face of Nahal Mishmar, a precipitous wadi running west from the Dead Sea. The entrance lay 165 feet below the plateau which enclosed Bar-Adon's camp site. A dull black layer of soot on the vaulted ceiling showed that camp fires had once been lit within, and on the floor were ancient potsherds, pieces of glass and straw and a human skull.

Bar-Adon, now in his early sixties, erect and robust with a flowing mane of white hair, projects an aura of serenity and vigour. He reminds one of a determined but gentle prophet, whose strength is the gift of the desert. He did in fact spend several of his early years in Palestine with Bedouin nomads, as a shepherd. 'The desert is the source of all things. You can no more explain it than you can explain love. . . ' The ancient path to Scout's Cave had long since fallen away. From the sheer edge of the cave mouth to the rocks below is a straight drop of 820 feet. Bar-Adon was lowered to the entrance on a rope, propelling himself into an arc like the weight on the end of a plumb-line and dropping heavily into the cave on the inward swing. 'You stave off terror only by keeping so busy there's no time to think about it. . . ' The team's efforts continually raised huge plumes of dust from centuries of dried bat dung which coated the cave floor like a thick carpet. Masks were impractical. Suffocating heat stifled them and the sweaty cloths over their mouths and noses were soon caked thickly with dirt. 'The only solution was to rotate. Part of the group worked inside while the rest dug at the cave mouth near the cleaner air. Every half hour, we changed places. . . '

The cave had twice been a haven of refuge. The upper layer of floor debris contained belongings of Jewish fugitives from Rome at the beginning of the Christian era. Beneath this layer, and three thousand years earlier in time, Bar-Adon found evidence that others had also hidden here. There were a large plaited straw basket for sifting grain, straw matting, a woven rope, spikelets of grain, cloves of garlic, pottery vessels and fragments decorated with the familiar incised herring-bone pattern—and the upper part of a bird

above Pesach Bar-Adon proudly examining the copper treasure
below Perhaps the outstanding object of the treasure—the ibex-headed 'sceptre'

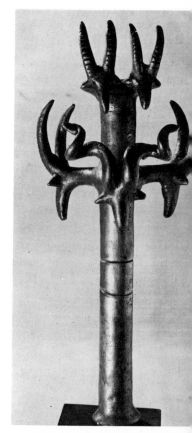

vessel: all perfectly preserved in the still, dry desert cave. After twelve days the work was halted, but the leaders of the cave search decided to remount the expedition the following year. Bar-Adon wrote at the end of his 1960 report: 'The resemblance of the objects found here with those from the Tuleilat, Ghassul and Beersheba cultures is remarkable.'

On the afternoon of 23 April 1961, one of Expedition C's volunteers, a student from Argentina named Ruth Pecherski, approached Bar-Adon at the mouth of Scout's Cave. She was literally shaking with excitement. . . ' 'I was frightened and thought she was seriously ill. 'Ruthie', I shouted, 'what's the matter?' A volunteer from the Israeli Army who had been digging with her, Freddie Halperin, approached the archaeologist with a gleaming piece of wrought copper in his hand. 'Bar-Adon', he said quietly, 'We have more.'

The elaborately decorated crown of the sceptre shown on the opposite page

The treasure lay behind a sloping stone which covered a natural niche in the north wall of an inner cave chamber. It was wrapped carefully in a large straw mat. Nothing could be touched until the next day when a photographer arrived. 'I remember it until today. For a month afterward, I couldn't sleep, but I never got tired. . . ' It took three hours to remove and record the objects—529 in all, including a number of metal axes and chisels. All but thirteen items were of pure copper ('We didn't even know what to call many of them. . . ') There were 240 'mace heads', some round, some oval, others flattened or shaped like discs. There were eighty wands or sceptres, some hollow. A similar sceptre had been found at Beersheba. There were ten 'crowns', two staffs, one shaped like a flower, and three copper jars. The skill of design and ornamentation in the new copper medium is amazing. The objects are decorated with spirals, parallel lines, concentric circles and herringbones, incised or in relief. In the entire collection there are no duplicates; each object is unique. One, for instance, is surmounted by figurines of birds, and what appear to be two portals or entranceways. Projecting from the portals, from the top of the rim, and from either side of a 'window' cut in the front of the rim itself, are the same knobs or nail heads which adorn the burial urns from Hadera and Azor. Other symbolic motifs are equally evocative. Two of the wands or sceptres are surmounted by human faces, dominated by exceptionally prominent noses. Bar-Adon comments: 'The nose. . . no doubt symbolizes the breath of life. The same is true of the fertility emblems which embody, with various nuances, the concept of revival and growth. . . All this implies a widespread belief in a life after death.'

The mystery of the pottery 'bird vessel' from Beersheba is solved to the satisfaction of most archaeologists. Here it is shown together with a goatskin milk churn still used by Bedouin. The similarity is remarkable

In 1954 the Tel Aviv archaeologist Jacob Kaplan produced a solution to the mystery of the bird vessels, after finding a perfect specimen on a dig near Jaffa. He recalled that the Bedouin use a device which is similarly shaped, but made of goatskin, to churn butter. It is suspended by a rope from a series of poles, and only a minimal amount of energy is needed to keep it swinging back and forth. The motion agitates the milk, slapping it against the blunt end of the vessel. A comparison between the ancient and contemporary versions bears out Kaplan's theory. The solution of the enigma had required over two decades.

Who were the people who made the copper treasure? Anthropologists who examined skeletal remains found both at Beersheba and in Scout's Cave identified two distinct racial types who had obviously been living side by side—the Mediterranoids of the old Natufian sites, and an intrusive strain called Armenoids. These Armenoids are characterized by a short broad skull, a large amount of hair, and a long nose with virtually no bridge which arcs prominently from the forehead.

Analysis of the copper showed that the ore from which the copper treasure was made was local in origin. But the copper in the axes and chisels contains a very high percentage of arsenic, similar to that found in the Caucasus or Iran. Bar-Adon has written tentatively: 'It seems, at this stage of research at least, that the connections of our culture point towards the north.' This conclusion also fits in with those drawn from Ghassul and Yarmuk.

One more vital archaeological landmark lies on our path— the lush oasis of En-gedi five and a half miles to the north—an arduous walk of perhaps three or four hours from Nahal Mishmar. On a rock terrace directly north of the spring, Israeli archaeologists working between 1957 and 1962 excavated a large building complex some sixty-six by ninety-eight feet, which they identified as the remains of a large temple. Usually religious sites of this kind are rich with finds. In this case, artifacts were strangely absent. It was as though all the material possessions of this obviously important shrine had been removed by its priests or worshippers. Only one fragmentary object of any importance was found, a ceramic figurine of either a donkey or an ox bearing on its back two butter churns similar to those identified by Kaplan.

The foundations of the En-gedi temple seen against the Judaean hills

Bar-Adon and others believe that the temple at En-gedi was the central place of worship for many of the peoples of the entire area—a site of veneration and pilgrimage for those as far away as Beersheba and perhaps even the plain of Sharon. Imminent danger impelled them, as it did the people of nearby Qumran four thousand years later, to hide their coveted religious treasures in the caves of the same area, with the intention of retrieving them when the threat had passed.

Like the later Essenes, the southern cultures of the copper age were never able to return. The light of civilized life was snuffed out at Beersheba, Ghassul, En-gedi and other southern sites in the late fourth millennium BC. However, similar immigrant groups had by this time established roots on firmer ground—on the fertile well-watered soil of the more hospitable north. From these crude settlements, the great fortified tells of Meggido, Gezer, Beth-shean and Lachish would slowly spring to dominate the countryside in biblical times.

From early Jericho onwards the foundations had been laid for an astonishing leap forward towards the world's first great social orders: metalwork and the inventions of pottery and weaving; the sophistication of the arts, architecture and irrigation; the growth of trade; the organization of primitive spiritual beliefs into religious systems; the development of urban administration and rudimentary legal institutions. Five thousand years ago man as we know him came to possess all the basic knowledge and skills he would ever have. Since then his techniques for exploiting resources and the use of materials have steadily improved. But the essential elements of what he is and has done emerged from the womb of Palestine and the Fertile Crescent even before the age of copper merged into the age of bronze. The culmination of this great process did not occur in Palestine. It was at either end of the green arc of the Near East that the light of civilization now began to blaze—in Mesopotamia and then in Egypt. Each in its turn would catapult Palestine into the dawn of history.

5 The Patriarchs and the World of Genesis

Clues which mark the passage of a handful of pastoral wanderers such as the patriarchal bands are as insubstantial as the breezes of the night: tents and jars of animal skin, vessels of wood, baskets of straw. Even today, the remains of an encampment of Bedouin are swallowed up by the desert only hours after they have taken down their tents and moved on.

A biblical archaeologist's job is not to prove that the Bible is true, but to identify those specific elements in it whose historical relevance can be established: not whether Abraham, Isaac and Jacob did exist, but whether they could have existed within the cultural, geographical and historical framework of Genesis. This they have answered with amazing thoroughness.

Recent decades have produced a deluge of evidence—much of it still being digested, deciphered and translated—which demonstrates, in the words of the historian John Bright: '. . . that the patriarchal narratives, far from reflecting the circumstances of a later day, fit precisely in the age of which they purport to tell.' Beyond this, archaeological discoveries have illuminated other facets of the lore of Genesis, revealing previously unknown aspects of the land from which the fathers of Israel came, and the profound influence of Mesopotamian culture on Hebrew institutions and ideas.

We know that as early as the late fourth millennium BC the Tigris-Euphrates basin was the cradle of a mighty civilization. A people called the Sumerians mastered the basic laws of hydraulics to irrigate their fields, invented writing and mathematics, created well-planned cities with lofty palaces and temples, and established great artistic and literary traditions. The light of art, science and the humanities burned bright in Sumer two thousand years before Israel became a nation. Records tell us, too, that as early as about

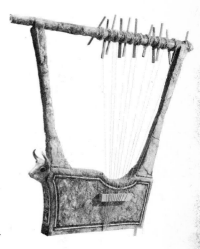

Lyre decorated with a bull's head from the royal cemetery at Ur in Southern Mesopotamia. It is believed that Semitic nomads carried the lyre to Canaan and introduced it to Egypt

opposite Upper part of a Sumerian male statuette (about 30 inches high) in diorite, dated to about 2,290–2,255 BC— shortly before the time of Abraham

Alabaster head of a man,
Imperial Akkadian period,
2,460–2,290 BC

2,400 BC. the leadership of the Sumerian world passed to the Akkadians—the first of two waves of Semitic infiltration from the desert which would sweep over the 'Land of the Two Rivers' before Abraham's departure from Haran in northern Mesopotamia for Canaan.

The first non-biblical evidence linking the earliest Hebrew tradition with Mesopotamian soil was found by pure chance. In 1862 the Keeper of Oriental Antiquities at the British Museum in London noticed a rather nondescript young visitor who had all but set up house in the galleries of Assyrian antiquities found at Nineveh by Austen Layard. George Smith was an apprentice printing engraver whose heart was hardly in his work. His lunch and dinner hours, as well as his holidays, were spent either in studying and restudying the Assyrian finds at the museum, or in reading the popular and scientific accounts of Layard and others in Mesopotamia. The museum official was so impressed by Smith's enthusiasm that he employed him to sort, catalogue and repair the immense collection of inscribed clay tablets from Nineveh.

These cuneiform texts constituted in large part the 'national library' of King Ashurbanipal of Assyria, who in the seventh century BC ordered them to be collected from every corner of the kingdom and stored in his own archives. They represented the sum total of the written heritage of Mesopotamian civilization, which had been copied and recopied by scribes for hundreds of generations, stretching back to the days of Sumer and Akkad in the third millennium BC. Layard and others had resurrected nearly twenty thousand tablets from the royal libraries of Nineveh, and for ten years Smith worked to put them in order, learning to decipher and read cuneiform in the process.

One day in 1872, Smith was studying a fragment, the now-famous Tablet XI. Suddenly, he sat bolt upright and caught his breath. He reread the passage. This is what it contained:

> I looked about for coast lines in the sea:
> In each of fourteen (regions)
>   There emerged a region (Mountain).
> On Mount Nisir the ship came to a halt.
> Mount Nisir held the ship fast,
>   Allowing no motion.
> One day, a second day, Mount Nisir held the ship fast,
>   Allowing no motion. . .
>   When the seventh day arrived,
>   I sent forth and set free a dove.

The dove went forth, but came back;
Since no resting-place for it was visible, she turned round.

'On reviewing the evidence', Smith announced to a stunned meeting of the Society of Biblical Archaeology, 'it is apparent that the events of the Flood narrated in the Bible and the inscription are the same, and occur in the same order.' One of the members of the group before whom Smith read his paper was the Prime Minister, William Gladstone. The date was 3 December 1872.

Newspapers thundered the news of Smith's discovery round the world. The young self-taught scholar became a celebrity. The *Daily Telegraph* and the British Museum enthusiastically underwrote three expeditions which sent Smith personally to Nineveh in a search for more cuneiform tablets. He turned up over three thousand. But less than four years after Tablet XI catapulted him to fame, Smith had died of amoebic dysentery in Aleppo.

He had succeeded in piecing together a complete version of the Mesopotamian flood saga before his death. It leaves us in no doubt about the connection of early Hebrew tradition with Mesopotamia.

What of the Patriarchs themselves? According to Genesis, the Mesopotamian town of Haran in the area that the Bible calls 'Aram of the Two Rivers' was where Abraham lived, and it was from there that he emigrated with his wife Sarah and his cousin Lot when commanded to go 'from your country and your kindred and your father's house to a land that I will show you'. From his 'country', which lay between the northern reaches of the Tigris and Euphrates, Abraham departed for Canaan. From here, a wife was brought for Isaac, and to the same area Jacob fled from Esau to spend twenty years with his uncle, Laban.

Excavations by David Storm Rice between 1951 and 1959, together with documents dated to the nineteenth and eighteenth centuries BC, the time within which the emigration of Abraham must be placed, show Haran to have been a flourishing city. Genesis says that one of Abraham's brothers was called Haran. The documents also speak of towns in the same neighbourhood called Nakhur (Nahor was the name of Abraham's grandfather and brother, and also the town from which Rebekah was brought to Canaan) and Til-Turakhi (Terah was the father of Abraham). In one text the word Laba-an is mentioned. Whether the names of Abraham's kinsmen were actually clan names which were given to or taken from these places is a riddle scholars may never solve. The point is that these ancient names are solely Mesopotamian in origin, as, Genesis tells us, were the Patriarchs themselves.

Ashurbanipal (668–627 BC, King of Assyria, hunting wild asses. This relief was found in the North Palace at Nineveh. The king, one of the world's first known antiquarians, assembled a vast quantity of the ancient records of Mesopotamia on cuneiform tablets

What is more, Professor Albright has brought together written evidence that the patriarchal names came into use from one end of the Fertile Crescent to the other in the second millennium BC. Beginning in northern Mesopotamia, there is the name Ya-ah-qu-ub-i-lu (Jacob) in a tablet dated to the late eighteenth century BC. In Canaan in the fifteenth century BC there was a town named after the head of a clan who had lived there previously; it was called Ya'qob-el, which means: 'May El protect.' El was the father of the Canaanite pantheon of gods. The name Aba(m)-ram(a) is also found in texts from the same period. And in Egypt in the nineteenth century BC the name Aburahana was used. There is no want of archaeological testimony that Asian nomads not only could but did follow the same route as that of Abraham—from Mesopotamia to Canaan to Egypt.

An alabaster vase from Uruk. It stands three feet tall, and is a product of early Sumerian art from the late 4th millenium BC

The fortunes of ex-engraver George Smith have a modern and equally exciting parallel. Like Smith, Dr Samuel Kramer of the University of Pennsylvania Museum in Philadelphia has devoted much of his life to extracting knowledge from a vast pool of cuneiform writing. Kramer's main interest has been the archives made up of thirty thousand clay tablets found over half a century ago at Nippur, which was the centre of a Sumerian cult to Enlil, the storm god, enforcer of the will of the divine pantheon. Nippur was also the seat of a flourishing scribal school, whose copyists were assigned to the preservation of the literature of Sumer.

In 1952 Kramer pieced together a literary puzzle from twelve fragments and tablets, stored in part at the Museum of the Ancient Orient in Istanbul, and also at his own museum in Philadelphia. Together they comprised the greater portion of a poem, based on a power struggle between the Sumerian hero Enmerkar, ruler of Uruk in about 2,600 BC, and the state of Aratta, which is believed to have existed somewhere in Iran. The poem describes Sumer's 'golden age', when:

Once upon a time, there was no snake, there was no scorpion.
There was no hyena, there was no lion,
There was no wild dog, no wolf.
There was no fear, no terror,
Man had no rival.

In this Utopia, the world thrived in peace, under wise leadership, and in security, and '. . . the people in obedience, to Enlil spoke in one tongue'.

There the poem ended, in mid-air. The final piece of the puzzle was still missing—about six concluding lines, Kramer judged. Where was it to be found? Kramer's literary trail led to the compact galleries of the Ashmolean Museum in Oxford. In 1967, fifteen years after he had assembled the main body of the poem, the missing fragment—no larger than three inches square—was found at the Ashmolean. It had been purchased in Iraq in 1924. As Kramer predicted, the fragment contained the missing six lines, which produced a sensation rivalling Smith's in every way. The missing portion read:

> Enki, the lord of abundance, of the true command,
> The lord of wisdom, the [?] of the land.
> The leader of the gods,
> Endowed with wisdom, the lord of Eridu,
> Changed the speech of their mouth. . .
> The speech of man that [until then] had been one.

From Ankara, Philadelphia and Oxford, to Genesis!

'Come', said the men of Shinar, 'let us build for ourselves a city, and a tower with its top in the heavens, and let us make a name for ourselves. . . 'And the Lord said, 'Behold, they are one people, and they have all one language; and this is only the beginning of what they will do; and nothing that they propose to do will now be impossible for them. Come, let us go down, and there confuse their language, that they may not understand one another's speech.'

Is there any basis for such towers as this 'with its top in the heavens', on which the authors of Genesis set their version of the pre-biblical

below The great *Ziggurat*, or stepped temple-tower, built by Ur-Nammu (2,250–2,233 BC) at Ur, and dedicated to the moon god Nanna. Such a building may have inspired the story of the Tower of Babel

myth? There are the soaring multi-tiered ziggurats which once towered over the great cities of Mesopotamia—for instance over Ur, Nippur, Uruk and Nimrud. The temple-tower which understandably most stimulates our wonder is Etemenanki in Babylon: the 'House of the Foundation Platform of Heaven and Earth', the resting place on his flights from heaven of Marduk, principal god of Babylon. Etemenanki was finished by King Nebuchadnezzar, who carried the people of Israel into their first exile in 587 BC. But it was begun by Hammurabi the Law-Giver, whose reign falls within the time of the earliest Hebrews, and it must have been a wonder of its age.

Though archaeology cannot produce a cuneiform document signed or witnessed by Abraham, Isaac or Jacob, it can bring us closer to the Patriarchs, help us to understand them in a more human way. In Genesis the reader faces a problem of identification. He might feel closer to the characters if only he had a better knowledge of the customs and social conventions that motivated their behaviour. Why would Sarah, Abraham's wife, give him her servant as a concubine? What lay behind the complex relationship which bound Jacob to his Uncle Laban for so long?

Again, it was Mesopotamia and archaeology which produced the answers. For some years the poor peasants of Kirkuk in northeastern Iraq near a northern branch of the Tigris River had been reaping a windfall, thanks to the eccentric tastes of rich Westerners. They were prepared to pay good money for tables of baked clay with mysterious wedge-shaped markings on them which native ploughs would turn up from time to time, or perceptive eyes would spot lying on the surface. In 1925, an Arab *fellah* trying to sell a sackful of these otherwise useless stones sparked off an expedition by Dr Edward Chiera, an accomplished American Assyriologist, which discovered ancient Nuzi. The town, whose origins could be traced back to about 3,000 BC, reached its zenith some 1,500 years later as the fiefdom of a wealthy aristocracy dominated by a non-Semitic people called *Huru*, who had begun spreading south and west from the area of Lake Van in Armenia in the last half of the third millennium BC. By the time Nuzi reached its prime, the Hurrians, as scholars call them, had become enough of a political and military factor in northern Mesopotamia, Syria and Palestine for their area to warrant the title 'Huru Land' or 'Hor' in contemporary Egyptian records. These people were the elusive 'Horim' or 'Horites' of the Bible, which places them as far south as Edom in southern Transjordan. Their centre of power,

A detail from the diorite stelae of Susa inscribed with the law code of Hammurabi (1728–1686 BC) in cuneiform

however, was farther to the north-east, where they adapted Akkadian writing to their own tongue, and borrowed certain aspects of Mesopotamian culture. But some of their traditions were unique, and this fact is central to the great interest they hold for us.

In Nuzi, the Hurrian nobles built a temple, an impressive palace with painted rooms, and large villas with archive chambers in

Two scribes holding clay tablets and writing sticks for making the tablets

A cuneiform tablet showing a seal impression as drawn in Layard's report on finds from Nineveh and Babylon published in 1858

opposite A collection of Canaanite jewellery including a necklace and bronze mirror found at Tel-el-Ajjul. Sir Flinders Petrie described them as *Hyksos* jewellery

which they assiduously stored the cuneiform records of their legal, social and business affairs. This was the source of the *fellahin* windfall. Chiera broke into the first of these private 'files' in the final days of the first season. They were the records of an enterprising noble named Tehip-tilla. In the seasons which followed, the excavators of Nuzi collected four thousand of these tablets, not only the dockets of the great families of Nuzi, but some public records of the palace as well.

This documentary profile of a lost Mesopotamian community, no less than the memorabilia of a dusty family attic, has a universal appeal. Their marriage contracts, deeds of sale, family quarrels, slave agreements and documents of adoption have brought us closer to the lives of the Patriarchs. For instance, there is the case of Shennima, who is given in adoption by his real father to an apparently well-to-do man of Nuzi named Shuriha-ilu. Shennima is named as heir of all his step-father's properties, but there is another important proviso. 'If Shuriha-ilu should have a son of his own, as the principal (son) he shall take a double share; Shennima shall then be next in order. . .' In Nuzi, it seems, a childless couple could legally adopt a younger acquaintance, stranger or even slave to tend their property, handle their affairs, look after them in their older years, arrange a proper burial and, in exchange, become their principle beneficiary. But if the couple were blessed with a son in the interim, the adopted party would lose his rights as primary heir. At last, readers of the patriarchal stories could understand Abraham's complaint: 'O Lord God, what wilt Thou give me, for I continue childless, and the heir of my house is Eliezer of Damascus. . . a slave born in my house will be my heir.' And God assures him: 'This man shall not be your heir; your own son shall be your heir.' It became immediately apparent that the adoption procedure of Nuzi was also practised by the Patriarchs.

The parallels continue. In the Nuzi agreement cited above, the adopted son Shennima is promised the hand of Shuriha-ilu's daughter in marriage. Her name is Kelim-ninnu. 'If Kelim-ninnu bears (children), Shennima shall not take another wife; but if Kelim-ninnu does not bear, Kelim-ninnu shall acquire a woman of the land of Lullu as wife for Shennima. . .Futhermore, Yalampa is given as a handmaid to Kelim-ninnu.' The modern conceit about romantic love has no place in the codes of Nuzi–or in those of the Patriarchs. The purpose of marriage was not only to preserve family status and property, but to beget children, preferably males. Kelim-ninnu would provide her husband with the handmaid Yalampa if she herself could not produce an heir.

Therefore, there was nothing immoral in concubinage, and we now understand the childless Sarah's seeming liberality toward Abraham in the matter of her Egyptian handmaid Hagar: ' "Behold now, the Lord has prevented me from bearing children; go into my maid; it may be that I shall obtain children by her". . . so. . . Sarah, Abraham's wife, took Hagar the Egyptian, her maid, and gave her to Abraham her husband as wife.'

A full understanding of the complex drama involving Jacob, his wives and his uncle Laban long evaded scholars, until they encountered the terse contractual arrangement at Nuzi involving the adoption of Wullu by a man named Nashwi:

> As long as Nashwi is alive, Wullu shall provide food and clothing; when Nashwi dies, Wullu shall become the heir. If Nashwi has a son of his own, he shall divide (the estate) equally with Wullu, but the son of Nashwi shall take the gods of Nashwi. Furthermore, he gave his daughter Nuhuya in marriage to Wullu, and if Wullu takes another wife he shall forfeit the lands and buildings of Nashwi. Whoever defaults shall make compensation with 1 mina of silver and 1 mina of gold.

Among his relatives in 'the land of the people of the east', Jacob enters into a relationship of service with the wily Laban, which involves not only his marriage to the daughters Leah and Rachel, but a share of Laban's estate, which he has helped create. 'I have learned by divination', Laban tells him, 'that the Lord has blessed me because of you; name your wages, and I will give it.' Jacob, like the adopted son of Nashwi, has obviously helped provide Laban with 'food and clothing'. In exchange, Laban seems more than willing to grant Jacob's request for a portion of his flocks.

In the absence of natural heirs, for none are mentioned at the beginning of the biblical tale, Jacob seems to be a counterpart of Wullu, who 'shall become the heir'. He has acquired wives, and, as in the case of Wullu, he is warned by Laban not to 'take wives besides my daughters. . . remember, God is witness between you and me'. After twenty years, however, sons of Laban suddenly appear on the scene, complaining that 'Jacob has taken all that was our father's'. Jacob is now clearly out of favour, because he in turn complains to his wives: 'I have served your father with all my strength; yet your father has cheated me and changed my wages ten times. . .' He seems to have been superseded as sole heir and, like Wullu, must legally give way to someone else.

He cunningly appropriates what he considers to be his rightful portion of Laban's livestock, and heads for Canaan. Rachel, too,

opposite The partly-gilded 'Copper Snake', or *nechushtan*, found at the ancient Egyptian temple to Hathor, the goddess of mining, at Timna in the Arava by Dr. Benno Rothenberg. It was the most coveted find of the dig, and links Moses and the tradition of Exodus to the itinerant Kenites, who played a central role in the pivotal Hebrew saga (see page 113)

appropriates something in a display of sympathy for her husband's sense of injustice. This is the pivotal point which few understood before reading the agreement of Nashwi and Wullu. Rachel 'stole her father's household gods'—small idols, called *teraphim* in the biblical story. Why were they so important? Examples of these idols have been found at Nuzi. The implication of the Wullu text is that these *teraphim* were the symbols of family leadership, the emblem of the right of patrimony for the man who inherited them. It is conceivable that they had legal standing, and that possession of the family gods was nine-tenths of the law. It now seems clear that Rachel steals them to guarantee this future role for her husband which has been formally challenged by Laban's natural sons.

'If Nashwi has a son of his own. . . the son of Nashwi shall take the gods of Nashwi.' 'Why did you steal my god?' thunders Laban at Jacob. We can now understand that this is a vital clash within the clan of Abraham over a point of law which goes far beyond mere theft. The question is whether the leadership of the Hebrews falls to those in Canaan, or those who stayed behind in Paddan-aram. It is also perhaps the final symbolic break by the Patriarchs of Canaan with the polytheism of the East, because Jacob angrily responds: 'Any one with whom you find your gods shall not live. In the presence of our kinsmen point out what I have that is yours, and take it.'

How, by whom or where these distinctive Hurrian manners and *mores* were transmitted to the Hebrews remains a mystery for scholars. There is no evidence of any patriarchal connections with Nuzi, though there is proof that there were Hurrians in Canaan. The Nuzi tablets have been dated to about 1,500 BC, though the customs they reveal could have originated much earlier. That there was contact, however, is clear, and it is more evident in the annals of the Patriarchs than in later parts of the Bible.

Shortly before 2,000 BC there occurred the second great Semitic invasion in the Near East. It came less as a sudden tidal wave than as a gradual flood—infiltrating bands of Semitic-speaking nomads from the desert fringes of the Fertile Crescent who flowed down the great funnel lying between the Euphrates and Tigris rivers. From there, they spilled westwards into Syria and Palestine, and even to the borders of Egypt itself. In all likelihood, nothing linked them but common trials in the desert, their language and their hunger for the green land. Culturally, they brought little with them. The settled peoples of civilized Mesopotamia called them *Amurru* (Westerners).

A life-size statue of a goddess holding a water pot. It was discovered in the palace of Zimri-lim (ca. 2,040–1,830 BC) at Mari

Scholars see these *Amurru* as the Amorites of the Bible, a term which the Old Testament authors often used interchangeably with 'Canaanites'. They did, in fact, overwhelm and merge with the original population of Canaan. And they brought an end to the golden age of Sumer and Akkad. By the eighteenth century BC, Amorite kings ruled every major city between the Tigris and the Euphrates.

Within the seething waters of migration, conquest, resettlement and dislocation were the Patriarchs. Can we discern them in the flood? The written texts of this period recovered by archaeologists may again help us. The Old Testament word for Hebrews is '*ibrim*' (singular '*ibri*'), from the Semitic root '*br*', which means 'to pass through', or 'to migrate from place to place'. In the entire text of the Old Testament, the word 'Hebrew' is used only thirty-four times—usually by Abraham and his descendants when speaking to foreigners, or by foreigners when speaking of or to them. They refer to themselves as '*Bene Yisra'el*', the sons of Israel. 'I was . . . stolen out of the land of the Hebrews', Joseph tells the chief butler of Pharaoh in the Egyptian prison. 'See,' complains Potiphar's wife, 'he has brought among us a Hebrew to insult us.'

Documents recovered by archaeologists from Ur to Egypt, spanning the beginning of the Amorite invasion at the end of the third millennium BC to the eleventh century BC refer to a kind or type of people called '*Apiru* or *Habiru*. Now, to reduce a highly complex etymological question to its simplest terms, many leading scholars relate this intriguing term to the same Semitic root, '*br*'. Professor Albright argues that a phonetic change occurred in ancient times in which the labial 'p' sound became a 'b', leading to a whole series of transliterated English spellings. What role do *Habiru* play in these various documents? The answer is not a simple one.

In a group of texts from Egypt listing the names of actual or potential rebel rulers and their cities within the Egyptian sphere of influence in the nineteenth/eighteenth centuries BC there appears the name of 'Apiru-'Anu, the ruler of Pella on the east bank of the Jordan opposite Beth-shean. The *Habiru* are to be found again within the cache of twenty thousand tablets recovered from the 250-room palace of King Zimri-lim, an Amorite who ruled the powerful city of Mari on the Upper Euphrates in the eighteenth century BC. In one letter the king is warned by a military aide that an Amorite ruler named Yapakh-Adad has 'made ready the settlement Zallul on this side of the bank of the Euphrates River, with two thousand troops of the *Habiru* of the land'.

A small terra cotta plaque with the figure of a seated woman wearing an elaborate flounced dress and mantle, and a high crown. Scholars ascribe it to the Sumerian or Old Babylonian period between the 22nd and 17th centuries BC. This type of small figurine may be similar to the *teraphim* mentioned in the Bible and the family gods referred to in the Nuzi texts

American archaeologist Dr. Nelson Glueck, who died in 1971, examining a so-called 'teapot' from the time of the Amorite invasion

Who were the *Habiru?* They seem to have worn a cloak of many colours, which suited a variety of roles. Some have called them merchant princes; others, untutored Bedouin. Scholars such as Professor Albright and the Israeli archaeologist Shmuel Yeivin maintain that they were probably semi-nomadic caravaneers who organized, provisioned and guided the slow-moving donkey caravans in the pay of traders who plied the trading lanes of the Near East in ancient times. In hard times they might have taken to pastoral pursuits, or hired themselves out as mercenaries, taken to downright robbery, or sold themselves as slaves. Others have classed them as stateless aliens, or rejected or displaced elements in the social whirlpool of Amorite times.

The name 'Habiru' was the symbol of second-class citizenship, the badge of inferior status conferred on those who refused, failed or were denied permission to settle in those turbulent days. This suggests that while all Habiru were certainly not Abrahamites, the Patriarchs may well have been classed among the *Habiru;* and, in time, the term came to apply to them.

If what we know about the Patriarchs in Mesopotamia is largely circumstantial, what we know about their entry into Canaan is virtually non-existent. But an adventuring American rabbi who found himself more at home in the desert than the synagogue gave us a good idea of when they arrived. After his ordination in 1923, the late Dr Nelson Glueck dedicated himself to biblical scholarship through archaeological exploration. By 1932 he was in Jerusalem under Professor Albright at the American Schools for Oriental Research. 'To me,' he once said, 'archaeology is like burning the mist off the Bible.' The object of his research was the *terra incognita* of the south Transjordanian Desert and the Negev. 'The more I thought about the Negev,' he wrote, 'the more my curiosity about it was aroused. Was it a real desert or only seemingly so? Was it actually as bare and barren and inhospitable as had for so many centuries been taken for granted?'

In the tradition of Edward Robinson, he set out to satisfy his curiosity, the only companions in his early travels being a Bible, an Arab guide and a camel. In twenty years of desert exploration, Glueck placed over 1,500 sites on the all but empty map of Palestine's southern desert. By studying surface ruins and their pottery fragments, he not only found a way to pinpoint the arrival of the Patriarchs, but also revolutionized our understanding of the dating of the Exodus.

Using his Bible as a historical atlas, Nelson Glueck hypothesized that the parched area of desert at the southern end of the Dead Sea must have contained thriving population centres in the time of Abraham. When Abraham and Lot decide to take their families and flocks and go their separate ways because 'the land could not support both of them dwelling together', Lot chooses Sodom and the 'cities of the plain' because 'the Jordan Valley was well watered everywhere' in the now desolate region of Zoar, Sodom and Gomorrah.

Glueck found that this area had been thickly dotted with strings of settlements in the twenty-first century BC, in all likelihood founded by land-hungry elements of the great Amorite invasion who failed to carve out living space in richer climes. Two hundred years later, these villages were suddenly abandoned as though a curtain had dropped on the desert stage, paralleling the mysterious disappearance of the Ghassul and Beersheba people a thousand years earlier. The arrival of the 'Abrahamites', therefore, must have occurred within these two hundred years. Glueck concluded: 'Either the Age of Abraham coincides with the. . . period between the twenty-first and nineteenth centuries BC, or the entire saga dealing with the Patriarchs must be dismissed, so far as its historical value is concerned, from scientific consideration.'

It can be argued that the biblical authors simply attached popular legends about the fiery destruction of Sodom and Gomorrah to the patriarchal narrative—a holocaust which scientists now ascribe to a great earthquake and ignition of natural gases which escaped from great fissures in the thin crust of the Jordan rift. The weight of evidence, however, points to the arrival of the early Hebrews within or near the time of the apocalypse that overwhelmed the 'cities of the plain'. Subsequent discoveries tend to support Glueck's conclusion that the Age of Abraham began in Canaan early in the second millennium BC.

The Patriarchs belonged to the epoch of the Amorite penetration, which moulded the features of the Canaan pledged to Moses and won by Joshua. Unlike their Semitic contemporaries, the Abrahamites were not yet ready to settle down. Their particular experiences had begun to fashion them into a people apart, who would always retain some of the essential qualities of the wayfaring *Habiru*. They would also convert the vicissitudes they had experienced into a system of socio-religious ideas and a will to survive which withstood the shocks of changing fortunes. And this process operated as invariably in their contacts with Canaan and Egypt as it had in Mesopotamia.

Two copper sword blades one still in its sheath found in a tomb at Ma'ayan Barukh in the Galilee

6 Sojourn and Exodus

Mighty Egypt knew Canaan for well over a thousand years before the Patriarchs knew either Canaan or Egypt. When the Ishmaelite caravan 'bearing gum, balm and myrrh' carried Joseph from Canaan to Egypt, caravans had been plying the commercial routes between Western Asia and the Nile Valley for centuries. Canaan and Egypt were already linked by a common history of commerce and war. Long before the time of Joseph the dynasts of the Nile had been extracting riches from the copper and turquoise mines of Sinai, while their armies had marched to the walls of squalid little Canaanite towns (in comparison with the grandeur of Egypt) demanding obeisance for Pharaoh.

Some of the most fascinating evidence of these connections has come from the arid Negev. In 1962, Arieh Eliav, now a prominent politician, was given the job of putting an ancient biblical name back on the map, of planning the new desert city of Arad. In the Book of Numbers it is the king of Arad who forcibly opposes the direct entry of Moses and the Israelites into Canaan, compelling them to make a roundabout journey. Now the descendants of these same Israelites were recreating Arad. In addition to town-planning funds Eliav had a budget for geological, climatological and archaeological research in the area. He asked the archaeologists Yohanan Aharoni and Ruth Amiran to investigate a double-humped hill of chalk about six miles to the west of the modern city site. Might this horseshoe-shaped tell have been the original Canaanite city mentioned in Numbers? The results were totally unexpected: only a few feet below a covering of wind-blown loess and scrub was not one early Arad, but two—neither the city of the hostile Canaanite king; instead, from the northern hump there emerged the remains of a large fortress-temple which guarded Israel's southern frontier in the days of Solomon.

opposite The majestic hills and sombre valleys of Sinai, testament to the tenacity of life and to those who have survived in this desolate land. Here was the crucible of Judaism, and according to the biblical account, the Children of Israel sojourned forty years in this desert before reaching Canaan— the Promised Land

overleaf A striking aerial view of the excavations of Tel Arad. The citadel excavated by Yohanan Aharoni is in the foreground and the early Canaanite city unearthed by Ruth Amiran is in the background

The southern mound revealed a much earlier city. Covering twenty-five acres, it must have dominated the trade routes of the Negev from the thirty-first century to the end of the twenty-seventh century BC. It was a city which flourished during the early days of united Egypt. Its plan, still clearly visible, was a triumph of function and forethought. Residential areas fanned out on the gently-sloping periphery of the town. Spacious rectangular houses of stone were grouped into orderly residential blocks, intersected by an extensive system of streets and open spaces. Along the easily defended ridge lines that encompassed the city ran the fortification wall—about 2,289 yards long and 7 feet 6 inches thick, which was separated from the houses by a wide street. At planned intervals of about every twenty-two yards, semi-circular bastions projected outwards from the walls, bringing attackers along its entire length under withering crossfire from defending bowmen on top of the towers.

Ruth Amiran has been able to prove that the earliest pharaohs of Egypt's Old Kingdom not only knew of Arad but had close commercial relations with it. The clues lay in the jugs, bottles and jars she found at Arad. Some of the pottery was 'Abydos' ware, named after a First Dynasty tomb site in Upper Egypt where it was first found in quantity. Archaeologists had long believed that this pottery had not been made at Abydos, but was imported from somewhere in Canaan. Now it had been shown that Abydos ware was also made in southern Canaan, and the pottery workshops of Arad itself might have exported some to Egypt. Side by side with this indigenous Arad pottery Ruth Amiran also found vessels of Egyptian origin. With this synchronization Canaanite Arad illuminated a vital piece of Egyptian history.

The Arad pottery found in Egypt and the Egyptian ware recovered at Arad were probably containers for the shipment of specific products. They reveal a brisk exchange of commerce between the two lands. Mrs Amiran thinks the Arad jars carried Canaanite olive oil and wine to the courts of the pharaohs of the First Dynasty. Possibly Egypt sent certain finished products in return. At any rate, Arad's fortunes seem to have been bound tightly to the pleasures of Egypt's rulers, as was to be the case with the future Patriarchs and their immediate descendants. It may well have been a decision of one of these pharaohs that sealed the fate of this city and led to its destruction and abandonment in the twenty-seventh century BC.

But early Canaanite civilization was not ended by the war machine of Egypt. It was destroyed by an endless army of land-

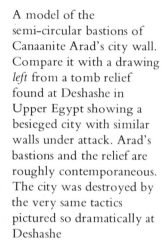

A model of the semi-circular bastions of Canaanite Arad's city wall. Compare it with a drawing *left* from a tomb relief found at Deshashe in Upper Egypt showing a besieged city with similar walls under attack. Arad's bastions and the relief are roughly contemporaneous. The city was destroyed by the very same tactics pictured so dramatically at Deshashe

hungry Semitic nomads, moving south and west from Syria and Mesopotamia. Encroaching waves of Amorites swept over the cities of Canaan at the dawn of the second millennium BC, cutting a deep swathe of destruction which is evident in virtually every major excavation in Israel. 'This', states Professor Aharoni, 'was one of the greatest and most decisive migratory movements in the history of Palestine.' The rock and mud fortifications of the insecure little cities melted before the torrent. Within this flood were the ancestors of the later Israelites.

In most cases, the Amorite invaders built anew on top of the ruins, laying the foundations for a flourishing new Canaanite culture. Other migrants, such as Abraham, Isaac and Jacob, moved only part of the way towards the new settled life. They camped on the outskirts of the cities, or on the stony terraces of the Palestinian hills, or they created crude seasonal settlements on land shunned by others on top of the bare and windswept mountains of the Negev. One such semi-nomadic colony is the remote site of Har Yeroham, which was discovered by Benno Rothenberg, and excavated by Moshe Kochavi of Tel Aviv University in the winter and spring of 1963.

Seen from the valley below, the tumbled rubble of Har Yeroham's huts and wall melt into their rocky surroundings. From their skyline village, the semi-nomadic shepherds and hunters commanded a breathtaking view of the undulating central Negev. No enemy could have crept up on the village unseen. The wind is chill at this height, even in summer, and must have penetrated the chinks of the rectangular stone hovels. They were crowded almost fearfully against the low rock fencing which encloses the lone acre of Har Yeroham. Flocks of sheep and goats were penned within circular corrals adjacent to the huts. The settlers must have cultivated their straggly patches of grain and collected their water, as Bedouin do today, on the flat fringes of a wadi at the bottom of the hill. They served their gods at a 'high place' on the spur of a prominent hill outside the main settlement. They buried their dead singly within crude cenotaphs of standing stone which dot the long ridge lines by the hundred, as far as the eye can see.

Though their surroundings were primitive, they were skilled craftsmen. They fired well-shaped and highly durable pottery vessels in a work area within the hamlet compound. They also knew how to work copper. It is tempting to imagine that, like the semi-nomads of Har Yeroham, the family of Abraham lived in semi-permanent Negev encampments at Beersheba and Gerar.

These copper ingots found at Har Yeroham offer evidence of the high technical skill attained by the Semitic nomads who settled it in patriarchal times

The prototypes of the semi-nomad chieftain Abraham were far from unknown to the pharaohs and aristocrats of Egypt in the early second millennium. Their artlessness must have made them an object of derision to the civilized Egyptians. But, as we can glean from Pharaoh's generosity and flattery towards Abraham in Genesis, they must also have been respectful and wary of the rough Semites who had toppled the walls of Canaan and apparently even threatened the borders of Egypt. 'I came up to the Wall-of-the-Ruler, made to oppose the Asiatics and to crush the Sand-Crossers', relates Si-nuhe, an Egyptian courtier. No doubt he was referring to a line of fortifications constructed on the eastern frontier of the delta along the line of the Suez Canal. Si-nuhe is the hero of a well-known Egyptian adventure classic of about 1,900 BC, the time of Abraham, according to Glueck. Out of favour after the death of Pharaoh Amenemhet I (about 1,971 BC), Si-nuhe flees across Sinai and into Canaan, taking refuge with a powerful Semitic chief named Ammi-enshi in a land called Upper Retenu. 'Ammi-enshi married me to his eldest daughter', narrates Si-nuhe, whose fortunes are now restored.

He let me choose for myself of his country, of the choicest of that which was with him on his frontier with another country. It was a good land, named Yaa. Figs were in it, and grapes. It had more wine than water. Plentiful was its honey, abundant its olives. Every (kind of) fruit was on its trees. Barley was there, and emmer. There was no limit to any (kind of) cattle. . . Bread was made for me as daily fare, wine as daily provision, cooked meat and roast fowl, besides the wild beasts of the desert. . .

Promoted to commander of Ammi-enshi's army, the valiant

Si-nuhe led raids on rival Amorite tribes. The hospitality of Ammi-enshi accords with that of Abraham towards his three visitors in the eighteenth chapter of Genesis: 'Then he took curds, and milk, and the calf which he had prepared, and set it before them; and he stood by them under the tree while they ate.'

Other Egyptian texts have come to light which link Hebrew tradition with the atmosphere of the Nile. There is the Egyptian stele which describes the circumcision rite of 120 Egyptian men. Those who are aware of orthodox dietary strictures (see the eleventh chapter of Leviticus) might be surprised at the Egyptian coffin text written several hundreds years before the time of Moses which details the mythological basis according to which the god Horus declared the pig unclean and the eating of pork taboo.

Hieroglyphic inscriptions describe the arrival of Semites from Canaan to seek the generosity of the 'domain of Pharaoh' and his burgeoning granaries during hard times. Consider the sons of Jacob, who tell Pharaoh that they 'have come to sojourn in the land; for there is no pasture for your servants' flocks, for the famine is severe in the land of Canaan; and now, we pray you, let your servants dwell in the land of Goshen.' This would appear to be far more than a dramatic device to help to sustain a biblical plot.

Is the story of Joseph, who rose in the service of the Pharaoh to become Prime Minister, also the invention of a romantic mind? What might logically explain the hospitality of certain pharaohs towards these Semitic visitors? Why a prolonged 'sojourn' by Jacob and his progeny, which begins so auspiciously and ends in bondage at some point within a period of up to four hundred years? The answer may possibly lie in a vital piece of political background to which the Bible alludes only in vague terms. The historical sciences have now filled in considerable portions of the puzzle. For instance, in the Book of Numbers Moses sends twelve men to 'spy out the land of Canaan'. Among other places they travel to Hebron, which, the Bible informs us for no apparent reason, was built seven years before Zoan in Egypt. As it has turned out, this has come to represent an important piece of historical information.

Let us now return to the saga of Si-nuhe to look at one fascinating detail. After he is made commander of Ammi-enshi's forces, Si-nuhe's Asiatic friends 'became so bold as to oppose the rulers of foreign countries'. In ancient Egyptian, the phrase 'rulers of foreign countries' is *Hequa-khasut*. In the days of Si-nuhe, in about the nineteenth century BC, Egyptians used the term to denote the leaders of roaming Amorite bands who refused to settle down

An early Canaanite painted pottery vessel found at Arad. This pottery is very similar to the so-called Abydos ware also found in the tombs of the earliest Egyptian pharaohs

at the tail end of the great invasion. As time went on, *Hequa-khasut*, transliterated into Greek by the historian Manetho as *Hyksos*, became a term which struck terror and dread into Egyptian hearts. By about 1,750 BC the *Hyksos*, or 'Shepherd Kings', had coalesced into a tremendous war machine which not only trampled the cities of Canaan underfoot, but broke through the Wall-of-the-Ruler and brought all Egypt to heel. The illustrious Middle Kingdom was smashed to dust. It was the detested foreign invaders, the Semitic *Hyksos*, who humbled and ruled once-proud Egypt. It would take nearly two centuries to cast them out again.

Twenty-five years after their expulsion, Queen Hatshepsut ordered an inscription to be carved on to the façade of a temple at Istabl Antar; recovered by archaeology in modern times, it hints strongly at the shame of that catastrophic event: 'I have raised up that which had gone to pieces formerly, since the Asiatics were in the midst of Avaris of the Northland, and vagabonds were in the midst of them, overthrowing that which had been made.' Avaris, in the delta, was the capital of the *Hyksos*, and the site has also been known as Tanis, Pa-Rameses and—Zoan!

A detail from an Egyptian tomb relief showing Semites bowing down in obeisance to an Egyptian official. One could easily imagine Jacob and his sons in such a scene

A relief from Tell el-Amarna, dated to the 14th century BC, showing a war chariot and horses. Their introduction created a revolution in the art of ancient warfare

A *Hyksos* horse-bit, one of the pieces of evidence linking the 'Shepherd Kings' to the introduction of the chariot in Canaan and Egypt

The 'natural inference' of the biblical reference to Zoan, suggests G. Ernest Wright, 'is that there must have been Hebrews who were connected with *Hyksos* activity and who were in Egypt when Tanis [or Avaris] was founded.' Many scholars go on to suggest that it was under the *Hyksos* pharaohs that their Semitic cousins, the Abrahamites, were welcomed with open arms into Egypt, under the *Hyksos* that a Semitic foreigner such as Joseph could have been awarded the mantle of power second only to the king himself, and under the Egyptian nobles who expelled the *Hyksos* with violence and loathing that the Hebrews were shorn of their privileges and impressed into bondage. Other Hebrews may well have escaped Egyptian revenge by joining the *Hyksos* retreat to Canaan (in about 1,550 BC), long before the biblical Exodus.

How could a swarm of 'vagabonds', as Hatshepsut so derisively called them, have swept through Canaan and into the very heart of Egypt? Scholars were baffled until archaeology produced several intriguing answers.

For sheer tactical innovation in warfare the *Hyksos* were virtually without parallel in Western Asia for perhaps two hundred years. It was they who introduced the horse-drawn chariot into combat in Canaan and Egypt. Archaeology has now strongly suggested that they also introduced the battering ram, a powerful siege engine whose invention has usually been attributed to the Assyrians eight hundred years later. Both the chariot and the battering ram were imports from Mesopotamia. The impact of this revolution on the art of warfare was enormous. In the open field, the chariot was the ultimate weapon of mobility and terror. Foot soldiers were totally defenceless against it. What unbuttressed wall of traditional design could withstand the ram? Little wonder that it took the Egyptians two hundred years to close the technological gap by finding ways to neutralize the advanced military capability of the *Hyksos* warriors.

The *Hyksos* are one of the lesser-known peoples of the ancient Near East, and yet one of the most fascinating. As intermediaries between Canaan and Egypt, they brought one of the richest periods of material culture to Palestine. After their expulsion, the founders of the New Kingdom under the illustrious Eighteenth Dynasty launched a fanatical campaign to wipe out all traces of the detested *Hequa-khasut*, thus depriving us of vital material evidence that could tell us more about this remarkable semi-nomadic people— or about how they may have affected the Hebrew destiny.

Of the Exodus itself, the heart of the profound spiritual and historical experience which is the rock of Israel, archaeology can find no trace. Few subjects kindle higher passions than the desert wanderings of the Children of Moses. Such disparate minds as Sigmund Freud and David Ben-Gurion have been drawn into the fray. Theories have become proprietary interests which scholars and sectarians covet like Midas his gold. Yet no one theory satisfies all the facts and conditions laid down by the biblical chronicle.

Unlike the patriarchal journey from Mesopotamia, there is no readily identifiable historical or archaeological context in which to set the Exodus, unless one links it to the consequences of the expulsion of the *Hyksos*. The biblical account states that about six hundred thousand men on foot, 'besides women and children', set out with Moses, giving us an estimated total of between two and three million for the journey. It is unthinkable that the barren Sinai could have supported a multitude of this order, or that Egypt could have survived such a drastic reduction of its slave labour force. Scholars have also calculated that such a body, marching in columns of four, would have stretched 350 miles—

Detail from an Assyrian relief illustrating the use of and defence against the terrifying battering ram, probably also invented by the *Hyksos* many centuries earlier. The defenders are trying to deflect the ram by means of chains. The attackers are attempting to remove the chains with grappling hooks

further than the distance by air between the Suez Canal and the Dead Sea! Surely, among the vast body of Egyptian texts we have, there would have been some mention of a migration even a tenth that size, particularly one which resulted in the loss of 'all Pharaoh's horses, his chariots, and his horsemen'.

Scholars have proposed at least four alternative routes for the Exodus. Similarly, there are more than a dozen candidates for Mount Sinai, including one in Saudi Arabia. The traditional site at Jebel Musa, near the southern apex of the Sinai peninsula, won pre-eminence only in the reign of Constantine, the first Imperial Roman convert to Christianity. Of all the modern identifications suggested for many of the forty-three stations listed in the most complete biblical itinerary of the Exodus (See Numbers 33), only two in Egypt and Sinai are unanimously accepted, and none can be positively identified.

There is also little agreement on the identity and character of Moses, or indeed whether Exodus is the tale of a single migration, of a synthesis of the sagas of a number of disparate Semitic elements united only by language, the tyrannies of Egyptian taskmasters, and the common dream of the landless in the promise of Canaan. One theory holds that only the priestly tribe of Levi endured the trials of Egyptian servitude, and returned to impose its authority, monotheistic theology and territorial ambitions on bands of disorganized Abrahamites who had never left Canaan. Somewhat similar views are passionately advocated by David Ben-Gurion, the former Prime Minister of Israel. There are archaeological clues which suggest that at least some Israelites were in Canaan during the period in which the Exodus must be placed.

The likely dating of the Exodus, in whatever form the march across Sinai took, is one of the few problems which archaeology really can solve. Once again, it is the old *Hyksos* capital at Avaris-Tanis-Zoan in the eastern Delta that holds the key. Most scholars identify it with the remains of a city found at a delta site called San el-Hagar. The excavations yielded not only the massive defences that are so characteristic of the Shepherd Kings, but a large stele in a later stratum dated the 'Year 400, 4th month of the third season, day 4'. Experts can relate this dating formula to our own calendar with some confidence, fixing it to the month of June in or about 1,330 BC.

The stele discloses that it was erected to commemorate a celebration attended by a vizier who was to become Pharaoh Seti I (*c.* 1,303–1,290 BC) marking the four hundredth anniversary of the

A commemorative stele erected by the Pharaoh Seti I at Beth-shean. It mentions an attack by an enemy called *Apiru* or *Habiru*, whom the pharaoh denounced as 'wretched Asiatics' (see page 128)

A colossal stone statue
of Rameses II in the great
courtyard of the temple at
Luxor. He is considered
one of the pharaohs of the
Exodus. Queen Nefertari
is shown in very small
scale beside him

founding of Avaris. So it is possible to calculate that the victorious
Hyksos built their new seat of government in about 1,730 BC.
This fits in with other chronological evidence about these Asiatic
invaders. We can infer that at least some Hebrews were present
in the Delta about that time.

It was Pharaoh Seti, and his son Rameses II, who systematically
set out to re-establish the great Asiatic Empire which Egypt lost
under the *Hyksos*. Symbolically perhaps, Seti began rebuilding
the city at San el-Hagar, the old *Hyksos* site. Tameses (*c.* 1,290–1,223
BC) enlarged the scheme, deciding to create a magnificent new
capital which would outshine Thebes. With characteristic pharaonic flourish, he named it after himself—Rameses, or Pa-Rameses
('House of Rameses'). Thirty miles to the south, at Tell el-Retabeh,
archaeologists have exhumed and identified the ancient remains
of Pithom, which is dominated by a great temple, also built by
Rameses. Both cities, Rameses and Pithom, are named at the
very opening of the Book of Exodus as the 'store-cities' built by
the enslaved Children of Israel over whom a 'new king. . . who did
not know Joseph. . . set taskmasters to afflict them with heavy
burdens'. In support of this, we know from other documentary
evidence that an earlier pharaoh, Amenhotep II (*c.* 1,447–1,421 BC)
returned to Memphis in triumph from his Asiatic campaign,
hauling a train of booty and plunder which included 3,600 '*Apiru*',
that Rameses himself encountered *Habiru* in Canaan, and that
some of them ended up hauling stones for his monumental public
works.

From these data, scholars can reckon that Seti, who began the
great work at Pa-Rameses, was the pharaoh who 'did not know
Joseph'; that Rameses II, who continued the project when his
father died in about 1,290 BC, was the hated pharaoh of the Exodus
from whom Moses exacted the release of the Children of Israel;
and that the turn of the thirteenth century BC was the very time
when the Israelites 'groaned under their bondage, and cried out
for help' at Pithom and the capital city of Rameses.

Now if the Israelites left Pa-Rameses some time after 1,290 BC
to begin their forty years of wandering, this would place them in
Canaan with Joshua after 1,250 BC. This coincides exactly with the
archaeological dating of the Joshuitic conquests in Canaan, which
we will discuss in the next chapter.

A departure date of some time after 1,290 BC also fits in precisely
with the tradition in Genesis that the sojourn in Egypt lasted for
four hundred years, and with that of Exodus, which lengthens
the stay slightly by thirty years. This takes us back to about 1,700 BC,

Objects and vessels formed or decorated in imitation of nature were popular in Canaan in the first half of the second millenium BC, the period of the Exodus. The beautiful alabaster fish was found at Tell-el-Ajjul

the era of the founding of Avaris, and the *Hyksos'* hospitality which greeted Joseph's kinsmen in Egypt. This is the only tangible thread of Exodus that can be traced with any reasonable hope of accuracy from Egypt to Canaan. The design of the entire fabric itself, however, remains indistinct. It is as though we had reconstructed the borders of a complicated jigsaw puzzle by first sorting out those pieces with straight edges, and then found ourselves unable to fit together the centre of the picture from the thousands of irregular pieces left over.

Dr Moshe Dothan, the energetic assistant director of Israel's Department of Antiquities, who has specialized in the archaeological problems of the Exodus and pre-Israelite Canaan, sums up one aspect of the puzzle as follows: 'If we are dealing with a written synthesis of separate migrations across Sinai by many small bands of fugitive Hebrew slaves, each travelling separate routes and meeting with wholly different sets of experiences and adventures, the whole question of the route of Exodus could well be a fantasy.' Let us assume, however, that one such group, led by an imaginative and forceful spirit named Moses, underwent a profound spiritual catharsis in Sinai which ultimately influenced a number of disparate Semitic elements, those who were enslaved in Egypt and those who remained in Canaan, creating one people who then forged a common Mosaic tradition which future generations came to accept as their own'.

If it is viewed in this way, is there anything more that archaeology and the other historical sciences can piece together from the biblical puzzle of Exodus? Firstly, Sinai Bedouin to this day harvest 'manna', shiny teardrops of sweet gum which form on the twigs and branches of the tamarisk tree in June and July. It is made and secreted by several kinds of scale insects which suck large quantities of tamarisk sap. Manna is eaten with unleavened bread, like honey or butter, 'a fine flake-like thing, fine as hoarfrost on the ground'. Secondly, when the Israelites complain to Moses of their spartan desert fare, a miracle occurs in which they are almost literally inundated by quail. Twice a year, in fact, the curving northern part of Sinai's Mediterranean coast is for a few hours the resting-place for coveys of exhausted quail. They carpet the sand on their outward winter migration from Europe to Arabia and Africa in September and October, and alight there again on the return flight in March. It is on this phenomenon that many scholars base their argument that the main route of the Exodus lay along the flat northern rim of the Sinai Peninsula, rather than by the more circuitous central passage, or a still more arduous march south by way of Jebel Musa—the traditional route of the Exodus.

This Bedouin boy in Sinai is licking sweet manna from a tamarisk, as the Children of Israel in all likelihood did many centuries before him

How do the arguments of the 'northern school' square with biblical details of the long march, including the chase and drowning of the hosts of Pharaoh? One of the most baffling elements of the Exodus has always been the miraculous passage through the Red Sea, or '*Yam Suph*' in Hebrew, whose nearest branch, the Gulf of Suez, is over eighty miles south of Rameses, the starting-point of the march. Yet the passage 'through the midst of the sea' occurred in the early stages of the journey. Today most scholars agree that 'Red Sea' is an early mistranslation of the biblical term *Yam Suph*, which actually means the Sea of Reeds, or the Marsh Sea. Thus the authors of Exodus may really have been referring to another body of water lying somewhere between Egypt proper and the bleak wilderness of Sinai. At this point, however, agreement again breaks down. The crux of the dispute is the biblical passage in which the Lord commands Moses to 'encamp in front of Pi-hahiroth, between Migdol and the sea, in front of Baal-zephon; and you shall encamp over against it, by the sea.'

The majority of archaeologists believe that the site of a temple to Baal-zephon, the Canaanite god of mariners, lay at Tell Defneh. This is south of Rameses near an arm of Lake Menzaleh called Lake Balah, which vanished with the digging of the Suez Canal. From here, Moses led his people south on the traditional route to Jebel Musa. Lake Balah, say the advocates of this theory, was the 'Reed Sea'.

However, Dr Moshe Dothan has armed the 'northern school' with a far more provocative premise, one originally suggested by a

Some of the probable routes of the Exodus from Egypt

French explorer named Kledat many years ago. Sixty miles due west of Rameses, a narrow shoal which we shall call the Serbonic Sands projects from the north coast of Sinai. It extends in a great arc of forty-five miles from north-east to south-east until it rejoins the coast near el-Arish, the biblical 'brook of Egypt', which marked the extreme southern limits of Canaan. This reef barrier encloses a broad shallow marsh called Lake Serbonis. The lake is actually a huge lagoon, connected to the Mediterranean by small shallow inlets which slice through the Serbonic Sands at three separate places. At some points the sand barrier is only about two hundred yards wide. But halfway along it the reef widens considerably. At this point stands its most conspicuous landmark, a prominent natural mound nearly a hundred feet high which the ancient Greeks called Mount Casion. To Phoenician sailors, plying the long sea route to Egypt without charts or compass, this lone peak, visible far out at sea, must have been one of the most welcome landmarks on the voyage. It meant that journey's end was at hand, safe harbour in Egypt, the renewal of the divine gift of life itself. Surely, Dothan reasons, the temple of the mariners to Baal-zephon could have stood here at or after the time of the Exodus. The theory is even more credible when one learns from early sources that there was another temple to Baal-zephon on the home coast of Phoenicia, and that it, too, was later called Mount Casion by the Greeks.

In the aftermath of the Six-Day War, Israel mounted a sweeping scientific study of the shoal, which included an archaeological survey team headed by Dr Dothan. Below the flanks of Mount Casion Dothan identified the remains of several ancient settlements, a late city dated to the Hellenistic period, and one going back to the twelfth century BC. The potsherds he found offered evidence of far earlier occupation, though none directly attributable to a temporary camp of fugitives on the run, who would have left few tangible traces behind.

Dothan's quick survey failed to locate the presence of a temple or shrine beneath the sands, which could be determined only by a thorough excavation. But it did establish that the first city was quite substantial, covering seven to eight acres—large enough to serve as a major port, and as a site of pilgrimage. Dothan thinks the actual temple or holy place of Baal-zephon may have been located on or near the peak itself, where priests probably maintained a fire beacon for ships at night. Whether the place was standing in Moses's time or not, it would certainly have been known to the editors of Exodus, who could have used the name anachronistically to identify the area to the audience of their time. The Bible often uses this device.

The fleeing Israelites would have found plenty of fresh water on the Serbonic Sands. Dothan located an ample supply, drinkable though brackish, at three wells used by the reef's small Bedouin population today.

The most intriguing feature of the long reef is the three inlets which intersect it, linking Lake Serbonis to the sea. When the wind blows freshly from the south or east, it lowers the water level of the lake appreciably, and the shallow inlets can easily be forded on foot. If the wind shifts to the north, the sea is carried back through the inlets into the lake, and anyone trying to wade across them will flounder in over six feet of water. Do we have here, in a capriciously turning wind, the reason why the fleeing Israelites could negotiate a passage which suddenly became a death trap for their Egyptian pursuers? 'Then Moses stretched out his hand over the sea; and the Lord drove the sea back by a strong east wind all night, and made the sea dry land, and the waters were divided. . . The waters returned and covered the chariots and the horsemen and all the host of Pharaoh. . .' Could Serbonis have been the Reed Sea?

An expedition to Sinai in 1913. The mountain looming in the background is Jebel Helal in central Sinai. Advocates of the 'northern route' of Exodus hold it to be Mt. Sinai, rather than the traditional Jebel Musa in the south

The northern rim of Sinai offered Moses the shortest passage from Egypt to Canaan, the same route as that followed by the great international highway, the Via Maris, along which caravans of riches and mighty armies marched between the lands of the eastern Mediterranean and Egypt. But the Egyptians guarded the way well, building a system of forts and guard-posts along its length. The way of the Serbonic Sands offered Moses a means of flanking these military installations as far as el-Arish, where he could then have turned inland to Kadesh-barnea—which is the only other fixed point (besides Rameses) in the wanderings on whose identification scholars are almost unanimous. There is an eminent candidate for Mount Sinai on this northern route as well —a great altar-like rock called Jebel Helal in north central Sinai, 'the wilderness of Shur', twenty-two miles west of Kadesh-barnea.

Yet even this theory cannot satisfy all the conditions laid down in Exodus. In all likelihood Dothan is right and the saga is a complex fabric woven of many separate strands. But above all the confusion looms the figure of Moses, whose own epic tale became the essential folk experience of Sinai. There is one more vivid circumstantial link between what Exodus tells us of Moses, and what archaeology has recovered from the covetous and silent Sinai. In the desert, a special relationship is established between the tribes of Israel and another Semitic people variously referred to as Midianites or Kenites. The ties ostensibly spring from Moses's marriage to the daughter of the Midianite priest Jethro, whose advice to his son-in-law in the desert, as related in the eighteenth chapter of Exodus, symbolizes the way Israel is transformed from a rabble to a people. The Semitic Kenites were itinerant coppersmiths and mine-workers who may have come from the copper-rich land of Midian, east of the Gulf of Eilat, today's Saudi Arabia. The root 'Keni' is derived from Cain, one of whose descendants, according to Genesis, was Tubal-cain, 'the forger of all instruments of bronze and iron'. Some scholars believe that there is a connection between our own gypsies and tinkers and these ancient wandering artisans in metal.

It is from the eastern desert—the flaming Arava and its fringes—that archaeology has turned up exciting traces of possible cultic and cultural connections between Moses and the Kenites. The tale of this discovery is a classic example of how archaeology leavens abstract science to create a rich human experience.

There could be no more spectacular setting for a discovery than the Pillars of Solomon in the Timna Valley, a broad corridor of yellow-pink sand bordered by awesome formations of many-hued sandstone, metamorphic schist, gneiss and sedimentary limestone. They are the sculptures of nature. Great geological forces moulded the pillars—towering columns of frozen Nubian sandstone that seem to support the heavens. Wind and sand were the masons which polished and fluted them and, with a final flourish, nature's chemistry tinted them with all the bright and subtle colours with which the sun touches the desert—cream, yellow, azure, red-pink and white.

Since his early days as a war photographer, archaeologist Benno Rothenberg of Tel Aviv University has taken little for granted, least of all what his eyes can tell him. Rothenberg relates how in the summer of 1969, 'I dug up a little Byzantine copper factory south of Timna. I had planned to work for three weeks, and I finished four or five days early. With a little extra time and money on my hands, I remembered that one particular site which had long ago struck me as a likely place of cult worship because of its unusual setting was at the Pillars of Solomon in the center of Timna. It was the only place in Timna where there were no metallurgical remains, no slag, for instance.

It was a small place, so I decided to spend just a few days making a trial trench. I was curious to see what we would find, even though tourists had trampled the spot for ages. On the second day, we

opposite The Egyptian temple discovered by Dr. Benno Rothenberg under only a few feet of sand at the foot of 'Solomon's Pillars' in the midst of ancient copper mining and smelting sites at Timna in the Arava

came on the little treasure. Despite the financial implications, I suddenly found myself with a major excavation on my hands.'

Rothenberg's 'treasure' lay in just a few feet of sand driven by the winds of centuries against an abrupt overhang of rose-pink rock at the foot of the eastern pillars. In surveying the area, he noticed what appeared to be three rough-cut niches low in the rockface. He ordered his digging team to start clearing the sand immediately below them. There emerged an ancient Egyptian temple, dedicated to the goddess of mining, Hathor, and dated by inscriptions to the reigns of Seti I and Rameses II, the pharaohs of the Exodus. In a region where the presence of the ancient Egyptians had never before been known or suspected, Rothenberg found a smaller replica of the great mining temple complex or Serabit excavated many years ago by Petrie in Western Sinai.

The temple court was thirty feet wide and twenty-three feet deep. Its entrance faced due east to the rising sun. Through it the pink early morning rays penetrated to light the interior of a small *naos* or holy of holies built against the pillar, and its finely-wrought face of Hathor. Her statue once stood within one of the niches which had caught Rothenberg's eye. Altars and standing stones, or *massebot*, were still in their places. There were ritual basins and larger works of art, including a sphinx and, as at Serabit, stone Hathor figurines.

The essence of Rothenberg's treasure hoard began to emerge the next day. The site was the *entrepôt* for thousands upon thousands of votive objects brought to Hathor by pharaonic emissaries and humble miners alike over a span of a thousand years.

There were two kinds of votive treasures. One huge group was obviously of Egyptian origin: scarabs, seals, beads of faience, stone vessels, ornaments of gold, amber and glass, wands, alabaster bowls with the lotus motif, cups and vessels to which remnants of turquoise glazing still adhered. But the mine workers, too, paid homage to Hathor. Their gifts bore a different stamp. Their currency of reverence was metal. With the tools of their craft— crude pit furnaces, pottery crucibles and moulds—they forged for the goddess thousands of copper rings, awls, needles, chain links and animal figurines. A few brought her even rarer stuff: tiny objects of soft iron, now fragile clots of rust, dating back to the thirteenth century BC, hundreds of years before the Iron Age dawned in Canaan. Rothenberg believes that iron was produced here in small quantities far earlier than the experts had originally thought, long before men learned how to harden it for practical everyday use.

A stone relief figure of Hathor, the Egyptian goddess of mining. Reverent pharaohs ascribed their wealth in turquoise and copper to the beneficence of this deity

The most important piece of the copper hoard is just under five inches long. It is a writhing serpent with a gilt head and eyes of lead, its body minutely textured with scales. In the palm of one's hand the undulating body seems to take on life and movement. This prized cult object is called a 'nechushtan'—in biblical Hebrew 'nachash ha'nechoshet', a snake of copper. It is interesting to note that in Hebrew both 'snake' and 'copper' are derived from the same root. At a number of crucial moments in the Exodus story, a nachash ha'nechoshet is the symbol of divine power. The rod of Moses and Aaron becomes a serpent, in a contest of the 'secret arts' with Pharaoh's magicians. The winged uraeus, or sacred snake, was also a well-known religious symbol of the ancient Egyptians. In Moses's hand, it brings plagues upon Egypt. And when the Israelites were beset by venomous reptiles in the Negev, perhaps not far from the general area of the Timna Valley itself, 'Moses made a bronze serpent, and set it on a pole; and if a serpent bit any man, he would look at the bronze serpent and live.' We cannot doubt that the serpent was a potent instrument of man's belief at the Timna metal complex, at the pillar temple, and in the Exodus drama. In time and in place, the nechushtan of Timna places us very close to Moses.

With the votive hoard Rothenberg found specimens of finely shaped and painted pottery, obviously not of Egyptian origin. Similar examples have been found in the southern Negev and in Midian, and Rothenberg ascribes them to the local Kenites. He believes that they worked in partnership with the Egyptians in the Timna mining venture, and were paid in copper, a portion of which they tithed to Hathor. With the nechushtan we see them clearly as intermediaries between the desert and the Israelites whom it tempered under Moses and Joshua. As Rothenberg has written:

An Egyptian-Midianite temple, built in the Arabah at a time close to the Exodus, and finds like the copper snake... are of great importance for our inderstanding of the cultic, cultural and social relationship between the tribes of Israel at the time of Moses and the Midianite-Kenites, through Jethro, the Midianite priest, father-in-law and adviser to Moses.

Though we may never fit all the pieces of the Exodus puzzle into a completed picture, archaeology has at least provided an intriguing framework within which to assemble what material clues there are. Beyond this, the empty Sinai itself can only hint at the rest.

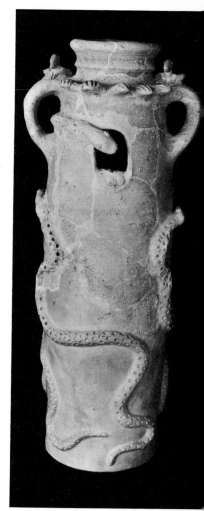

An incense burner of the Israelite period adorned with writhing snakes. This same symbol, in the form of Moses' rod, unleashed the plagues upon Pharaoh. The duality of this ancient emblem, as the sign of healing and the incarnation of evil, makes it one of the more fascinating of ancient signs

7 The Distant Wake of Joshua

One day in the summer of 1950, over three thousand years after the Joshuitic legions of ancient Israel had carved their historic claim upon the hard and uncompromising land, a group of Israeli military officers walked beneath the grass-covered flanks of silent Hazor. They and their troops were on a field exercise in the north near the sensitive borders with Syria and Lebanon. Once, their senior officer mused, it had been this commanding tell which held the key to the strategic control of the northern region. Lying at the junction of the teeming roads from Phoenicia to the east and from Damascus to the sea and Egypt, ancient Hazor had given her rulers dominion over Canaan's Palestinian northland. Little wonder, Yigael Yadin, Chief of Staff, pondered, that the Book of Joshua paid such deference to this place. 'For Hazor', the passage reads, 'formerly was the head of all those kingdoms.' From his strategic point of reference Yadin could also appreciate the military logic behind the brutal extinction of the city by Joshua, who took Hazor. . . and put to the sword all who were in it, utterly destroying them. . . But none of the cities that stood on their tells did Israel burn, except Hazor only. . . ' The total reduction of this vast urban fortress complex must have broken the back of Canaanite resistance in the area and ratified the claim of the land-hungry tribes of Israel upon the fertile rolling heartland north of the Sea of Galilee.

Historic accident had cut short Yadin's preparatory years as a student archaeologist, diverted him into the Haganah, harnessed his intellectual talents as chief military planner in the 1948 War of Independence, and placed him in overall command of the fledgling defence forces in the aftermath of victory. He felt a unique sense of continuity as he stood at the foot of Hazor.

What traces of the Joshuitic Conquest, if any, remained locked

This unique silver-plated bronze cult standard was found in the potter's storehouse of Hazor. It has a tang for fastening to to a pole

opposite The pottery workshop discovered in Canaanite Hazor in which were also found a cult mask and a basalt potter's wheel. It was destroyed by the armies of Joshua

within the mound of deserted Hazor? Might the archaeological evidence yield the precise date of the Israelite campaign against the city? Could the spades of excavators help to clarify the tangled biblical accounts of the Conquest related in Numbers, Joshua and Judges? 'On that day in Galilee,' Yadin recalled, 'I decided to excavate Hazor. I had no doubts that it was the only place to begin.' He was now to drop his military responsibilities to take up once more his chosen vocation, archaeology.

The Bible itself seems more of a hindrance than a help in attempts to reconstruct the entry of the Children of Israel into the lands of the Divine Promise. From the several biblical versions of the chronicle of conquest, we encounter a number of bewildering contradictions. Numbers alone clearly embodies at least two different sagas. In one, the Israelites march in a seemingly unopposed passage from Kadesh-barnea in Sinai east across the Arava to Transjordan, and then turn north along the famed King's Highway through Edom and Moab to the plains opposite Jericho. In another, they are forcibly blocked in their attempts to take the most direct northerly routes from Sinai to Canaan. First they try to storm Canaan via the Negev and are met in battle by the King of Arad, who defeats them at Hormah. Then they trudge far to the south, crossing into Transjordan at Eilat. Again they meet opposition. The Kings of Edom and Moab refuse them permission to travel north along the King's Highway, forcing them to take a circuitous journey through the desert well to the east of Canaan. Only by fighting their way west again through the kingdoms of Og of Bashan and Sihon of Heshbon do they arrive at the banks of the Jordan overlooking Jericho and the Promised Land. Surely at least two different traditions have been included in the Book of Numbers? The same duality becomes apparent to the careful reader of the other biblical accounts of the Conquest.

One of the anomalies which particularly vexed Yadin and his colleagues concerns the battle of Hazor, whose conquest is intimately connected with the biblical campaign of Joshua's warriors and is therefore central to an understanding of it. The Book of Joshua relates Joshua's violent confrontation with the forces of the northern Canaanite coalition under the command of Hazor's King Jabin, 'by the waters of Merom'. The Canaanites were routed. Following their crushing victory, the Israelites turned violently on Hazor itself, slew Jabin, and put the city to the torch. 'None of the cities that stood on their tells did Israel burn, except Hazor only. . . ' The contradiction can be pinpointed in the Book of Judges, which relates the stormy history of young Israel during the several hundred

years after Joshua. The figure of Jabin enigmatically arises again in the stirring battle of the prophetess Deborah. The people of Israel have been sold 'into the hand of Jabin King of Canaan, who reigned in Hazor'. Deborah summons Barak as general over ten thousand warriors from the tribes of Naphtali and Zebulun. They triumph over the nine hundred chariots of Jabin's commander, Sisera, and 'destroyed Jabin king of Canaan' in a battle far to the south-west of Hazor.

A Canaanite man and woman depicted on potsherds from the tell of Beth-shean

Which is the real Jabin: the adversary of Joshua, or of Deborah and Barak some hundred or so years later? When did the great city of Hazor really die: in the time of the Joshuitic Conquest, or of the consolidating struggles of the later Judges? From at least the Middle Ages, scholars of biblical history have wrestled with this inconsistency. There seemed as many theories as Jabin was alleged to own chariots.

Though much of the legend of the Conquest still hangs on conjecture, archaeology has found the trail of Joshua's stern and ragged legions. The evidence is mustered most dramatically against the backdrop of the epic discoveries prised from the tell of Hazor by Yadin. His certainty that the burgeoning mound beneath Mount Hermon could unlock some of the baffling riddles of the Conquest grew during 1953 and 1954, after his retirement from the Israeli Army. The four campaigns of excavation carried out from 1955 to the end of 1958, ultimately cost £250,000. The word 'campaign' is not used lightly. The former chief of staff planned his excavation like a military campaign. He appointed a ranking military officer to look after the drudgery of administrative details, from erecting staff prefabs to labourers' pay, to housing arrangments at a nearby kibbutz guest-house for forty-five expedition archaeo-

logists and their student assistants. The military administrator
proved himself magnificently, Yadin recalls, leaving him almost
completely free to deal with the scientific substance of the dig.
But some intervention was necessary. Lacking a full appreciation
of archaeology, the administrator budgeted for the use of a bulldozer
as the most efficient way to remove the mound of Hazor at a cost
of 'several scores of thousands of pounds'! The bulldozer was
cancelled.

The tell of Hazor is not only one of the most impressive, but
certainly one of the most formidable in Israel. It leaps in two giant
stages from the surrounding Hula Plain. On its north, west and
east there is a vast elevated rectangular plateau about three-quarters
of a mile long and roughly 750 yards wide. On three sides it was
protected by deep natural ravines. To shore up its vulnerable
low-lying western perimeter the *Hyksos* first carved out a gigantic
dry moat 660 yards long and 87 yards wide at the top. At the same
time earth from the digging of the moat was laboriously hauled
to the adjacent western slope and pounded into a rampart 765
yards long, 98 yards wide at the base, and nearly 50 feet high.
On the south the tell rises abruptly from the plateau to a bottle-
shaped acropolis twenty-five acres in area.

Despite the size of the enterprise, Yadin had to limit his exca-

An aerial view showing
part of the mound city of
Hazor. Note the grid
system into which
excavations are divided. On
detailed drawings, it
permits a precise reference
for every building and
object found

vations to relatively small, carefully selected areas: three on the high mound, and seven on the lower rectangular plateau. The first problem he aimed to solve was the nature of the Canaanite city which Joshua had conquered. During a brief excavation at Hazor in 1928 the British archaeologist Professor John Garstang came to the conclusion that the large plateau had been a fortified camp of temporary structures rather than a permanent community. For Yadin the answer came within hours. Spades had barely penetrated three feet into the soil of the plateau when a dense collection of wall stumps began to appear, the remains of stone buildings. 'What we had', says Yadin, 'were the remains of solid permanent buildings. This was the first great surprise of the dig. Wherever we dug, we encountered a city, with houses and buildings of stone all well-built, and sophisticated drainage systems.'

The plateau was a far cry from Garstang's temporary military enclosure. It had been part of a sprawling, bustling, densely-populated Canaanite conurbation covering the entire mound and culminating in the high twenty-five acre tell. Yadin quickly labelled the broad plateau the 'Lower City of Hazor', a well-engineered metropolis founded on bedrock by the *Hyksos* in the eighteenth century BC. And on top of the ruins of the first *Hyksos* Lower City lay the remains of four more.

The second great surprise of the dig was not long in coming. Garstang had dated Joshua's conquest of Hazor to about 1,400 BC, a finding which created a storm of controversy. He claimed as evidence the absence of a unique type of imported pottery called Mycenean IIIB, which he would have expected to find among the debris had the destruction occurred after 1,300 BC. The pottery began to be imported only after that date. Therefore Garstang reasoned that the conquest of Hazor must have occurred earlier. Here was the very dating evidence Garstang in his haste had missed; Yadin's teams found it in each of the seven excavation sections opened into the Lower City. Not only could Yadin now confirm that Joshua had stormed Hazor late in the thirteenth century BC. He also determined that this northern city against which Joshua triumphed had been the largest metropolis of its day in Canaan, with a population not of four thousand, as Garstang had claimed, but closer to forty thousand. Thus the compiler of the Book of Joshua could accurately state of its one-time grandeur: 'For Hazor formerly was the head of all those kingdoms.'

Though Hazor was later to be restored by the Israelites under Solomon, they restricted reconstruction to the smaller high tell on the southern edge of the plateau. The great Lower City of the

This jar, found at Hazor, was imported into Canaan from Mycenae, home of one of the earliest Greek high civilizations. It is of the type which helped provide the vital clue to the date for Joshua's conquest at Hazor and other sites

The 'Stelae Temple' of Hazor during excavation. All of the standing stones were found upright, but an idol had been 'decapitated', presumably by the zealous conquering Israelites

opposite The ancient Egyptian mining temple of Serabit el-Khadem in the austere heights of western Sinai at which Hathor was worshipped. From the Serabit mines came highly-prized turquoise which Israelites may have toiled to mine

plateau itself was never rebuilt after its destruction by Joshua. Even before Joshua's time, Yadin found, the magnificence of the city had begun to decline. Yet her vaulting fortification walls, temples, buildings and bustling streets, the never-ending procession of pedestrians, caravans and chariots at her impressive north-eastern gate, must have intimidated the dusky men of the desert whom Joshua dispatched to reconnoitre the approaches to the great city. One can recall the report of the twelve spies sent into Canaan by Joshua from the wilderness of Paran: '. . . The people who dwell in the land are very strong, and the cities are fortified and very large. . .' Yadin cannot tell us how the Israelites over-whelmed the mighty defence of Hazor: whether by siege, ruse or direct assault. Yet the archaeological evidence of their furious onslaught is eloquent enough.

Near the far north-western corner of the Lower City, Yadin uncovered one of the most imposing gate complexes ever found in Israel. Its walls still stood to a height of ten feet. On either side of a well-cobbled entrance stood three pairs of pilasters, which once supported the inner and outer entrance and the ceiling of the passage. The gate structure had been flanked by twin two-roomed towers. This complex had been reduced to a ruin by a tremendous fire, which left vivid scorch marks on the brickwork. Deep piles of powdery grey ash from the timbers of the gates and the beams of the tower lay thickly on the floors. '. . . None of the cities that stood on their tells did Israel burn, except Hazor only . . .'

Evidence of fiery ruin lay everywhere, but the savaging of Hazor's great temples produced the most dramatic traces of Israel's wrath. In the Stelae Temple, so named after an impressive group of stone slabs found in it, there were signs of sudden and violent devastation. Far across the mound to the extreme north lay perhaps the most emphatic witness to the Joshuitic whirlwind. In what was later designated Area H, one of Yadin's associates had retreated to what had become a personal privy. He haphazardly eyed a serried rank of stones which appeared above the surface, examined them with greater interest, and reported his chance observations to Yadin. An excavation team was sent to the area, and from it there slowly emerged one of the prize finds of the entire campaign.

The sensation it was to produce was not immediately obvious. Two to three inches beneath the surface emerged a line of finely dressed basalt stones which archaeologists call 'orthostats'. After several weeks Yadin found that the orthostats belonged to a rather large three-celled building, in which they served as dados for a

superstructure of brickworks which had long since disintegrated into mud and silt. Strangely, the excavators prowling within the perimeter of the building ruins were unable to turn up a single fragment of pottery or any other artifact in the topmost layers of the rubble. After examining the site Yadin quickly thought his way through the problem. The detritus was formed of a thick carpet of powdery ash. Evidently the conflagration that devoured the building became a fire storm which weakened the beams supporting the ceiling, until the entire roof collapsed into the structure. Signs of the charred beams had begun turning up. Clearly, if the labourers continued to dig beneath the debris of the roof, they would find remains of what the building contained under the thick layer of destruction.

That is precisely what happened. Beneath the ruins stood intact the stone furniture and paraphernalia of a vast temple—perhaps the most complete set of ritual implements ever found in Israel. In a later chapter, we shall take a closer look at the parallels between this Canaanite shrine and the magnificent Temple of Solomon in Jerusalem. The temple was equipped with a magnificent incense altar, a large basalt basin, earthenware pots and dipper juglets, offering tables, and a small basalt statue of a seated figure bearing a goblet in his hands. Scattered along the floor were bronze figurines, cylinder seals, beads of faience and lapis lazuli, and the shattered remains of a complete set of ritual earthenware vessels.

A statue of the temple's god, minus his feet, was unearthed in front of the temple entrance. Later, in the same general area, excavators found a basalt fragment of a bull, with two feet firmly planted on its back. Fitted together, the two pieces comprised the figure of the Canaanite storm-god Hadad riding on top of his emblematic animal, the bull. They had been severed as if by a sword blow. Below the south-west corner of the temple porch excavators encountered another eloquent testament to the religious fervour of the conquerors—a basalt orthostat 6 feet 6 inches long. Sculptured at its head and along its sides was the beautifully wrought figure of a majestic lion, nearly life-size. It had once served as part of the door jamb of the temple, but had been deliberately buried by the Israelites and then entombed beneath a pile of stones.

The temple of Hadad was the last of four sanctuaries erected one on top of the other, over a period of four hundred years. The long history of the holy site ended with the Israelites, who in an angry orgy of smashing and burning avenged the spirit of their One God against the 'abominations' of the Canaanites. 'And the Lord said. . . "When you pass over the Jordan into the land of

opposite The tell of Hazor dominates this aerial view of magnificent northern Galilee. Note the pillars of a public building

Canaan, then you shall drive out all the inhabitants of the land from before you, and destroy all their figured stones, and destroy all their molten images, and demolish all their high places. . ."'

The Israelite Conquest is a classic example of the seemingly eternal cycle of destruction and regeneration so characteristic of this tormented land, in which primitive outcasts have banded together to swallow up and be swallowed up in their turn by the forces of civilization. Nelson Glueck called the process the struggle between the Desert and Sown.

In Yadin's trenches at Hazor, Glueck's abstract phrase is vividly translated into concrete terms. Stratum XIII is the graveyard of high Canaanite civilization. Locked in a mortice of its own ruin and ash are the amputated shells of soaring towered temples, pitiful stubs of great fortification walls, broad houses and cobbled streets, earthenware masterpieces with which local potters delighted the design-conscious ladies of the day.

This last Canaanite city is entombed beneath Level XII—the squalid detritus of the victorious Israelites. Excavation uncovered circles of rude stone foundations where tents and sheepfolds stood, crude pits or silos scratched into the ground for storing grain or pottery, rudimentary ovens often roughly fashioned out of large jars. Hazor had become a mocking shadow of its former self—a settlement of primitives planted on a carpet of disaster. The civilizing process would start again with Joshua's army of nomads from the desert.

Thus Israel claimed Hazor and secured uneasy mastery of northern Galilee. Through Mycenean IIIB pottery and other dating evidence, Yadin confirmed that Joshua most probably stormed across the land in the latter half of the thirteenth century BC, refuting Garstang's contention about Hazor's fall. In all likelihood, Yadin believes, the battle of Deborah, 'at Taanach, by the waters of Megiddo', in the twelfth century BC did not involve Jabin at all. The long-dead 'King of the Canaanites' was a dramatic anachronism inserted by an imaginative later editor of the Book of Judges.

Yadin's dating of Joshua fitted in neatly with the findings of Albright at Debir, Starkey at Lachish, and excavations at Shiloh, Bethel, Gibeah and other sites. What of the walls of Jericho which, Garstang had claimed, came tumbling down in about 1,400 BC? Archaeologists have now shown that his Jericho 'of Joshua' was actually a thousand years older. Unhappily nothing remains of the Jericho captured by the Israelites. It has been completely eroded.

Two other pieces of evidence should be mentioned, which also

Small seated bronze figurine of a Canaanite deity found at Hazor

opposite The 'Stelae Temple' has been transported in part to the Israel Museum, Jerusalem. In the foreground, the seated figure of a deity. Note the stele with arms raised in supplication to the sacred symbol of a sun disc within a crescent

A bronze representation of a Canaanite from the 16th or 15th century BC

opposite, top One of the impressive basalt lions carved in relief which flanked the entrance way to the temple of orthostats at Hazor
below Several jars containing the bones of children were among the objects disinterred from the graves at Hazor. The burials pre-date the coming of Joshua by over 400 years

seem conclusively to link the late thirteenth century BC with the epoch of the Joshuitic Conquest. The first was provided by a boastful Egyptian pharaoh, Merneptah, who reigned from about 1,236 to 1,223 BC. He erected a great stele at his mortuary temple at Thebes, discovered by Sir Flinders Petrie. The long text was a paean to his triumphs in battle. Part of its conclusion reads:

> The princes are prostrate, saying: 'Mercy!'
>   Not one raises his head among the Nine Bows.
> Desolation is for Tehenu; Hatti is pacified;
>   Plundered is the Canaan with every evil;
> Carried off is Ashkelon; seized upon is Gezer;
>   Yanoam is made as that which does not exist;
> Israel is laid waste, his seed is not. . .

This is not only the first but the only mention of the name Israel in ancient Egyptian texts. It has been dated to about 1,230 BC. Scholars point out that the hieroglyphic determinative sign for a people rather than a land is used with the word Israel, which is the only name in the text so treated. Thus we have direct evidence of the presence of the Israelites in Palestine in the second half of the thirteenth century BC, though not yet as a settled nation. This fits in precisely with the rest of the archaeological evidence.

Let us take, for instance, the results of the ambitious survey of archaeologically unknown Transjordan in the thirties by Rabbi Nelson Glueck, which gave scholars their first scientific insight into the dating of the Patriarchs (see Chapter 5). Working his way 'square mile by square mile' through Transjordan, examining surface ruins and potsherds as he went, Glueck was able to establish that the ancient kingdoms of Edom, Moab and Ammon were not in existence before the thirteenth century BC. Thus, in his own words:

> It became clear. . . why, being denied permission to travel via the King's Highway through the center of Edom and Moab, in spite of their specific promise to deviate neither to the right nor left of it, the Israelites of the Exodus had no choice but to heed the refusal. Their enfeebled forces would have been over-whelmed by the armies of these entrenched kingdoms. They therefore took the desert route northward around the eastern borders of Edom and Moab before turning westward to cross over the Jordan and enter the Promised Land at Gilgal and Jericho. The Exodus through easternmost Transjordan could thus not have taken place before the thirteenth century BC. If it had occurred earlier, the wanderers would have found neither

Edomites nor Moabites with sufficient strength to say yea or nay with regard to anything.

For the first time since the advent of the Patriarchs, the mists obscuring the beginnings of the Hebrews part. With the age of Joshua, we have found the identifiable trail of Israel—in potsherd, stone, ash, and the written word as well.

But some aspects of the Conquest must always remain in shadow. The diplomatic archives of two Eighteenth Dynasty pharaohs, recovered from Tell el-Amarna near Cairo, and known as the Amarna Letters, suggest that some Israelites could already have been in Canaan by the fourteenth century BC, as much as 170 years before the fall of cities such as Hazor. They paint a portrait of the city-states of Canaan reeling under a great invasion by the elusive *Habiru* or *'Apiru*. Their rulers begged the Egyptian suzerain for reinforcements, complained of the activities and depredations of the *Habiru*, in some cases claiming that rival rulers were in league with these mysterious peoples, and that some cities had fallen to them.

The tale of Joshua contains the intriguing assumption that portions of the hilly central zone of Canaan were at least partly in control of the Hebrew tribes before the Joshuitic Conquest. After his victories at Bethel and Ai, Joshua summons 'all Israel, sojourner as well as home-born', to a holy congregation of thanksgiving and rededication on Mounts Gerizim and Ebal, which overlook the ancient city of Shechem (modern Nablus), in the central mountains thirty-two miles north of Jerusalem. When the Conquest is complete, Joshua again calls the 'elders, the heads,

Three of the Tell el-Amarna Letters, written in Akkadian cuneiform, the diplomatic *lingua franca* of their time, by the feudal princes of Canaan's city-states to their pharaonic overlords in the 14th century BC. Such missives as these complained about the *Habiru* menace

the judges, and the officers of Israel' to Shechem for a last peroration against foreign gods and a reconfirmation of his people's covenant with the Lord. Yet we never read of the capture of Shechem, though it holds the key to control of the hilly zone and the special status of tribal cult centre for the conquering Israelites. The passage suggests that Shechem had all along been in control of a body of Israelites, who either never went to Egypt or were perhaps part of an earlier pre-Mosaic migration back to the Promised Land, where they waited to greet the main body of migrants from Egypt late in the thirteenth century BC.

Archaeological evidence confirms that Shechem suffered no destruction in the thirteenth century BC. In short, as G. Ernest Wright, Shechem's chief excavator, puts it: 'The kingdom of Shechem. . . entered the Israelite tribal federation by treaty and not by conquest.'

Most scholars now accept that the biblical saga embodies the traditions of not one but at least two waves of Israelite migration. The first is the journey referred to in Numbers 33, which could have occurred in connection with or after the *Hyksos* expulsion from Egypt some time between the sixteenth and fourteenth centuries BC. In this tradition, there is a relatively easy march directly north along the King's Highway in Transjordan, which must have taken place before Edom and Moab became settled states in the thirteenth century BC. For the second wave, access to the King's Highway was blocked; the Israelites were forced to make the northward transit by way of the eastern borders of Edom and Moab, finally fighting their way across Gilead and into the Promised Land.

Biblical scholars maintain that it was the advance wave which moved into the relatively unsettled central mountain area at the time of the Amarna Letters, leaving some turbulence in its wake, but wreaking nothing like the carnage with which the second wave pressed its settlement claims in places like Debir and Hazor. Is it sheer coincidence that in the Amarna Letters 'Abdu-Heba of Jerusalem continually complains that Lab'ayu, the ruler of Shechem, and his sons 'have given the land of the king to the *Apiru?* We may never have a definitive answer. But taken together with the biblical evidence of an Israelite *entente* at Shechem, and a tortured later history of north-south schisms within the Israelite nation which seem to reflect two totally different backgrounds, it seems reasonable to accept that the Israelites who burned Hazor upon its tell in the thirteenth century BC were not the first of their kind to settle in Canaan.

8 From Judges to Kings

The twelfth and eleventh centuries BC embraced a time of storm and stress not unlike our own epoch. Empires rotted and fell, or lost grip of their outlying dominions. Suppressed or oppressed minorities arose to exploit the collapse of the old order. Others, made homeless by barbaric invaders, formed great waves of migration which rolled across the Mediterranean. With the breakdown of Egyptian, Hittite and Mesopotamian supremacy Canaan, Syria and Asia Minor became vulnerable to infiltration by nomadic raiders. The states of Ammon, Moab and Edom were now established in Transjordan, Phoenicia in north-west Canaan, and Aram.

The turmoil of the times, in which the Hebrew invaders shared, is the dominating theme of the Book of Judges. Even after Joshua's conquest Canaanites clung stubbornly to many of the strategic cities of the plains. Egypt tried desperately to maintain her vital lines of communication through Canaan. There were depredations from Mesopotamia, from Ammonites, Moabites, Amalekites and Midianites against the Israelite newcomers in the central hills. At times, internecine struggles among the Hebrew tribes cast them into perils as great as those they faced from without. Dominating the ranks of Israel's mortal enemies, however, were the Philistines. So profound was their influence across the land that, ultimately, it would come to bear their name: Palestine.

This complex and intriguing period has lured biblical archaeologists since the earliest days of the science, though not always to its further advancement. Much of the work of those who rushed enthusiastically to 'find the Israelites' at the turn of the century has had to be reinterpreted and corrected. Slowly, scientists and scholars have constructed a coherent portrait of a disintegrating Canaan, and the Israel which slowly took root among the ruins in the days of the legendary Judges.

opposite This early Israelite jewellery hoard from Beth-shemesh is shown in the original pottery jug in which it was found. The hoard contained more than 200 objects, including beads and earrings in gold, silver, jasper and cornelian, as well as a typical Byzantine gold chain, proving that the jug had been looted in Byzantine times

Figurine of the fertility
goddess Astarte

Beth-shemesh, guarding vital access through the Vale of Sorek
to Jerusalem from the coastal plain, had been a flourishing Canaanite
city. The citizen of Beth-shemesh might derive a certain sense of
security from the great gate which dominated the southern wall
of the town, and from the wall itself: a massive affair nearly eight feet
wide, containing stones maybe three feet across. The wealthy
Canaanite lived in an ample, well-built home of stone and mud
brick. Its floor and walls were finished off with lime plaster, undoubtedly decorated by a skilled artisan. An ample number of
waterproofed cisterns and lined silos kept him comfortably supplied
with water and grain. The town was well drained.

Some of Beth-shemesh's prosperity undoubtedly came from
copper smelters which excavators unearthed. The Canaanites
had a taste for luxuries: imported ceramic ware from Greece and
Cyprus, plaques and pillared figurines of the fertility goddess
Ashtoreth (Astarte), even Egyptian antiques such as jewelry and
magnificent diorite bowls dating from up to 1,500 years earlier.
One scholar has suggested that Egyptian tomb robbers had perhaps found a booming market among avid Canaanite 'collectors',
a phenomenon not unknown in later times.

With the Israelite newcomers came a marked deterioration in
the quality of material life, an abrupt break with the Canaanite
past, not only in places like Beth-shemesh but in the new villages
which they founded in the more secure central mountain country.
Their houses were poorly and hastily built of ill-fitting stone, with
smaller rock or pebbles sealing the chinks. There was no town-
planning; streets and house walls were laid without rhyme or
reason. City walls were thin and weak, or else the newcomers made
do with the old Canaanite defences, in a poor state of repair.
Among the loosely organized Israelites in the days of the Judges,
there were no slave gangs to undertake vast public works, and
'every man did what was right in his own eyes'. Pottery was
crudely fashioned and fired, and there was hardly time or resources
for the support of art or artists.

But the Book of Judges speaks of another important category
of cities, those against which Joshua's sword was never raised,
which were quite peaceably absorbed within the Israelite con-
federacy. These include most notably the important religious
centre of Shechem, which we discussed briefly in the previous
chapter, and the league of cities led by Gibeon, whose population
cleverly inveigled Joshua into making a peace covenant. Gibeon
became a part of the Hebrew nation through negotiation rather
than war. The Gibeonites obviously came to adopt the religion of

opposite A group of
Phoenician amulets from
the Israelite period

48-642

the Hebrews, and their city, like Shechem, apparently enjoyed a special status within the religious rite of the early Israelite nation. It was to Gibeon in the central mountains eight miles north-west of Jerusalem, 'for that was the great high place', that Solomon later came to sacrifice, and to offer up his moving prayer for wisdom.

Thus an archaeologist delving into the ancient mound beside the village the Arabs call el-Jib should not have been surprised at the absence of the destruction layer which commemorates the tide of Joshuitic conquest at such places as Hazor, Bethel, Lachish and Debir. That is precisely the archaeological picture which James B. Pritchard revealed at the sixteen-acre site of Gibeon between 1956 and 1962. In fact the absence of destruction levels stretching back before the Patriarchs created serious dating problems for the Pritchard expedition. Gibeon seems to have boasted a long-standing tradition of pacifism and non-involvement, sparing it from those cyclical ravages of destruction so common to Palestine. It does not even seem to have had a fortification system before Israelite times.

Joshua's price for sparing the Gibeonites was that 'some of you shall always be slaves, hewers of wood and drawers of water for the house of my God'. It is known that great forests crowned the ridges of the central hills at this time. The second part of Joshua's sentence takes on dramatic perspective against two of Pritchard's discoveries.

In 1956 and 1957 excavations revealed that Gibeon possessed not one but two great water systems. One is an enormous cylindrical 'pool' on the north side of the tell. It is thirty-seven feet in diameter and thirty-five feet deep. Its engineers cut a great staircase five feet wide round the rim of the pool which spirals clockwise towards the bottom. But the steps do no end there: they continue downwards below the pool's bottom into a corkscrew tunnel which descends yet another forty-five feet, ending at a cavernous reservoir which marks the water table deep inside the hill. In all, the Gibeonites skilfully chiselled seventy-nine steps out of the living rock, not to mention the core of the gigantic pool itself. All told, Pritchard estimates that three thousand tons of limestone had to be quarried—a truly mammoth engineering project which he believes was carried out in the twelfth and eleventh centuries, that is, just after Gibeon had been amalgamated into the Israelite tribal confederation.

There is one remarkable facet to the discovery of this 'pool of Gibeon', which readers of the Old Testament will instantly ap-

opposite The pool of Gibeon was excavated in 1956 by James B. Pritchard of the University of Pennsylvania. It may date to the time when the city was peacefully absorbed into the Israelite tribal league *below* This jar handle of the Israelite period was discovered in debris during the excavation of the pool

This Canaanite pottery mould was found at Shechem. It was used for casting tools and weapons and shows two bronze tools which exactly fit the mould

preciate. Two violent episodes in Israelite history actually took place beside such a pool in this very city. In II Samuel, the forces of Abner, commander of Saul's army, take part in a grotesque series of single combats against the young warriors of Joab, David's military leader. 'The battle was very fierce', we are told. The men of Saul are routed. And in Jeremiah, at a much later date, another epic battle is joined 'at the great pool which is in Gibeon' between the forces of Johanan and Ishmael. If Pritchard's dating is correct, the pool would have been a familiar landmark at the very time when both events took place.

We have mentioned two great water systems discovered by Pritchard and his University of Pennsylvania Museum expedition at Gibeon. The second complex, which lies surprisingly close to the pool, represents an even more ambitious feat of engineering. It begins in a long tunnel of ninety-three steps over 167 feet long. The tunnel descends beneath a substantial city wall which was erected after Gibeon joined Israel and ends in a rock-cut cistern room. Water was delivered to the cistern room by a horizontal feeder tunnel from a spring 112 feet inside the bowels of the hill on which the city lay. In times of security, the cistern room was reached directly through an entrance which lay outside the city. But in times of siege the external entrance could be blocked and concealed, with safe access to the cistern room beyond the city still assured by the stepped tunnel under the very noses of any enemy.

Pritchard believes that the tunnel system was constructed in about the tenth century BC, while the pool complex remained in use until the sixth century BC. Thus for some centuries the Gibeonites apparently boasted dual water sources, an achievement in which their reputations as 'drawers of water' must have become a matter of civic pride. Why Gibeon needed two water systems remains a puzzle. The engineering standard they display, however, is breathtaking for their time. Discoveries from a later era attest that these exceptional skills of engineering and hydraulics by no means remained a monopoly of the Israelites of Gibeon. As the relatively meagre archaeological record attests, the times of Saul and David were not for builders, but for warriors. We need only think of the less than grandiose remains of a shattered building which had in all likelihood been nothing less than the first royal residence of ancient Israel—the fortress home of Saul at Gibeah. The royal seat, a rustic farming village, for that is what it was, stood on top of a prominent hill three miles north of Jerusalem, commanding the main road through the hill country of Benjamin, Ephraim and Manasseh. The highway still flanks the base of the hill to the west, a hill crowned today by the half-finished West Bank villa of King Hussein of Jordan; its foundations have destroyed the little that remained to be seen of Saul's Gibeah.

In 1922, when the director of the American Schools of Oriental Research, William F. Albright, began sieving through the detritus of the derelict town, the hill had already been scoured of most of its burden by three thousand years of wind and storm. On its summit, however, clung the stumps of the south-west tower and some of the walls of what had been a primitive stone fortress. Its dimensions were imposing, measuring as much as 170 feet long and 115 feet wide. Albright dated it by pottery and stratification to the late eleventh century BC, which would have been the time of Saul. The citadel, prototype of the forts to be built by the Romans along their Negev lines of communication a thousand years later, was probably two storeys high, built of rough-cut stone with a wooden superstructure, with stout defence towers at each corner, and surrounded by double walls, the outer one perhaps as much as six and a half to seven feet in thickness.

The citadel could claim no kingly architectural stature beyond size. The archaeological finds within it give a picture of humble tastes and a spartan existence in accordance with Saul's rural background: rough, undecorated pottery, grinding stones, utilitarian storage jars and bronze arrowheads. There was one foretaste, however, of a revolution in the making—a ploughpoint of durable iron. The citadel was sacked and destroyed, most probably by the Philistines, who took the life of Saul and his son Jonathan on Mount Gilboa.

Archaeologically, there is hardly any more to tell of the stormy, though fruitful time of King David. At Debir and Beth-shemesh there are fortification walls ascribed by Albright to the time of David; at Megiddo, which finally fell to Israel in about 1,100 BC, there are signs of settlement in David's reign; in Jerusalem there are remains of a wall built by the Jebusites, which were incorporated by David into his own defences for the city he conquered and made Israel's capital (see Chapter 13).

At Tirzah in the north, however, Father Roland de Vaux of Jerusalem's Ecole Biblique has vividly sketched an archaeological portrait of a developing Israelite city which speaks eloquently of growing stability and the beginnings of a social system which would become one of Israel's greatest contributions to its heirs:

... Houses appear which stand in an orderly fashion along

The interior of the south tower of Gibeah excavated by William F. Albright in 1922

opposite Fragment of
another Philistine jar with
characteristic decorations
drawn from nature. The
Philistines, misrepresented
in later ages, were among
the most aesthetically
gifted peoples in Palestine

well-marked streets. The plan is always the same; from the
street one enters a courtyard, on each side of which are one or
more rooms. All the houses follow more or less the same arrangement and have roughly the same dimensions. Each represents
the home of an Israelite family, and the very uniformity of the
dwellings shows that there was no great social inequality among
the inhabitants.

The age of Egypto-Canaanite feudalism was on the wane in
Palestine. The question of what would replace it—the rudimentary,
theologically based egalitarianism brought from the desert by the
Israelites, or the autocracy of the 'overlords' (*seranim*) who ruled
the mighty Pentapolis on the coast, the league of Philistine city-
states—hung in the balance for two hundred years, from the beginning of the twelfth century BC, when the Judges ruled the autonomous tribal league of Israel, to the tenth century BC, when David
came to power.

In fact it was the Philistine struggle which forced on the Israelites
the unhappy necessity of abandoning their autonomous tribal
structure for the centralized direction of a monarch. 'Why has the
Lord put us to rout today before the Philistines?', cry the anguished
elders of Israel after the battle of Aphek. 'We will have a king
over us who will go out before us and fight our battles', demand
the distraught people of Israel of a reluctant prophet Samuel,
who can only warn them of the consequences.

A Philistine pottery jug
found in 1968 in a tomb at
Tel Eitun

The seriousness of the Philistine threat can be measured by the
utter hatred in which they are held by the biblical authors. Of
all the enemies of Israel who people the Old Testament, none are
the object of so much scorn as the masters of Philistia, who, intones
Ezekiel, 'acted revengefully and took vengeance with malice of
heart to destroy in never-ending enmity. . . ' So central were they
to Israel's awareness of its own history that the compiler of Genesis
anachronistically inserted the Philistines into the patriarchal
traditions of some eight centuries earlier. And so influenced were
biblical readers in the West by the biblical fulminations that to
be branded a 'Philistine' has become one of the worst of insults.
Its connotation of an uncultured boor, a priggish embodiment of
bad manners and bad taste, appeared relatively early in our culture.
At the beginning of the century, an influential British clergyman,
quoted by the archaeologist R.A.S. Macalister, gave vent to the
sum of his 'knowledge' about the Philistines in a popular journal:
'The Philistines were of a gigantic size and of herculean strength. . .
brutish size and brutish strength of body, brutish grossness and

brutish stupidity of mind and heart. . . These were the outstanding characteristics of the Philistines.' Macalister responded to this on behalf of all those archaeologists and fascinated amateurs from his time on, who have insisted that rarely has a race of people been so unfairly treated, 'for the most artistic objects found in all the excavations in Palestine come from them'.

For the better part of a century, archaeology has been collecting and collating scraps of evidence which might broaden and deepen the one-dimensional biblical portrayal of the Philistines and carry an understanding of them somewhat beyond that of our turn-of-the-century clergyman.

We might well pick up the archaeological trail of the Philistines in the Shephelah or 'Lowland', the gently undulating country of low-lying hills between the southern coastal plain and the Judaean Hills. Here, for two years between 1898 and 1900, the American archaeologist F.J. Bliss, assisted by R.A.S. Macalister, surveyed a number of ancient tells. Two in particular are relevant to our inquiry: Tell el-Judeideh, most probably Moreshet-gath, the town of the prophet Micah; and Tell es-Safi, thought to be ancient Gath of the Philistine Pentapolis. In their report, Bliss and Macalister noted down their discovery of 'a hitherto undescribed branch of ancient art'. Among the debris of the lower strata were fragments of painted pottery decorated in a manner quite unlike any of the indigenous types they knew. Among its unique features were 'natural motifs' of flowers and graceful birds enclosed by decorated metopes, patterns of fretwork, triangles, graceful spirals and combinations of lined and chequered patterns. Brown or black and 'Indian red' were the colours most often used. Though unable to classify the culture which produced the ware, Bliss and Macalister noted: 'The art just described does not bear exact comparison with any other ancient system of the Mediterranean area. The spirals suggest perhaps Aegean or Mediterranean analogies . . .

Some years earlier, Sir Flinders Petrie, excavating at Tell Yehudiyeh twenty miles north of Cairo, had found specimens of the same ware, which he labelled simply 'foreign pottery'. It was clear that the matter would not rest there. Excited scholars could now link the presence of 'exotic' pottery, possibly of Aegean origin, to other facts they already knew—from Egypt, Crete, and even a few objective details from the Old Testament.

From perhaps the fifteenth down to the end of the twelfth century BC, the Aegean world was shocked by violent change. Minoan Crete collapsed virtually overnight, to be supplanted by the power

opposite An aerial view of 'Armageddon', the great tell of Megiddo. From the times of the pharaohs to the First World War, it figured in battles for control of the fertile Jezreel Plain. Here King Solomon erected one of his great military and administrative centres, and King Ahab housed a great fleet of chariots

of Mycenae, whose trial of strength at Troy in turn carried the ferment to Asia Minor. Having over-extended themselves in their Trojan adventure, the Myceneans fell prey in turn to hordes of barbaric Dorian invaders from the north. Wave upon wave of homeless and displaced people washed across the shores of the Mediterranean basin, from Italy, Sicily and Sardinia in the west to Egypt, Palestine, Syria and Anatolia in the east. Those harbingers of trouble, the Tell el-Amarna Letters of the fourteenth century BC, which we first encountered as a prelude to the Joshuitic Conquest,

opposite A Philistine clay statuette of a goddess dubbed 'Ashdoda', dating from the 12th millennium and found at Ashdod. The goddess is shown seated, her body forming part of the chair

This interesting Philistine ritual stand made of clay dates from the 10th century BC, the time of Saul, David, and Solomon and was found at Ashdod. Its plinth is decorated with five musicians and three animals are incised above the windows

were also contemporary with the end of the Minoan civilization. They speak of coastal raids against Cyprus and Syria by plundering tribes called Lukku, Sherdanu and Danunu. Scholars encountered such tribes again in Egyptian records from the reign of Rameses II a century later. A number of them had allied themselves with the Hittites against Egypt, while the Sherdanu were now being paid as mercenaries to fight for Pharaoh Rameses. His successor Merneptah was also plagued by such tribes, whom he descriptively calls 'People of the Sea'.

It was in the reign of Rameses III, however, that the floodtide of Sea Peoples broke from the north over the coasts of Egypt's Canaanite dominions, even over Egypt itself. This pharaoh had the artistic sensibility to show us what they looked like: on the walls and pylons of his great fortified temple near Thebes, Medinet Habu, were found great sculptured reliefs in which Pharaoh's artist immortalized a massive sea-and-land invasion by the Sea Peoples and their repulsion by Egyptian warriors. The event can be dated from evidence in the accompanying hieroglyphic text to about 1,196 BC, roughly coinciding with the fall of Troy. In the scenes depicting the great naval battle, one of the most graphic and revealing illustrations of ancient warfare ever found, Egyptian biremes carrying bowmen close in on the invaders' oarless sailing craft. Armed only with spears and swords, the Philistines are raked and decimated by the superior firepower of the Egyptian archers. Their boats capsize. Rameses III boasted: 'They were dragged in, enclosed, and prostrated on the beach, killed, and made into heaps from tail to head. Their ships and their goods were as if fallen into the water.'

The same fate awaited the land expedition of the Sea Peoples. In another scene, we see it being spearheaded by three-man chariots, and behind them, two-wheeled carts pulled by snorting oxen carrying women and children. They have obviously come in search of land on which to settle. All are grist for Pharaoh's war machine. Those who are not killed are taken captive. The accompanying text also lists the elements of the Sea Peoples' tribal invasion alliance: the Sherdanu, Danunu, the Shekelesh, Zakhala, Washasha—and the Pelastu. In the Old Testament, the latter name is reflected in the Hebrew *Pelistim*, the Philistines.

What became of the survivors? Ironically, we are told in the Harris Papyrus I recovered from the records of Rameses III, they were granted their wish—a homestead in the land they had come to conquer—in exchange for mercenary service under Pharaoh: 'I settled them in strongholds, bound in my name. Their military

The great naval battle showing the defeat of the Philistines and other Sea Peoples by the Egyptians. The drawing is made after a relief on the wall of the Temple of Rameses III at Medinet Habu near Thebes

classes were as numerous as hundred-thousands. I assigned portions for them all with clothing and provisions from the treasuries and granaries every year.'

For archaeologists, the friezes at Medinet Habu contained one other vital piece of information, a portrait of these Philistines—clean-shaven, bare-chested and wearing a short pleated kilt. Most important of all, however, is their unique headdress or helmet, plumed with an upright row of feathers. Its head band is decorated with circle motifs, zig-zag lines or horizontal stripes. Hardened seamen and soldiers? Yes. 'Brutish' goliaths? Hardly.

With the pottery finds in the Shephelah and the data from Egypt, scholars now linked what they knew with several other vital pieces of information. In the Book of Amos we learn something about the origin of the Philistines. 'Did I not bring up Israel from the land of Egypt, and the Philistines from Caphtor..?' Scholars generally accept that Caphtor derives from the ancient Egyptian name Keftiu, which stands for the region of Crete. There is supporting archaeological evidence of primary connections between the Philistines and Crete, even if we accept that their ultimate assault against Canaan was not launched from there.

In 1908 an Italian antiquarian named Federico Halbherr launched his excavation of the great Minoan palace at Phaestos, on the southern coast of Crete. One of his most important finds remains one of archaeology's biggest puzzles. It is a terracotta tablet, roughly circular in shape and a little over six inches in diameter. Dated to about 1,500 BC, it is called the Phaestos Disc. On both faces, spiralling in continuous rows from its centre toward the outer rim, runs a text in picture writing, as yet undeciphered. The 119 pictograms impressed on face I and the 123 on face II are composed from a basic syllabary of forty-five different characters. The most common symbol is the head of a man wearing a plumed headdress or helmet virtually identical with those worn by the Sea Peoples, (or, generically, Philistines) pictured in the battle scenes at Medinet Habu.

The Bible contained another vital piece of information for early Philistine-hunters. The Book of Joshua tells us: 'There are five rulers of the Philistines, those of Gaza, Ashdod, Ashkelon, Gath, and Ekron. . . ' The discovery of those 'exotic' painted pottery specimens at sites within Philistine territory as delineated by the Bible, taken together with the historical data, pointed to the Sea Peoples as the likely source of the ware. The same beautiful pottery was also discovered in cities on the fringes of the Philistine plain, such as Gezer and Beth-shemesh, which the Sea Peoples

The mysterious terracotta tablet known as the Phaestos Disc discovered by the Italian Federico Halbherr in Crete. The symbol of the warrior with plumed headdress connects the Philistines with the Aegean area

did not own, but must have controlled economically.

A young archaeologist named Duncan Mackenzie came to excavate Beth-shemesh for the Palestine Exploration Fund in 1911. Several years earlier, a German scholar, Herman Thiersch, had published a paper definitively linking the pottery found at Tell es-Safi and Tell Yehudiyeh in Egypt with the Philistines. Mackenzie's special field of knowledge was the Aegean. He had served under Sir Arthur Evans in Crete, and now had come to Palestine to find more of this 'Philistine ware' in order to study the question of its possible connection with Aegean sources. He found the specimens he sought in the ruins of Beth-shemesh, concluding that, while they had been produced locally, their inspiration clearly lay outside Palestine. He paid particular attention to the characteristic spiral design of the Philistine ware. Mackenzie noted that it bore a striking resemblance to the 'Cretan manner of the Third Late Minoan Period' (i.e. about 1,400 BC, when Minoan civilization abruptly ended). However, Mackenzie noticed that unlike the Cretan spirals, these were not connected but discontinuous, as were the designs on the pottery of Cyprus and Rhodes in the same period. Could it have been from these islands that the Philistines brought their pottery? Mackenzie tentatively suggested in his report that Cyprus and Rhodes might well have been the last stations of the Philistine exodus to the shores of Western Asia.

Philistine pottery again provides the clue to the date when these Sea Peoples arrived. Experts can demonstrate that the last Cypriot and Rhodian designs to influence Philistine ware produced in Palestine date from late in the thirteenth century BC. From that time on the influence of Cyprus and Rhodes ceased. The arrival of the Sea Peoples can thus be fixed to the beginning of the twelfth century BC, which coincides exactly with the documentary evidence of Medinet Habu and Rameses III's confrontation with them in about 1,196 BC.

Philistine pottery figurine of a woman in mourning found at Azor. The lower portion of the figurine is sharpened to a point, possibly for insertion into a ritual cup. The mourning woman is also a common motif found at sites in the Aegean

A study of the distribution of their pottery and other data throughout the ruins of Israel provides the archaeological equivalent of a geo-political map showing Philistine holdings at the height of their power. They extended over a wider area than that of the biblical Pentapolis. Their control stretched from south of Gaza along the Palestinian coast to the port of Dor, extended east across the strategically vital plain of Jezreel to the great mound city of Beth-shean, and perhaps southwards from there to encompass a portion of the Jordan Valley. We can now understand the despair of the Israelites: the Philistines had cut their territory in half.

It was in this black hour, in about the year 1,000 BC, that the body of King Saul was found and mutilated by the victorious Philistines on the battlefield at Mount Gilboa. 'And they cut off his head. . . put his armour in the temple of Ashtaroth; and they fastened his body to the wall of Beth-shean.' Thanks to the archaeological findings there can be no doubt that the Philistines actually held the fortress of Beth-shean, first in the service of the Egyptians, and then for themselves in the decline that followed the death of Rameses III.

Between 1922 and 1926 the excavators of that city recovered fifteen cylindrical sarcophagi from the cemetery on the northern precincts of the mound. They represent one of the most singular burial customs in the material record of Palestine. They were just large enough to receive the corpse, through a hatch-like aperture cut at head-and-shoulder level in the coffin. It was in the lids of these apertures that the singularity lay, for on them in high relief were moulded stylized heads and arms, with hands as though folded on the chest in repose. It is not the artistic merit of these coffin 'hatches' that arrests the eye, but the headdresses painstakingly rendered by the artist on top of each head—the helmet of feathers with the decorated headband first seen by archaeologists in the depiction of the Sea Peoples at Medinet Habu.

On the edge of encroaching sand dunes and sunflower fields which rim the shores of southern Israel, and some two and a half miles from the sea, an expedition now headed by Dr Moshe Dothan (with the help of his wife Trude) has been probing into the reddish-brown mudbrick ruins of Ashdod since 1962. It was one of the greatest cities of the Philistine Pentapolis—the city to which the Philistine army brought its prize, the Ark of the Covenant, after the victory at Aphek. In its prime it was a vast community of ninety acres, comprising a seventeen-acre acropolis and a teeming lower city. Wind and water have remelted much of the mudbrick into the thick clay soil it once was. For several centuries Arab villagers nearby have dredged its rich earth for fertilizers and clay to shape and bake into mudbrick once again. The dig at Ashdod represents the first full-scale archaeological study of a major Philistine city, the full yield of which will take some time to harvest and evaluate.

Evidence at Ashdod appears to confirm an arrival in the twelfth century BC of the Sea Peoples, a violent one to judge by Dr Dothan's finds. They camped on top of the ruins of the great Canaanite city they levelled, later rebuilding a portion of the old Canaanite fortress and walls and incorporating them into their own

above A cemetery of the Sea Peoples at Beth-shean. Several anthropoid sarcophagi are shown

defence system. Their ceramic ware represented a departure but in all else they adopted the ways of the land — borrowed the Canaanite deities Dagon and Ashtoreth, based their temples on the Canaanite model, ultimately adopted the Canaanite language, and were absorbed and lost within its turbulent history.

In 1968 the Dothans discovered a transitional link to Philistine origins. In the earliest Philistine layer they found a number of clay vessels which were not locally produced, but seemed to the Dothans to have been brought to Palestine with the first wave of Philistine settlers. The style is closely related to ceramic ware excavated at

Philistine ritual vessel composed of a hollow clay ring adorned with various (objects) connected to the ring. These vessels are known as *kernoi*. Liquid may have been circulated through it to represent 'the water' or 'fountain' of life

Sinda in Cyprus and ascribed by archaeologists there to the Sea Peoples. This seems to provide confirmation that Cyprus was most probably the final jumping-off point for the sea migration to the east. Other objects which have come to light, including striking hollow kernoi rings used in 'water of life' fertility rites, and sensitive figurines of mourning women, are clearly traceable to similar examples of ceramic art found in Cyprus and the Greek mainland towards the end of the Mycenean epoch.

Earlier in this chapter we mentioned the discovery of a rusted iron ploughpoint in the ruins of Saul's Gibeah, dated to the tenth century BC. The appearance of iron deserves more than a casual mention, particularly in measuring the full impact of the Philistines on Canaan and Israel. In the south-eastern sector of Tell Ashdod, dubbed by Dr Dothan the 'industrial area', his excavation team unearthed from Philistine strata a huge quantity of iron slag, telltale evidence that experienced iron makers had been busily at work there. This discovery dovetailed neatly with highly suggestive evidence from earlier excavations; among them were an iron spear from a Philistine tomb in Egypt, an iron dagger blade and an iron knife from Philistine graves at Sharuhen (Tell el-Fara'h) in southern Palestine, and an iron knife in one of Macalister's 'Aegean' graves at Gezer, iron implements from Tell Qasile and Megiddo. These finds have been dated to the twelfth century BC, the time of the Judges, and represent the earliest appearance of the new metal in an identifiable context in Palestine. They herald the arrival there of the age of iron, a far more durable and plentiful metal than bronze for the manufacture of weapons and farming implements. They have convinced a large number of archaeologists that it was the Philistines who introduced the new technological revolution to the country.

These discoveries quickly recalled to scholars this passage from the Book of I Samuel:

> Now there was no smith to be found throughout all the land of Israel; for the Philistines said, 'Lest the Hebrews make themselves swords or spears'; but every one of the Israelites went down to the Philistines to sharpen his ploughshare, his mattock, his axe, or his sickle. . . So on the day of the battle there was neither sword nor spear found in the hand of any of the people with Saul and Jonathan. . .

This passage, together with the fact that no artifact of iron appears at an Israelite site until two hundred years later, suggests to many experts that the Philistines must have maintained a monopoly on iron-making and jealously guarded the secret of its manufacture for many years. Here, they believe, lay the real Goliath of the Philistines. More than the economic stranglehold it gave them over Israel, monopoly of the iron market was their insurance that the balance of power in weapons technology would remain in their favour, a strategic device we have seen in operation in our own nuclear era.

The Rameses III texts suggest that the Sea Peoples descended upon the Syrian and Palestinian coasts from the north, Anatolia in Asia Minor, the land of the Hittites. Here they could have landed from Cyprus and the eastern Aegean, acquiring the secret of iron making from the Hittites, who seem to have possessed it as early as 2,000 BC.

The Philistines' proprietary interest in iron was broken with the victories of King David and the consolidation of power by King Solomon. For the Sea Peoples, iron had been but an advantage of the moment. The balance was finally turned by the determination of a united Israel, focused in the centralized leadership of able monarchs, and David's alliance with the Phoenician King Hiram of Tyre, who successfully challenged the Philistines' supremacy at sea. The rise of Solomon would hasten the Philistine decline and fall. Beyond that it would mark the establishment of Israel as a new and growing nation and usher in the long awaited 'golden age', a period of peace and stability whose duration was all too brief.

An iron knife from a tomb on the Palestine coast. The Bible attributes great importance to Philistine metal workers who established a monopoly in Palestine for the production of iron implements

9 The Gates of Solomon

In the tenth century BC a new historic order is established in the land. King Saul has united a loose confederation of tribes into a single nation. King David has assured its survival, breaking the back of Philistine power with its monopoly on ironmaking. The direct beneficiary is the Israelite farmer: his land is safe, and a free market in durable iron tools has given him the power to cultivate it more efficiently.

David has established a great capital at Jerusalem on the borderland between north and south round which the contentious tribes of both regions can unite. Israel now controls the great trade routes which pass through her territory, and her partnership with the Phoenicians on land and sea affords her a share in the great commercial wealth of the Near East. For a relatively brief moment Israel lies unmolested by the great powers on her periphery and expands to fill the vacuum. The inheritor of this golden moment is King Solomon: 'For he had dominion over all the region west of the Euphrates from Tiphsah to Gazah, over all the kings west of the Euphrates; and he had peace on all sides round about him. And Judah and Israel dwelt in safety, from Dan even to Beersheba, every man under his vine and under his fig tree, all the days of Solomon.' According to the Bible, he built store cities, and 'cities for his chariots and the cities for his horsemen, and whatever Solomon desired to build . . . ' In partnership with the Phoenicians he established an Israelite merchant fleet. Israelite middlemen dealt in horses and chariots 'from Egypt and Kue', which they in turn exported 'to all the kings of the Hittites and the kings of Syria.' In establishing the great Temple and his palace, the House of the Forest of Lebanon in Jerusalem, Solomon also created a mystical bond between a capital city and its people that would be unique in world history.

Few Old Testament kings were blessed with the gifts which

This splendid ivory box carved with lions and sphinxes was found at Megiddo in 1937

opposite 'Solomon's Gate' —the main entrance portal of the great Israelite city of Megiddo. This depiction is from a scale model showing different periods of settlement at Megiddo. In all, excavators unearthed strata representing the ruins of 20 superimposed cities

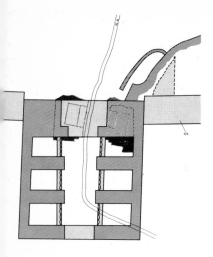

A plan of the Solomonic
six-celled gateway
at Megiddo

history accorded Solomon, and, for that reason, none would ever equal his reputation as a builder. For that reason, too, none have captured the imagination of biblical archaeologists as has Solomon.

Two important discoveries are relevant here. The first was made by the expedition of the Hebrew Union College, which set out in 1964 to re-examine and bring up to date the findings of R.A.S. Macalister, who excavated a large portion of the mound of Gezer at the turn of the century. In 1965 a team opening up a new excavation area in the south central area of the axe-shaped tell, called Field II, encountered what the Archaeological Director, William G. Dever, called a 'a dramatic destruction level—black ash, chunks of charred timber, calcined plaster, tumbled stones, and mudbrick debris—reaching a depth of twenty inches.' The scorched pottery sorted from this swathe of devastation could be dated to the middle of the tenth century BC—early in the reign of Solomon. Excavators quickly recalled that singular passage in I Kings in which 'Pharaoh king of Egypt had gone up and captured Gezer and burnt it with fire, and had slain the Canaanites who dwelt in the city . . .' This same Pharaoh then gave Gezer as a dowry to this daughter, whom he presented to King Solomon as a bride. In this bizarre fashion the last great Canaanite city to withstand the Israelites was absorbed into the dominion of Jerusalem.

The excavators identified Solomon's generous benefactor, who was also the perpetrator of Gezer's destruction, as the Pharoah Siamun, whose reign is assigned to the very same period as Solomon, from 960 to 930 BC. The Israeli historian Abraham Malamat has pointed out that this is the only instance in the historical record in which a great Egyptian pharoah deigned to give his daughter in marriage to a foreign monarch—eloquent evidence of the relative stature of Solomon among his Near-Eastern peers.

The second find plays the central role in a fascinating story of archaeological discovery which begins in 1925 and ends nearly half a century later, encompasses three of the greatest cities in King Solomon's dominion, and marks one of the most revealing trails in the archaeological investigation of the Holy Land.

The story starts at Megiddo, the lofty thirteen-acre mound which looms like a sleeping sentinel above the western end of the broad and fertile Jezreel Valley. In its day Megiddo was one of the most strategically important cities in the Near East. In its dual role as fortress and bustling commercial centre, it guarded the mouth of the Wadi Ara, the narrow eight-mile pass connecting the coastal plain with the Jezreel Valley. Thus the city constituted a formidable man-made barrier to great armies and caravans alike along the road from Egypt to Phoenicia and Mesopotamia. Little wonder that it was the victim of a tormented history, reduced so often to char and rubble by invading armies that legend transmuted it into the Armageddon of the Book of Revelations in the New Testament, the setting for the final battle between the forces of Good and the satanic forces of Evil.

As the founder of the Oriental Institute of the University of Chicago in 1919, and the man who pioneered modern American research into the antiquities of the ancient Near East, James Henry Breasted was determined to excavate Megiddo on a scale as yet unmatched in Palestinian archaeology. It would be a model of modern scientific technique. It would embody the very latest technological devices and methods. His dream was to excavate the seventy-foot mound *completely* over a twenty-five year period, stripping off each of its twenty superimposed cities dating from the fortieth to the fourth century BC.

Breasted's ambitious project received the backing of the oil millionaire and philanthropist John D. Rockefeller Jr., and he was able to launch the Oriental Institute expedition in 1925— 'with resources', wrote Professor William Albright, 'which dwarfed all preceding archaeological enterprises.' The entire tell was purchased from the Arab farmers who tilled it, and Breasted lured Dr Clarence Fisher from the Beth-shean expedition undertaken by the University of Pennsylvania Museum to head the Megiddo excavation. It was the wonder of its field and its time. A large stone building was constructed as staff headquarters, an unheard-of luxury to archaeologists used to tents or makeshift huts. The building was fitted with drafting rooms; advanced filing systems for artifacts, plans and photographs; a modern darkroom; a telephone system to connect offices with the excavation site; a spacious kitchen with a grand cast-iron stove (it is still to be seen in the building now used as the Megiddo Museum, a glorious antiquity in its own right) and a staff tennis court!

The Megiddo expedition introduced aerial photography to Palestinian archaeology. 'The advantages of viewing excavations from a height directly above have long been realized', wrote the excavators. First, they tried taking overhead views of the dig in progress from the top of a thirty-three foot extension ladder. When this proved unsatisfactory, they purchased a huge weather balloon and hoisted it above the mound bearing a camera with an electrically operated shutter.

But there was still a number of problems that affluence and technology could not overcome adequately: malaria caused a rapid turnover of staff and this affected the results; the Depression, coupled with the death of Breasted in 1935, brought on a financial crisis which forced the excavators to abandon the dream of their late organizer to peel away every layer of the mound; the dig was restricted to selected sections, the standard method employed today as befitting the limitations of scientific precision, and the feelings of modern excavators that large areas of a tell should be preserved for the advanced techniques of future archaeologists.

The Megiddo excavation continued until 1939, when the Second World War brought it to an end. In fifteen years of digging it had cost nearly a million dollars. The archaeological contributions of the Megiddo excavations were enormous. However, much of the dating and identification of strata, particularly the Israelite sequence was incorrect, thus creating serious problems, as we shall see.

As the layers of the tell gave way to the spades and picks of the work-gangs, there emerged from the northern flank an impressive fortified gate complex. This gateway merits some description, for it is central to our story. A visitor to this ancient city on foot, donkey or chariot first ascended from the plain on a broad ramp or tell traversing the north face of the mound. He entered a guarded foregate whose roof was supported by two small flanking towers. Having passed this security point, he approached a broad cobbled plaza or square large enough to accomodate the turning radius of a chariot or cart. In this entrance plaza much of the business of the town was conducted—elders holding impromptu discussions on community affairs, officials holding court, children watching the comings and goings of citizens, soldiers and visitors, peddlars hawking their wares.

Edging his way through the bustle, our traveller turned sharply left, and found himself before the imposing main gate, a large roofed structure about twenty-five feet deep fronted by twin two-storey towers. The entrance between them was over fourteen feet wide. He entered the imposing gate chamber, and the pair of great wooden doors (perhaps covered with bronze plating) swung back on stone sockets into great recesses in the chamber. Then he passed the final security hurdle before entering the city. The entrance passage was flanked by three pairs of pilasters forming three cells on each side. Within each recess, guards could take their stations during a siege, ready to spring from behind the protective piers with swords drawn to obstruct any enemy who succeeded in breaching the huge wooden doors.

To the Megiddo excavators, this six-celled gateway was unique in Palestine, as was the masonry technique used to build it. Massive

blocks of stone, well-drafted and cut almost perfectly true, were fitted together without the use of mortar. So tightly did the stones fit that it was impossible for the excavators to insert a knife blade between them. The spaces behind the stone faces were packed with rubble and clay fill. The fine stonework was typical of the masonry techniques of the Phoenicians, recalling the biblical information craftsmen to assist in his great building enterprises. The excavators that Solomon called on King Hiram of Tyre for skilled builders and confidently ascribed the Megiddo gate complex to King Solomon, and this judgment has withstood the subsequent tests of science.

After studying its unique design Professor William Albright came up with an exciting piece of scholarly insight. In the fortieth chapter of the Book of Ezekiel, the prophet in the twenty-fifth year of the Babylonian exile has 'visions of God' in which he minutely and eloquently describes details of the Temple in Jerusalem. Early in this mystical flight Ezekiel approaches the eastern gate of the temple enclosure, and says: 'And there were three side rooms on either side of the east gate; the three were of the same size . . .' This description accorded exactly with the six-celled northern gate of Megiddo. Could the architects of Solomon's Temple also have had a hand in planning the great gate of Megiddo?

Ezekiel also gives the precise dimensions of the Temple's eastern gate in the ancient measure called a cubit. While the exact value of the Israelite cubit is unknown, archaeologists presume that it approximated to that of the Egyptian common cubit, whose length is 17.7 inches. If we apply this formula to Ezekiel's measurements, the width of the Temple gate would have been 14 feet 9 inches. The width of the Megiddo gate was found to be 13 feet 9 inches. The length of the Temple gate is given by Ezekiel as fifty cubits, or 75 feet 9 inches. The gate of Megiddo was 66 feet 7 inches long. Surely the similarity was not just coincidence, thus increasing the likelihood that the builders of the two great Solomonic works were one and the same.

The great gate of Megiddo was not the only construction assigned by the excavators to Solomon's city, and here the plot thickens. Seemingly bonded to the gate was a solid stone fortification wall which encircled the crest of the mound for a length of over half a mile. The wall, perhaps twelve feet thick, was composed of a series of alternating recesses and salients, known as offerts and insets, which allowed defending bowmen on top of the wall to bring attackers under withering crossfire.

Contemporary with this wall were four structures which represent the most spectacular find in Megiddo—complexes which could

only have been used as stables. Recalling the statement in the Book
of I Kings that Solomon had built 'cities for his chariots' and 'cities
for his horsemen', the archaeologists ascribed the stables to him, as
well. Near the stable complex on the southern side of the mound
lay the ruins of a great fortified palace which seemed to be Solomonic too. Its masonry style was Phoenician, as were two proto-
aeolic capitals found lying in the rubble. Once they had crowned
the tops of pilasters attached to the walls of a large room or corridor. They are fashioned from a triangle within two volutes—
a stylized palm tree. Not only would the proto-aeolic capital
become a trademark of royal construction under the later Israelite
kings, but the Greeks would borrow it from the Phoenicians in the
eighth century BC. In Ionia and Cyprus it would evolve into the
graceful Ionic capital so familiar in the West.

But this so-called southern palace of Solomon created a problem
for the excavators. On top of its ruins ran the offset-inset wall
which had also been credited to the same king. How could *both*
be Solomonic? They proposed two alternative explanations.
Either the palace had been built by David as an isolated administrative centre or fortress when the city was unoccupied, and then
destroyed by Solomon to permit the erection of his wall; or Solomon had ordered its construction early in his reign, destroying it
when he decided to raise the fortification wall of offsets and insets.
The latter theory has a rather desperate ring to it. It seems unlikely
that the king would have approved a plan for the wall which spelled
destruction for one of the most impressive buildings of his reign.
Scholars were clearly disturbed by these suggestions, and they were
debated for years. Surely something was wrong—but what?

In 1939, the archaeologists of the Oriental Institute supervised
the final packing up of their equipment and the closing of their
sumptuous camp after fourteen long years. The mound again became the domain of weeds, wild grasses and lizards.

During and after the days of the great Megiddo expedition, other
scholars conducted surgical probes of Israelite layers among the
tells of Palestine, seeking to isolate and identify the lost cities of
Solomon, but with limited success. When Professor Yigael Yadin
chose to excavate Hazor, he was armed with the following tools:
precise information about tenth century BC pottery, the findings
of the Megiddo excavators, and a brief passage from the Book of
I Kings. Of the quotation, Professor Yadin has written: 'Hardly
ever in the history of archaeological digging has such a short verse
in the Bible helped so much in identifying and dating actual remains

An ivory plaque
showing a Canaanite
woman from the Megiddo
ivory hoard

found by the spade.' It reads: 'And this is the account of the forced labour which King Solomon levied to build the house of the Lord and his own house and the Millo and the wall of Jerusalem and Hazor and Megiddo and Gezer . . .' Did this account of Solomon's building activities represent merely a haphazard grouping of cities, or did the biblical authors intend it to convey a particular meaning? Had the king built in all these places as part of a single grand design?

Hardly a trace remained of Solomon's Jerusalem. At Megiddo, the Oriental Institute expedition had produced a Solomonic city which included a gate, stables, palaces, a wall and a hornet's nest of archaeological contention. Yet R.A.S. Macalister, digging at Gezer in the early 1900's, had made no claims at all for any discoveries attributed to Solomon. Might Hazor help to shed light on that cryptic verse in I Kings? 'It was . . . natural enough', wrote Yadin, 'that we hoped to succeed in uncovering Solomon's city as described in the Bible, which would in turn help clarify his building enterprises elsewhere.'

A bronze cult stand of the Israelite period

In the second season of the dig, in 1956, the field team of Area A near the centre of the bottle-shaped upper mound uncovered a fortification wall of the design which archaeologists call case-mating. It lay on the tenth stratum from the top, a layer whose pottery and stratigraphic position led Yadin to believe it might be the Solomonic city of Hazor. What emerged there the following year proved to be one of the outstanding discoveries of the dig. Yadin was hastily called to Area A. In clearing the casemate wall, the labourers had encountered the edge of a structure to which the wall was bonded. A gatehouse? Yadin seemed tense with excitement. At first, few who watched realized what Yadin had in mind when he ordered an assistant to bring the scientific report of the old Megiddo expedition from his office. Creative intuition, or a 'hunch', which is so essential a part of this man, led him to decide that this was the moment to apply the acid test to that verse from I Kings.

When the volumes arrived, Yadin asked for the measurements of the Solomonic gate discovered at Megiddo so many years before. He gave a few quiet commands and suddenly the nature of his experiment began to dawn on his staff, who had streamed from the other areas of the dig to watch. With tape-measures, pegs and twine, they laid down the exact plan of the Megiddo gate on the ground which shrouded the suspected Solomonic gate of Hazor. When it was done, Yadin turned quietly to the workmen and said: 'Now, dig here and you will find a corner. Dig here and you will find a wall. Then dig there and you'll see another corner. There

Israelite horned altar found at Megiddo dating from the 10th or 9th centuries BC

will be rooms here, here, and here.' Then pointing to two of the longest pieces of taut string, he said: 'That will be the length of the entryway, and this will be its width. Please, start to dig.' Nothing could be heard but the soft sound of spades in yielding earth.

Yadin was correct on every count. The massive ruined gate which emerged was virtually identical in every detail with the plan. It was the exact twin of the Solomonic gate at Megiddo.

We referred above to another singular aspect of Solomonic construction at Hazor, the casemate design of the wall. It consists of a double wall, a stout outer bulwark and a thinner inner one. The walls are divided at regular intervals into cells or compartments by a series of cross-walls or partitions. When empty, the cells could be used to store military equipment and house soldiers within the actual line of defence without disturbing the civil peace of the town. Under the shock of the battering ram, the cells could be filled with rubble or earth. Having breached the outer barrier, the enemy would be forced to clear away the fill and begin battering the second wall, under withering fire from defenders on the broad parapet above.

In the light of his Solomonic discoveries at Hazor, Yadin's curiosity quickly shifted to Gezer and Megiddo. If that short verse in I Kings were totally accurate, there should have been a six-celled

A manger and hitching post belonging to Ahab's vast stable complex at Megiddo. The Megiddo excavators mistakenly ascribed them to King Solomon

gate at Gezer, but Macalister had reported none. And at Megiddo, the Solomonic gate should have been joined to a casemated wall, not a solid one of offsets and insets. 'Gezer', Yadin wrote, 'was a mystery, and Megiddo a fly in the ointment.'

Back in his Jerusalem study, Professor Yadin tackled the problem of Gezer. Still operating on his 'hunch', he began to pore through the three-volume report which Macalister had published after his dig at Gezer in 1909. His eyes were quickly drawn to the plan of a massive structure on the south central perimeter of the mound which Macalister had identified as the 'Maccabean Castle' from the Hellenistic period; i.e. the second to first centuries BC. 'In the drawing of that so-called castle', Yadin announced to his astonished colleagues, 'it was easy to see immediately a casemate wall like ours at Hazor and half a gate which was exactly like ours at Hazor and the one at Megiddo. They were absolutely identical in plan and in dimensions. The intent of the verse from I Kings was correct. They all had been built by the same royal engineers of King Solomon's Court, according to the same blueprint!'

Yadin facetiously likes to say that he never went to Gezer with a spade to prove his discovery 'because subconsciously I didn't want to destroy my own brilliant theory'. But in 1969 the conclusive proof was provided for him. Under Dr Dever's direction, the Hebrew Union College Expedition re-excavated Macalister's 'Maccabean Castle'. From it emerged the other half of the Solomonic gate and casemate walls, exactly as Yadin had predicted. What is more, the stratum contained fragments of red-burnished Israelite pottery characteristic of the late tenth century BC. Thus Dr Dever was able to report 'Yadin's hunch was correct—Solomon did indeed rebuild Gezer!'

That left only the 'fly in the ointment', Megiddo. And in three short campaigns of re-excavation on that site, in 1960, 1966 and 1967, Yadin produced dramatic proof that the great biblical city also fitted exactly into the Solomonic pattern uncovered at Hazor and in his 'paper' re-excavation of Gezer. Clearly visible beneath Megiddo's solid offset-inset wall was a rampart of casemates which the earlier excavators had overlooked. It was this wall which had originally been bonded to the Solomonic gate, as at Hazor and Gezer. It followed that the stables and solid fortification wall of Megiddo were not the work of Solomon but of another Israelite king, most probably Ahab, who reigned over half a century later. The riddle of the southern palace was thus neatly resolved. It was clearly contemporary with the six-celled gate and casemate wall— a royal residence fit for and obviously built by Solomon.

But it was by no means the only one. On the first day of the 1967 season, Professor Yadin's team discovered the foundation walls of what proved to be another palace in the northern sector of the mound, a building complex even more monumental than its counterpart to the south. Labelled on Yadin's plan as Palace 6,000, it was a rectangle covering 6,458 square feet of ground. On entering from the south, a visitor in Solomonic times found himself in a broad central courtyard bounded on three sides by spacious corridors and rooms. At one corner of the complex rose a single guard tower. Within the palace, Yadin found a large amount of pottery truly befitting a royal pantry—hundreds of storage jars, dishes, juglets and cooking pots—all of them typical of the tenth century BC, the time of Solomon.

The architectural design of this impressive northern building is known from Phoenician sites, where such edifices served as ceremonial palaces. The northern palace of Megiddo may also have 'served ceremonial purposes and perhaps even the King himself whenever he visited the city', suggests Professor Yadin. 'This fact is particularly interesting, because it adds further evidence to the biblical assertion of Phoenician influence on Solomon's building activities.' King Solomon's close collaboration with the Phoenician King Hiram was far more than a business partnership. The sophisticated traders of Sidon and Tyre whose travels took them to every corner of the ancient civilized world acquired, synthesized and retransmitted to Israel a cultural inheritance which leavened the spartan Hebrew culture of the desert in the tenth century BC, just as Phoenician contacts with the Western world would help to produce the brilliant civilizing light of the Greek city-states several hundred years later. But the cosmopolitanism bequeathed to Israel by the Phoenicians also played a fundamental role in sparking off the conflict between prophetic advocates of the uncompromising Hebrew faith and the more wordly ruling classes of Judah and Israel which lies behind so much of the tragedy of later biblical history.

Where does historical fact about Solomon end and legend begin? His vast wealth is very much a part of present-day mythology. It is based on the Bible's tales of 'silver and gold, garments, myrrh, spices, horses, and mules'—brought as gifts from 'all the kings of the earth', imported by Israelite merchants and traders from Arabia, borne by ship from distant lands. A generous fillip of modern romance was added by Rider Haggard with his popular African adventure tale *King Solomon's Mines*, published at the end of the nineteenth century. Then from out of the southern desert in the

This bronze weight, shaped like a monkey, holds an apple-like object in one hand and covers an eye with the other. It was discovered by Prof. Yadin's expedition to Megiddo in 1969 and dates from the second half of the twelfth century BC

late thirties came the archaeologist Nelson Glueck with a sensational report which lent an aura of scientific credibility to it all.

While exploring the Arava, the roasting valley between the rose-pink mountains of Transjordan and the Negev, he discovered a long forgotten copper-smelting and mining site called by the Arabs 'Khirbet Nahas', the Copper Ruin. At another mound of ruins just five hundred yards from where the Arava slopes beneath the turquoise Gulf of Aqabah, a place called Tell el-Kheleifeh, he excavated a large building which he took to be a great smelting complex for Solomon's copper industry. To his collective package of copper finds in the Arava, Glueck applied the romantic and all-inclusive title of 'King Solomon's Mines'. He also identified Tell el-Kheleifeh with the legendary biblical port of Ezion-geber, 'which is near Eilat on the shore of the Red Sea'. Here Solomon had with the help of King Hiram built his fleet, which brought gold and precious stones from Ophir, and 'gold, silver, ivory, apes and peacocks' from Tarshish. Glueck's discoveries were enthusiastically incorporated into the standard fare of travel guides and archaeologists alike.

Beginning in 1960, Dr Benno Rothenberg, whom we first encountered in connection with the discovery of the Egyptian mining temple at Timna, published a series of papers criticizing Glueck's findings. Rothenberg has himself specialized in the archaeology of the Negev-Arava region, and for a time served

Domestic Israelite pottery, *left to right* Jars and jug with spout, pilgrim's bottle and oil lamp. These objects were found in the excavations at Tel Amal

Monumental pillars of natural rock at 'King Solomon's Mines' at Timna in the Arava just just north of Eilat. Some authorities dispute whether 'Solomon's mines' as such ever existed

A general view of Jezirat Far'un which may have been the home of Solomon's trading fleet

as Dr Glueck's assistant and chief photographer. He convincingly argued that the building at Tell el-Kheleifeh, rather than serving as the copper smelter which produced the bronze for Solomon's Temple, had in fact been only a storehouse or granary. In 1965 Glueck graciously accepted Rothenberg's contention as correct. But both he and the Israeli Ministry of Tourism still clung tenaciously to the theory that 'King Solomon's Mines' lay somewhere in the Arava.

Rothenberg, however, basing his argument on what he insists is a misreading of the pottery evidence, is adamant that the Arava and the Negev were never mined for copper in King Solomon's time—in short, that there are no 'King Solomon's Mines'. He cites verses in II Chronicles as evidence that the vast stocks of bronze used by Solomon for the fixtures and fittings of the Holy Temple came

from material collected by his father King David expressly for that purpose, by conquest and Phoenician trade: 'With great pains I have provided for the house of the Lord a hundred thousand talents of gold, a million talents of silver, and bronze and iron beyond weighing . . .' Finally, he argues that Tell el-Kheleifeh cannot be the lost Solomonic port of Ezion-geber, which would have had to be at the water's edge. In fact the tell lies five hundred yards from the actual shoreline, and there is no evidence indicating that there has been a dramatic change in the waterline since 1,000 BC. Glueck himself conceded 'that the shoreline has experienced no great change' since the days of Solomon.

Where, then, is the lost Ezion-geber, the home port of Solomon's great fleet. This is just one of the many mysteries awaiting the picks and spades of future archaeologists.

The ghostly remains of the medieval castle known to the Crusaders as the Isle de Graye. Arabs call the island Jezirat Far'un, the Isle of the Pharaohs. Just south of Eilat on the Sinai coast, it is believed by some scholars to have been the site of King Solomon's great port of Ezion-geber

10 A House Divided

In June 1961 there occurred one of those archaeological finds that are common in a land so thickly scarred with the leavings of man. On the western slope of the Judaean range, about three miles east of Lachish, a bulldozer widening a cutting for a road uncovered the mouth of a burial cave which had been sealed for 2,500 years. Joseph Naveh, who is both a specialist in ancient writing and a staff archaeologist for the Israel Department of Antiquities, was called to carry out a 'rescue operation', a rapid but thorough excavation of the cave before the priority road project erased all traces of the tomb. Naveh dated it to the late eighth century BC. For the most part the finds were typical of a pre-exilic tomb: skeletons on benches of stone lying amid a jumble of votive pottery objects and a few personal possessions.

In one respect, however, this burial cave was different. In the face of all tradition, inscriptions and drawings had been etched in the soft limestone walls of the ante-chamber, perhaps by members of the family of the deceased, perhaps by strangers seeking shelter or refuge. There were carvings of a man playing a lyre, and another raising the palms of his hands in a gesture of prayer. A third etching was that of a man whose dress and headgear seem to identify him as a priest or Levite. Naveh translated three brief but moving inscriptions which he found incised on the walls:

Yahweh is the God of the whole earth; the mountains of Judah belong to him, to the God of Jerusalem.
The Mount of Moriah Thou hast favoured, the dwelling of Yah, Yahweh.
Yahweh deliver us!

Surely something beyond piety lay behind these inscriptions.

opposite Detail of a panel from the palace of Sennacherib at Nimrud portraying the siege and destruction of Lachish (see page 184)

Among the finds at Tell Dan was the so-called 'Chariot Krater', bearing a beautiful depiction of a painted chariot of Mycenaean origin. It was found in the tomb of a Mycencenaean dignitary, attesting to the international importance of Dan in Canaanite times

They are the only ones known in pre-exilic tombs. They contain the earliest mention of Jerusalem from a non-biblical source in Israel, and the only mention of Mount Moriah to appear before the literature from the days of the Second Temple. They, and the drawings, fly in the face of the biblical injunction against graven images. Frozen in stone is a desperate plea for salvation by terror-stricken men in an hour of mortal danger: perhaps, Naveh suggests, the advance of the warlord Sennacherib of Assyria upon Jerusalem in the reign of King Hezekiah in 701 BC. Whatever the crisis, that short entreaty is full of dramatic anguish.

In about 922 BC Solomon's arrogant son and heir, Rehoboam, went to Shechem to receive the loyalty of the northern tribes. They demanded release from the levies imposed by Solomon to support his building projects and sumptuous court. Rehoboam refused, and the land was split in two. 'Look now to your own house, David', said the men of the north, rallying under the leadership of their own king, Jeroboam. With their secession, Rehoboam was left with Jerusalem and less than half a nation, the southern tribes of Judah and Benjamin. His kingdom was called Judah. Jeroboam's northern kingdom retained the name Israel, the greater share of the population and fertile land. The border lay just north of Mizpah, about nine miles from Jerusalem.

From the break-up of the Solomonic Empire emerged two second-class states, at a time when only unity could have assured the nation's survival. Great powers, dormant in the age of Solomon, were again seeking territorial adventures and expansion—Egypt, Assyria and the kingdom of the Arameans, Damascus. Megiddo would be levelled four times in two hundred years. Jerusalem would be held to ransom or sacked at least six times in just over three centuries. In fratricidal feuding, petty power struggles, clashes between impious kings and zealous prophets, disastrous alliances, together with the insatiable greed of neighbouring aggressor states, there lay but one tragic outcome—the total extinction of both kingdoms and the banishment of virtually an entire people. The Near East has never been charitable towards weakness.

The early stamp of the new northern kingdom emerges at Tell Dan, a magnificent mound some fifty acres in extent and sixty feet high. It erupts from the Hula Plain amid a forest interlaced by brooks, rivulets and cascades fed by the melting snows of nearby Mount Hermon. It was the secessionist King Jeroboam who earned the undying enmity of the biblical authors and prophets of Judah by erecting 'calves of gold' in high places at Dan and Bethel to rival the Temple in Jerusalem.

Digging into the great tell of Dan since the summer of 1966, an expedition led by Dr Abraham Biran, Director of Israel's Department of Antiquities, has found Jeroboam's gate. It is a monumental structure of brown basalt stone with four guard chambers and an entrance eighty-five feet across—the largest gateway ever found in Israel—fully worthy of a king anxious to create a northern religious and administrative centre which would dwarf the achievements of the line of the House of David. A 'processional royal way' up to about 29 feet wide led from the gate into the city. In addition, in the north-western corner of the mound, which has abundant rivulets of crystal-clear spring water, Biran's team has found a high place of well-drafted ashlar stones on a platform of basalt. This may well have been the sanctuary which housed Jeroboam's golden calf of Dan.

Entrance post of King Jeroboam's Gate at Tell Dan leading to the processional royal way into the city, which housed one of the 'golden calves' erected by the rebellious monarch to rival the Temple in Jerusalem

The honours for the first great building tradition of the Divided Kingdom fell not to a member of Judah's Davidic line but rather to a royal dynasty of the north, founded in 876 BC by an army commander—turned-usurper named Omri. The biblical authors of Judah viewed Omri with a jaundiced eye, devoting only a handful of verses to him in the Book of I Kings, in which they described him as a man who 'did more evil than all who were before him'. In particular, they held Omri responsible for marrying his son Ahab to the infamous Jezebel, the daughter of a Phoenician priest-king named Ethbaal, in order to restore the great trading alliance with Sidon and Tyre originally established by David and Solomon. Jezebel chose to bring her pagan gods to Israel, wherein lay the particular grievance of the biblical editors and prophets. Nonetheless, Omri established the most famous and powerful dynasty of Israel and founded the new capital of Samaria. His son Ahab was the greatest builder of the Divided Kingdom.

Samaria, or 'Shomron' in Hebrew, means 'watch tower'. Isaiah called it 'the proud crown of Ephraim on the head of a rich valley'. Omri chose well. Rearing three hundred feet from the fertile undulating plain some six miles north of Nablus, Samaria is not a tell but a natural hill, standing in unchallenged command of the countryside. Today its rounded summit is crowned with orchards of olive and fruit trees where the crenellated towers of Omri and Ahab once stood. From them one could look north to the great Jezreel Valley and Megiddo, and west to the Plain of Sharon and the Mediterranean Sea.

Between 1908 and 1910 Samaria was excavated by George A. Reisner and Clarence Fisher, who headed an expedition sponsored by Harvard University. It was the first major American effort in

Palestine, amply backed by the banker-philanthropist Jacob Schiff. Between 1931 and 1935 their work was continued and clarified by another historic expedition, the united effort of Harvard, the British Academy, the Palestine Exploration Fund, the British School of Archaeology in Jerusalem and, for the first time on a major dig, the fledgeling Hebrew University, which was represented by Professor E.L. Sukenik. The Omride architects planted their buildings in trenches cut into bedrock, so that their outlines can in part be traced. Scholars now generally agree that the first phase of construction was begun by Omri and completed by Ahab. The fortified palace complex lay in a huge courtyard on the summit enclosed by a well-built inner wall five feet thick and a huge outer fortification of casemates, towers and bastions a full thirty-three feet in breadth. The perimeter of the city which lay round the palace is marked by traces of a wall to the north and south which seems to have encircled an area of about twenty acres. Some experts think that plots were reserved for farming within these walls, allowing Samaria to withstand the protracted sieges she was to endure at the hands of the Aramaeans and Assyrians.

The stumps which remain of the walls of the Israelite acropolis represent one of the finest examples of masonry in the land. Courses of well-drafted, tightly fitting stone lie on deep foundation walls in the Phoenician manner of Solomon's reign. The ashlar stones of the foundation are bordered by a perfectly shaped frame on several sides and a large projecting boss in the centre. It is believed the Phoenicians used the vertical and horizontal edges of the frames to ensure that the foundations were laid straight and true. The roughly bossed faces of these foundation stones were then concealed

A corner of the excavations of Samaria. In the right foreground can be seen remains of a wall of the Israelite period, stones from which were used in the Herodian structure on the left *opposite* This photograph was taken at the start of excavations at Samaria in 1931

with earth. Much later, Hellenistic builders would convert this masonry technique into an aesthetic dressing, a familiar trademark of Roman times still visible in the retaining walls of the Temple Compound in Jerusalem.

The remains of an Israelite gate were found on the eastern slope of the hill at Samaria, along with developed examples of proto-aeolic capitals which may have crowned the piers of the entrance—capitals of the same design as those used by Solomon at Megiddo. It may have been at this very gate that Ahab and Jehosophat of Judah consulted the prophets on whether to attack the Aramaeans at Ramoth-gilead; and that the wild food riot took place when the long siege of Ben-hadad of Aram-Damascus was finally lifted.

As a builder Ahab left his mark on two other places which are familiar to us: Hazor and Megiddo, great cities of the northern kingdom. Under him, the character of Solomonic Hazor changed radically. Whereas Solomon's city had been restricted to the western half of the high mound, Ahab's city now expanded to include the entire upper tell. His engineers filled in the casemates of Solomon's wall with earth and stones, converting it into a solid construction better suited to withstand the punishment of the improved battering rams of the rising new power to the east, Assyria.

Ahab also raised a monumental citadel on the high western rim of the mound. In 1956 Professor Yadin found a structure 82 feet long, with walls up to 6 feet 6 inches thick and deep foundations 9 feet 9 inches beneath the floor. Some of its ashlar stones were up to 5 feet long. The imposing fort had great cellars, a second storey and annexes to the north and south which were undoubtedly living quarters for the garrison. So sturdily was it built that the fort remained in use for over a hundred years.

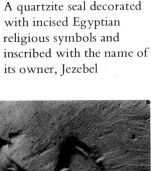

A quartzite seal decorated with incised Egyptian religious symbols and inscribed with the name of its owner, Jezebel

Thanks to Yadin's clarification of the work of the Oriental Institute expedition at Megiddo, we now know that the solid wall of recessed panels and salients and the great complex of stables at Megiddo were not the work of Solomon, but most probably of Ahab. A visitor will be struck by the remains of the stone hitching posts with pierced tie-holes tilted crazily against the background of the broad valley beyond. There were four stable structures in all, each about eighty feet long. The hitching posts, which also served as roof supports, stretched along either side of a paved central passage. The horses stood facing each other in double rows of stalls. Between each pair of hitching posts was a manger hollowed from a block of limestone. Excavators calculated that the entire complex held 480 horses, with teams of two hitched to Ahab's war chariots. Under him, Megiddo was thus a permanent camp of 240 chariots.

Though the Bible does not say so, Ahab must have possessed many more chariots than this, if the report of Shalmaneser III of Assyria is accurate. Shalmaneser was the first of Assyria's leaders to launch a campaign of expansion against Syria and Palestine. So great was the Assyrian threat that Ahab apparently declared a truce with the Aramaeans for a time to join them in a great coalition of twelve Near-Eastern kings against Shalmaneser. They met the Assyrian expedition near the town of Qarqar on the River Orontes north of Damascus. We learn this not from the Old Testament, but from an account of the actual battle on a victory stele found in 1861 lying in a ruin called Kurkh on the banks of the Tigris. In his recital of the enemy legions leagued against him, Shalmaneser lists '2,000 chariots and 10,000 foot soldiers of Ahab, the Israelite (A-ha-ab-bu Sir-i-la-a-a)'. In the coalition's battle order as detailed Shalmaneser, Ahab's is the largest formation of chariots in the field. This is the earliest mention of an Israelite king outside the Bible.

The Battle of Qarqar, fought in 835 BC, apparently ended indecisively for Shalmaneser, despite his boasts of victory, for on

Details from the giant bronze doors of Balawat in Assyria show a military expedition of Assyrian King Shalmaneser III. On such campaigns as these he tried to bring the Israelite kings to heel

this attempt he failed to establish a permanent presence in the lands of his enemies.

It is in relation to the time of Ahab that we read vivid biblical accounts of a siege. If an enemy could not breach, undermine or scale a fortification wall, his only recourse was to throttle the city slowly but deliberately by girdling it with his forces and starving its inhabitants. An essential objective in this operation was to capture the water supply, which was usually a spring issuing from the foot of a tell outside the city walls. It was in their scheme to deny an enemy this objective that Ahab's engineers most dramatically displayed their technical brilliance. Whether Gibeon served as their example we do not know.

In the early years of this century, R.A.S. Macalister uncovered a huge vertical shaft at Gezer nearly thirty feet deep. From its bottom, at a slope of about forty degrees, branched a hand-cut tunnel which ended in a large chamber 130 feet below the surface of the tell. The chamber was clogged with fallen rock, silt and mud, but when Macalister probed through the debris he found water. The engineers of this ancient system had bored through solid rock until they reached the water table, which maintained an unfailing supply of water in a pool formed at the bottom of the chamber—always accessible in times of siege. The pioneer archaeologist attributed the project to the Canaanites, dating the system's use to the period between 1,800 and 1,400 BC.

About three decades after Macalister's expedition, P.L.O. Guy, directing the efforts of the Oriental Institute team at Megiddo, also encountered one of these seemingly bottomless pits at the end of a narrow postern which ran through the bottom courses of the great 'Solomonic' inset-offset wall on the western edge of the mound. Inside the city itself, in the western sector almost immediately beside one of the stable complexes, his diggers hit another sterile zone without buildings, walls, floors or any other remains of occupation. Recalling Macalister's discovery at Gezer, Guy ordered

The tunnel of Megiddo's monumental water system

his labourers to dig straight down. He too found a spectacular water system, even more sophisticated than Macalister's.

The engineers of Megiddo had dropped a great vertical shaft through eighty feet of earth and soft limestone, cutting a staircase round its perimeter. The shaft eased to a gradient of forty-five degrees and ended at the mouth of a tunnel arched in a Gothic manner. Their work crews had then chiselled a tunnel 165 feet long which ended in a pool of cold water fed by a spring lying beyond the city wall. In gouging the tunnel the crews had worked towards each other from either end, presumably without the knowledge that we take for granted in modern tunnel engineering. Only for the last thirty to forty feet could they have been guided by the sounds of each other's chisels. Yet they met with an error of something less than three feet! The irregularity is visible to the visitor as a gentle splaying at one point on the tunnel's northern face.

Before the tunnel was built, the women of Megiddo had walked out of the city to reach the spring and fill their water jars. When enemy harassment made this hazardous, the narrow postern must have been dug to the water source. But this still left the spring vulnerable to capture, as witness the macabre scene which Guy found in what must have been an alcove for a guard just inside the external entrance to the spring—a battered skeleton curled on its right side showing clear evidence of violent death and then burning. As the excavators put it, it was clear that the watchman had 'died with his boots on'.

To some unknown technical genius came the only acceptable answer to the defence of Megiddo's spring. The external entrance was blocked and concealed, and the tunnel was dug to it from inside the walls. Even at the height of a siege, the women of Megiddo could safely reach the water supply.

Who were these phenomenal builders? Like Macalister, the Megiddo archaeologists also ascribed their water system to the Canaanites, but of a much later period than those of Gezer. They dated the postern passage to the early twelfth century BC, and the great shaft and tunnel to the middle of the same century, several decades before Joshua's arrival in Canaan.

Once again our tale hangs on the intuition of Professor Yadin. His first hunch was that Hazor, too, had boasted a water system similar to those of Gezer and Megiddo. But during his four seasons of excavation in the 1950's he had been unable to find it. His second hunch was that the Megiddo excavators might have misdated their system, as they had their 'Solomonic' city wall and stables. The task

The great water storage pool of Hazor and part of the hewn staircase leading to it. Its discovery in 1968 was due to a hunch of Prof. Yadin

of dating a water shaft can be tricky. It is relatively easy to ascertain when it went out of use from the latest object associated with it, usually a broken pitcher or water jar. Determining when it first came into use is a problem of a different order, since the tunnel has no readily identifiable structures attached to it, and its construction has destroyed whatever buildings once stood there.

Yadin considered the problem. Surely the answer was to find and date the topmost layer destroyed by those who cut the shaft. Applying that formula to the postern gallery during his session of 'problem solving' at Megiddo, Yadin excavated an area adjacent to it and found near the surface a building that had been 'cut like a knife'. It was clearly related to the layer immediately preceding that of Solomon's city. This, together with other evidence, including the familiar 'fingerprint' of Phoenician masonry in the stones of the gallery, led Yadin to conclude that it could only have been built by the engineers of Solomon. Since the shaft and tunnel had replaced the postern, they were dug later and had to be the work of a northern king, most probably Ahab.

The final step was to resolve the nagging mystery of Hazor's water supply. This was one of a number of problems left unsolved by Yadin's 1955-58 expedition. To test his hunch, he and a team of excavators revisited Hazor ten years later in July 1968.

Resources were limited, and the kernel of the problem was where they were to start. From a study of air photographs Yadin was drawn to a large circular depression on the southern edge of the mound. It had, significantly, been used as the site of a latrine by his earlier expeditions because the abrupt drop in ground level afforded relative privacy. His suspicions were heightened by the fact that springs still issue into the wadi at the southern foot of the ancient tell immediately below the circular depression. 'It was still circumstantial,' Yadin recalls, 'just another hunch.'

After weeks of fruitless digging through sterile soil, excavators began to call the site 'the depressed area'. There were only two weeks to the end of the special season, and Yadin was aware, not unnaturally, that his reputation was at stake. 'I did what no archaeologist is supposed to do. I hired a digging crane at a hundred dollars a day.' Its shovel swallowed an entire cubic yard at a time.

Within several days, with everyone's nerves taut, a stone retaining wall and a man-made rock-cut shaft began to appear. What emerged is the largest known water system in Israel. Its vertical shaft is 935 feet square and ninety-eight feet deep. Five broad flights of steps cut from live rock cling to its walls. From its bottom the tunnel plunges eighty-two feet into the rock, but away from the springs in a south-westerly direction. It ends in a quarried pool filled with water. As at Gezer, the engineers of Hazor had spared themselves the rigours of digging a long tunnel to the water source. They quite simply bored unerringly to the water table, of whose existence they were aware and on which they had clearly counted.

Applying the same dating formula as at Megiddo, Yadin was able to attribute the Hazor water system to Ahab as well. Though the present excavators of Gezer disagree, Yadin is convinced that a re-excavation of Macalister's tunnel will place its construction in the reign of the same monarch. The biblical authors and the prophet Elijah have nothing but scorn for Ahab. But his material works leave little doubt that he was outdone only by Solomon as a master builder among the monarchs of Old Testament Israel.

During the reign of Ahab's son, Jehoram, the Bible speaks of a successful rebellion against Israel by Mesha, King of Moab. In the last half of the nineteenth century, this event was sensationally confirmed—by Moab's sovereign himself.

It was during 1868 that a German church missionary named F.A. Klein made a brief exploration of Transjordan. It was, he relates, 'a country little travelled by foreigners at that time.' At Dhiban, Klein was told by a local sheikh of a large black basalt stone with strange writing on it, which was less than a ten-minute ride from where he had pitched his tent. Klein found a slab with a rounded top a little over nearly four feet high and two feet wide. Within a carved framework surrounding its worn face, he counted thirty-four lines of monumental writing in a cursive style which he could not identify. There was no break in the precise alignment of the letters, but dots were used to separate them into words or groups of words. Klein had no idea of the importance of the find and merely copied a few words, together with a sample of all the symbols used. Armed with his drawing, he went to the German consulate in Jerusalem and persuaded a diplomat to communicate with the Berlin Museum for instructions on whether to open negotiations with the Arabs for the purchase of the stone.

Even at that early date the Bedouin were aware of the European appetite for antiquities; in order to push the price as high as possible they leaked word through their contacts in Jerusalem of the stone's availability, to produce as many bidders as possible. Two who needed little urging were Captain Charles Warren, 'the indefatigable and accomplished agent' of Britain's Palestine Exploration Fund, and the equally ubiquitous Charles Clermont-Ganneau.

The writing on this black basalt stele erected by King Mesha of Moab around 830 BC confirmed in startling detail the biblical account of Mesha's successful revolt against Israel. Moabite script is almost identical to ancient Hebrew. The stele today stands in the Louvre

Given the dearth of inscriptive material in Palestine, Clermont-Ganneau was astonished that Klein had failed to make a complete copy or paper 'squeeze' of the text. He wasted little time, and made a bid of £375 for the stone. At the same time he secretly dispatched a confidant named Selim el-Kari to copy the text. Meanwhile a number of sheikhs, not to mention the Turkish governor of Nablus, began squabbling over who had the right to sell it.

Convinced that without either the stone or the money a blight would fall on their crops, the Arabs who were in possession of it heated it on a fire, and then plunged it into cold water, shattering the stone. They distributed the fragments and hid them in their granaries. In a stroke, they had destroyed what a thousand years had been unable to destroy. Clermont-Ganneau managed to locate and purchase two large fragments and eighteen smaller pieces. Together with the squeeze which el-Kari had managed to make before the destruction Clermont-Ganneau was able to reconstruct the stone, which now stands in the Louvre.

When it was translated, the slab proved to be nothing less than a stele erected by Mesha to commemorate his victory:

I (am) Mesha, son Chemosh-[. . .], king of Moab, the Dibonite . . . As for Omri, king of Israel, he humbled Moab many years, for Chemosh was angry at his land. And his son followed him, and he also said, 'I will humble Moab.' In my time he spoke (thus), but I have triumphed over him and over his house, while Israel hath perished forever!

Chemosh was the god of Moab. The stele is dated to the second half of the ninth century BC.

The reign of the Omride Dynasty was ended by another regicide, Jehu; with the blessing of the Prophet Elisha, he rose to kill Jehoram, end the life of his mother Jezebel, and ruthlessly slay the Baal worshippers of Samaria. The Bible does not record the return of the legions of Shalmaneser, who by about 840 BC was apparently able to force Jehu to ransom the safety of Israel. The source of this information is the famous Black Obelisk, recovered from the palace at Nimrud by Austen Layard. Beneath a carved panel showing the Israelite king bowing in submission before the Assyrian monarch are these words: 'The tribute of Jehu (Ia-u-a), son of Omri (Hu-um-ri); I received from him silver, gold, a golden *saplu*-bowl, a golden vase with pointed bottom, golden tumblers, golden buckets, tin, a staff for a king, (and) wooden *puruhtu*.' How ironic that the man who butchered the descendants of Omri should be called 'son

A basalt statue of King Shalmaneser III in Istanbul's Archaeological Museum

A carved panel of the Black Obelisk shows Israelite King Jehu bowing in submission to Shalmaneser. It is the first known depiction of a Hebrew monarch

of Omri'! The phrase is used in the sense of 'of the House of Omri'. The Omride line must have earned so high a reputation in the Near East that Shalmaneser identified the usurper Jehu by associating him with it.

Assyria was not the only source of trouble in this period. Destruction at Megiddo, Samaria and Shechem is associated with depredations by King Hazael of Aram-Damascus. Judah also suffered at his hands. And yet, despite the escalating crises which slowly begin to sap the strength of the sundered House of Israel, the archaeological record presents a richly textured profile of daily life in the Divided Kingdom. The great cities and smaller towns heal their wounds and expand. The population flourishes. Those who dwelled amid the splendours of Ahab's court in Samaria, for instance, had come a long way from the desert austerity of their forefathers. Typical of their cosmopolitan tastes were the remarkable carved ivory plaques found in the ruins of Samaria. The Harvard excavators came across some of these carved ivory pieces lying in the courtyard, and later the united expedition recovered about two hundred in a building complex west of the palace. In them lay the accumulated traditions of thousands of years of ancient art. Egyptian gods and goddesses set in a delicate landscape of lotus flowers, palm trees, lilies and bulrushes, lions, bulls, stags and mythological cherubim held forever in a pearly universe tinted by evanescent reflections of light on overlays of gold or enamel, minute facets of lapis lazuli and coloured glass—

opposite Another of the Samaria Ivories

the Egyptian imagination captured by the deft hand of the Phoenician artist, here in Samaria gracing the exquisite wooden furniture of Israelite kings as panels and insets.

Could those upholders of the desert tradition, the prophets, have been anything other than repelled by such opulence, trading as it did not only in an alien display of materialism but in the symbols of a pagan religion? Ahab's epitaph in I Kings indicts him as the king who built 'the ivory house'. And Amos, speaking in the name of the Lord, forewarns that he will 'smite the winter house with the summer house; and the houses of ivory shall perish. . .'
Such a house surely stood in Samaria.

Lavishness of a lower order was also reflected in the house of the affluent merchant or farmer Makhbiram at Hazor. It stood near a long pillared public storehouse, an older structure, in which royal officials collected taxes for the king—olive oil, wine and grain. The pillared storehouse at Hazor has its counterparts at other major sites, and seems to be the forerunner of the basilica. Yadin discovered Makhbiram's name incised on a jar in the ruins nearby. His home was in a wealthy residential area and projects an aura of grandeur, but little privacy. He lived in an attached residence whose outer walls were all shared with the houses next door. It had six rooms on the first floor, surrounding a central paved court. A row of pillars on one side of the court, the trademark of the Israelite house, helped support a second storey where in all likelihood the family lived. The open unit screened by the pillars and partly open to the courtyard was used either as an animal pen or as a 'workshop' —perhaps for selling produce, baking, weaving wool or flax, drying figs or dates, making pomegranate juice or producing fine oil for ritual or medicinal purposes. A stone press to squeeze the oil from the olives was found in the courtyard. The house was rich in pottery, instruments and tools. Archaeology illustrates the continuing struggle of the prophets and their instruments, such religious purists as Jehu of Israel and Josiah of Judah, against the inroads of heathen cults. Ceramic pillared figurines of the fertility goddess Astarte, or Ashtoreth, are frequently found in the ruins of houses at both Israelite and Judaean sites. They were the sex symbols of their day, the 'source' of blessings upon field and family, a popular superstitious hangover from the Canaanites which was embraced by the Hebrews until the last days of Israel and Judah. One unforgettable moment came for me when I watched Professor Yohanan Aharoni gingerly lift a small Astarte figure, incense-burner and offering table from a layer of destruction in the room of a residence at Tell Beersheba. He stared at them for

An entire tomb of the Semitic *Hyksos*, found at Jericho by Kathleen Kenyon and re-created in detail at the Rockefeller Museum, Jerusalem. A skeleton on the bench wears a gold scarab ring. Other skeletal remains have been pushed toward the wall. In the foreground, votive gifts for the dead; pottery, bowls containing the remains of food, even a wooden table, portions of which have survived for over 3,000 years

seconds in silence, brushed their charred surfaces to remove the dust and then said in the tradition of the prophetic giants, 'God was angry.' Yet it is fascinating that archaeologists have yet to unearth a representation of Yahweh. Hebrew culture accepted the efficacy of its idols over olives, grain and wine. But the universe beyond was the province of the One God, and the taboo against rendering Him in physical form was scrupulously honoured.

The well-to-do buried their dead in a form that could be traced back in its essentials to at least the Hyksos of the eighteenth century BC. In a belt that usually girdled the outskirts of a city beyond the walls, families had caves laboriously tunnelled into the living lime-stone. The typical family burial unit consisted of a chamber with three slabs or shelves of rock, one opposite the small square-cut entrance and one each on the walls at either side.

Burials were simple: no coffins, no inscriptions, with the single exception referred to earlier. Custom called for only one indulgence: the bodies were laid out on the stone shelves together with pottery, often containing food, and a few possessions, usually personal seals and occasionally jewelry; beverage juglets were grouped near the shoulders; oil lamps were left in niches cut in the walls. When the shelves were needed for new burials, the bones were cleared and placed in a common repository pit dug deeply into the rock near the back wall of the cave.

The burial cave is the most dramatic testimony we have to the strength of the 'family contract' in biblical times. The family was the basic unit of responsibility, security and survival—in life and death. Not to have one's bones 'collected unto one's fathers' in a proper family burial—the prospect of dying far from home— must have been seen as the Hell of its day. For at this stage in the evolution of Mosaic theology, the concepts of Heaven and Hell, of judgment and resurrection and salvation of the soul would not yet have been developed, awaiting Jeremiah and Isaiah, the later prophets, and the cataclysms of intertestamental times.

In these burial caves, with their food and drink and other bare essentials, lay a rudimentary belief in a physical transmigration to a Land of the Dead, the Underworld—Sheol—where departed members of one's family awaited in a plane of existence that was but a reflection of the former life. Hence the food and drink, for the journey to Sheol.

Of a different order of interest is the tomb which clings to the eastern scarp of the Kidron Valley across from the City of David. Today it is surrounded by the houses of an Arab village called Silwan, which shares the hillside with it. It is a structure cut in a monolithic piece from the rocky slope. In its face, ancient masons carved a once-beautiful facade with a gabled roof and a rectangular door which led into the vault. Traces of its 'foreign' Egypto-Phoenician derivation are immediately apparent.

The rock-hewn tomb thought to belong to Shebna, chief minister of King Hezekiah of Judah (c. 715 to 687 BC). The tomb now lies beneath an Arab house in Silwan, Jerusalem

The first man to take active notice of the tomb was the French archaeologist Clermont-Ganneau in 1870. His attention was instantly drawn to an engraved three-line inscription cut into a sunken rectangular panel just above the door. The inscription had been badly damaged at some point, and it appeared to the Frenchman that someone had deliberately defaced it with a hammer. He could not decipher the text, but to preserve it for further study he had it cut out of the facade and shipped to the British Museum. Despite a few half-hearted attempts to decipher it the meaning of the inscription remained hidden for years. In 1952, a German scholar wrote: 'The reading of this much-damaged inscription, now in the British Museum, is impossible.'

Deciphering ancient texts is one of the many special interests of Professor Nachman Avigad of Hebrew University's Institute of Archaeology. He began to study photographs and a 'squeeze', or paper impression, of the text, which he had requested from the London museum. 'I immediately saw much more than could be read before', he recalls. He at once made out the phrase '*Asher al ha-beit*'—'He who is over the House.' At once Avigad knew that he was on biblical ground. This ancient royal title can be taken to mean 'Royal Steward', chamberlain, or Prime Minister. Unfortunately the name of the royal official on the epitaph was lost. A hole had been hammered through it, leaving only the theophoric suffix '*yahu*'. This is how Avigad deciphered it: 'This is [the sepulchre of]... *yahu* who is over the house. There is no

British archaeologist Sir
Austen Layard (1817–
1894)

silver and no gold here but [his bones] and the bones of his slave-wife with him. Cursed be the man who will open this!'

The peculiarities of the script dated it to about 700 BC. The style of the tomb struck a chord that sent Avigad to the Book of Isaiah:

> Thus says the Lord God of hosts, 'Come go to this steward, to Shebna (Shebanyahu), who is over the household and say to him: "What have you to do here and whom have you here, that you have hewn a tomb for yourself, you who hew a tomb on the height, and carve a habitation for yourself in the rock? Behold, the Lord will hurl you away violently, O strong man."'

Shebna served under King Hezekiah of Judah, who reigned from about 715 to 687 BC. It is certainly not too speculative to imagine the violent reaction of the prophetic school to the raising of this foreign tomb in so prominent a location. Most scholars now accept the parallel, agreeing with Avigad's identification of Shebna as the owner of the tomb in Silwan.

This world was destined to end. The Divided Kingdom died slowly. The architects of its doom were the kings of Assyria and the new Babylon—of the land from which Israel's forefathers had come. The prophets saw them as human instruments of God's will. History sees them as tyrannical megalomaniacs, like so many before and after them, to whom Israel and Judah were merely a nuisance on the vital road to Egypt, lands which could, like the other petty nations of Western Asia, be bled dry of tribute when the occasion merited and the royal treasury was low. Inscribed panels and clay prisms recovered from their palaces by Assyriologists, notably the great Botta and Layard, chronicle the story of the architects of the Divided Kingdom's doom.

The first of these was Tiglath-pileser III, the hated Pul of the Bible, who reigned from about 745 to 727 BC, and 'came against the land' on bloody campaign after campaign. The Assyrian monarch informs posterity in his records that he overwhelmed King Menahem of Israel 'like a snowstorm', that Pekah his successor was overthrown, and that Hoshea was installed in his place as an Assyrian puppet. A large number of Israelites were led into exile in Assyria. This early use of mass-deportation is a device which would plague the Jews again and again in their later history.

Tiglath-pileser also demolished to its foundations the great citadel of Hazor which had stood since Ahab's days. Yadin found amid the ruins a wine jar bearing the words: 'For Pekah, Semadar.'

This was apparently a fine wine, translated in the Song of Songs as 'tender grape'. Had this been a royal portion for Pekah the king? Great Hazor, founded as early as the twenty-seventh century BC, was never to rise again but for a small settlement at Hazor and an Assyrian fortress in the seventh century BC. The site was to be used for the last time by the British for a pillbox in the Second World War to protect the Tiberias-Metulla road from possible attack by the Vichy French in Syria. Tiglath-pileser also extended Assyrian sway over tiny Judah. In a text badly scarred with lacunae he boasts of how he exacted heavy tribute from King Ahaz. This event, too, is confirmed by the Bible.

Final eclipse now came speedily for the northern kingdom. Hoshea withheld both loyalty and tribute from Tiglath-pileser's successor, Shalmaneser V, and sought help from Egypt. The capital of Samaria was besieged for three years. The horror of such prolonged suffering can only be imagined. Shalmaneser died suddenly, and we learn from Assyrian records that it was his heir, Sargon II, who ended the agony of Samaria, and, with it, the life of Israel: 'I besieged and conquered Samaria, led away as booty 27,290 inhabitants of it. I formed from among them a contingent of 50 chariots and made the remaining (inhabitants) assume their (social) positions. I installed over them an officer of mine...' In another text, Sargon II adds this information: '[The town I] re[built] better than (it was) before and [settled] therein people from countries which [I] myself [had con]quered.' What does the Bible say of this event? 'And the king of Assyria brought people from Babylon, Cuthah, Avva, Hamath, and Sepharvaim, and placed them in the

Israelites of Lachish being led into captivity by the soldiers of Assyrian King Sennacherib. This detail is taken from panels found in the ruins of the monarch's palace at Nimrud

cities of Samaria instead of the people of Israel; and they took possession of Samaria, and dwelt in its cities.'

From the ancient records, it has been determined that Israel died in August or September 722 BC. The fate which now befell the tiny southern kingdom was tragically similar.

The Bible tells us what occurred. 'In the fourteenth year of King Hezekiah, Sennacherib king of Assyria came up against all the fortified cities of Judah and took them.' Forty-six cities and towns in all fell before the Assyrians. One of the mightiest was Lachish, which guarded the route from the lowlands of the Shephelah to Hebron and thence to Jerusalem. Archaeology has recovered dramatic evidence of how Lachish died, in 701 BC, the most important piece being a picture of the actual event.

It was excavated by Sir Austen Layard during his excavations of ancient Nimrud on the east bank of the Tigris below Mosul between 1845 and 1851. Girdling the walls of an inner room within the ruins of what Sennacherib had called his 'Palace without a Rival' was a truly remarkable triumphal relief in thirteen panels depicting the attack and capture of a great city. Even before its short text had been translated, Layard knew that it was 'an undoubted representation of a king, a city, and a people, with whose names we are acquainted, and of an event described in Holy Writ'. The Bible tells us in only the barest outline that the Assyrian king besieged Lachish and evidently used it as his headquarters, for it is from here that he moved to reimpose his hegemony over Jerusalem and Hezekiah. The great bas-relief, on the other hand, is a panorama of pictorial art so detailed and vivid that the diligent eye is continually engaged in an adventure of discovery.

In one series of panels appears the city, surrounded by a double set of offset-inset walls, under assault by Assyrian troops. They wear crested helmets and skirts, and carry large shields, spears and bows. A powerful battering ram has been pushed up an earthen ramp to demolish an isolated defence tower. The people of the town stand on the battlements returning the fire of the Assyrians with slings and bows. They hurl blazing torches at the wooden siege engine. The Assyrians pour water on the burning brands to protect the vital ram. In another section, a procession of Judaean captives is being herded through the city gate by the Assyrians, while two enemy warriors impale three of their captives on sharp stakes. Another part of the bas-relief details the end of the struggle: Assyrian soldiers carry out the spoils; oxcarts are heavy with the belongings of the exiled prisoners; among the objects carried by the troops we can identify a Judaean chariot and cult vessels. The As-

This delicate ivory gazelle's head was found in a hoard of ivories within the ruins of a Canaanite temple at Lachish

syrian king sits on a throne watching a column of prisoners. To the left of the king's head is an inscription eloquent in its brevity: 'Sennacherib, king of the world, king of Assyria, sat upon a *nimedu*-throne and the spoil from Lachish passed in review before him.'

Starting in 1932, a brilliant British archaeologist named James Leslie Starkey directed excavations at Lachish which have shed vivid light on the last days of Judah. There is still much work to do there because the expedition was brought to a tragic close in 1938 when Starkey was murdered by fifteen Arab terrorists while being driven to Jerusalem to attend the official opening of the Palestine Archaeological Museum.

This photograph of archaeologist James L. Starkey, excavator of Lachish, appeared in the *Illustrated London News* together with the announcement of his murder by Arab terrorists

Starkey had been convinced that under the mound called by the Arabs Tell ed-Duweir lay the remains of the biblical city of Lachish, and he set out to prove it. The discovery of a large group of ostraca, containing the name of the city, and known as the Lachish Letters, established that Professor Starkey was indeed right. He also found other evidence that linked the mound indisputably with the very city portrayed in its death-throes by the artists of Sennacherib. Lachish had in fact been surrounded by two lines of walls, the first girdling its summit nearly twenty feet thick, with a revetment of stone and brick thirteen feet wide planted in the slope below it. Both walls had been constructed in alternating panels of recesses and salients, which, as we have seen, are known as offsets and insets, and were lined with defence towers. There were clear signs that the city had been taken and burnt; the evidence included heaps of carbonized wood, possibly from the wide superstructures built on top of the battlements to support large numbers of defenders. Against a bastion in the lower wall were the remains of large earth ramps constructed by attackers to support assaulting battering rams. And from the debris along the outer wall came one of the most sensational finds of all, the mount of a bronze helmet crest identical with those worn by the Assyrian soldiers. From every standpoint, the remains found by Starkey fitted exactly with the details in the bas-relief in Sennacherib's palace.

Evidence of the human toll of Sennacherib's conquest awaited Starkey on the north-west slope—a mass burial pit into which had been flung the bodies of at least 1,500 people, most of whom were clearly young. Many bones displayed traces of burning.

Sennacherib turned next to Hezekiah and Jerusalem. Of this grave moment the Bible tells us two things: that Sennacherib

Another of the beautifully executed Lachish Ivories. This one was used as a jar cover

One of the clay prisms relating in Cuneiform script the triumphs of Sennacherib. In such chronicles as these was found the Assyrian King's description of his siege of Jerusalem

demanded three hundred talents of silver and thirty talents of gold, and that the Judaean king 'gave him all the silver that was found in the house of the Lord, and in the treasuries of the king's house', together with the gold fittings of the doors and doorposts of the Temple. But we also read that Sennacherib withdrew from the walls of Jerusalem because his forces were decimated by a plague. Sennacherib's own annals, recovered from inscribed prisms of clay, clarify the events somewhat:

> Himself (Hezekiah) I made a prisoner in Jerusalem, his royal residence, like a bird in a cage. I surrounded him with earthwork in order to molest those who were leaving his city's gate. . . His towns which I had plundered I took away from his country . . .Hezekiah himself. . .did send me later, to Nineveh, my lordly city, together with 30 talents of gold, 800 talents of silver, precious stones, antimony, large cuts of red stone, couches (inlaid) with ivory, *nimedu*-chairs (inlaid) with ivory, elephant hides, ebony wood, boxwood (and) all kinds of valuable treasures, his (own) daughters, concubines, male and female musicians. In order to deliver the tribute and to do obeisance as a slave he sent his (personal) messenger.

It is interesting to note that the thirty talents of gold claimed by Sennacherib is the same amount as the Bible says was demanded of Hezekiah.

The final act of Judah's destruction did not fall to the Assyrians, however. A new power arose in the east—Babylon, which inherited the hegemony of Assyria among the lands of Syria and Palestine. Its claim was pressed with urgency by Nebuchadnezzar, whose vision was of a new Babylonian Empire. King Jehoiakim of Judah at first submitted. But in about 599 BC he rebelled, profiting little from the experience of Hezekiah before him. Nebuchadnezzar and his mighty army quickly moved to tame the tiny upstart nation. Tame it he did. One of the cities against which he directed his wrath was Lachish, which had scarcely recovered from its pulverizing by the Assyrians a hundred years before. Miss Olga Tufnell, an associate of Starkey, described the city's mortal wounds as they were found:

Masonry, consolidated into a chalky white mass streaked with red, had flowed in a liquid stream over the burnt road surface and lower wall, below which were piled charred heaps of burnt timber. In the angle below the north wall of the bastion and the west revetment, breaches which had been hurriedly repaired with any material available were forced again; indeed, evidence of the destruction by fire was not difficult to find anywhere within the circuit walls.

This time the Holy City of Jerusalem itself was added to the list of the invaders' conquests. A portion of the famous Babylonian Chronicle, found by the German archaeologist Robert Koldowey amid the ruins of Babylon itself, records in a matter-of-fact manner: 'Year 7, month Kislimu. The King of Akkad moved his army into Hatti land, laid siege to the city of Judah (Ia-a-hu-du) and the King took the city on the second day of the month Addaru. He appointed in it a (new) king of his liking, took heavy booty from it and brought it into Babylon.' The date would have been 15 or 16 March 597 BC. The remaining treasures of the Temple were among the spoils, according to II Kings, and also 'all the princes, and all the mighty men of valour, ten thousand captives, and all the craftsmen and the smiths; none remained except the poorest people of the land.'

High-stemmed Israelite bowls thought to have been used as incense burners. They date from the 10th or 9th century BC

Against the strenuous advice and baleful warnings of Jeremiah, King Zedekiah, too, tried to lead a rising against the Babylonian overlords. Nine years after his departure, Nebuchadnezzar returned to Judah for the last time, determined to be rid once and for all of this thorn in his side. The devastation was total. There is not an excavated tell of Judah that does not bear the deep scars of Israel's last agonies: the charred rubble of gates, fortification walls, houses—and the great Temple of Solomon, the magnet of Jerusalem's greatness and the focus of her pride for 360 years, torn from its foundation as by the hand of a giant. Not a single identifiable trace remains. Six centuries after the coming of Joshua, in 587 BC, 'Judah was carried captive out of its land' into her grieving exile in Babylon. 'Israel is a hunted sheep driven away by lions.'

What can I say for you, to what compare you,
       O daughter of Jerusalem?
What can I liken to you, that I may comfort you,
       O virgin daughter of Zion?
  For vast as the sea is your ruin;
       who can restore you?

11　Tide from the West

In 537 BC, half a century after Nebuchadnezzar had all but wiped her out, Israel began to rise from the dead. Cyrus of Persia swept away the empire of Nebuchadnezzar and his heirs, and with calculated charity shrewdly proceeded to erect his empire on the good will of his vanquished enemy's victims. In a victory proclamation recorded on clay Cyrus tells how he gathered the exiled remnants of the peoples whom Babylon had conquered and deported, 'and returned their habitations' and also resettled their gods back 'in their sacred cities'.

So thorough was the Babylonian destruction, so pitiable the existence of those who remained behind in Judaea, that there is barely any archaeological trace of their existence. But for the wind that soughed across their surfaces and their heaps of ruins, most of the great biblical tells stood silent and empty. At Lachish, for instance, there is no evidence of a single house that can be dated to the sixth or early fifth centuries BC. Although a descendant of the House of David, Zerubbabel ('Offspring of Babylon') and a body of priests returned from Babylon to begin raising the Second Temple in 520 BC, it was not until perhaps seventy-five years later that exiles started following in significant numbers in the train of Nehemiah, the great Jewish governor appointed by Artaxerxes I. Even then Nehemiah speaks in the Bible of a bleak Jerusalem and piles of rubble over which his horse could not pass. We can imagine the first exiles to return to Zion squatting among the debris, or in rude huts built from the fallen stones.

The new Judaea, now the Persian province of Yehud, was an enclave extending perhaps from Ramat Rachel, the biblical Beth-haccherem, a few miles north of Jerusalem, to just below Beth-zur near Hebron. Its neighbours were noticeably hostile to the exiles' return. In the north these included a motley population of Jews, and the descendants of foreigners settled forcibly in Samaria by the Assyrians in the eighth century BC; to the east, equally un-

A small gold earring in the shape of a ram's head. It is probably of Persian origin (6th to 4th century BC). Excavators found it in the crack of a wall in Ashdod

opposite A group of elegant red-burnished jars and a painted mask—the work of the Phoenicians whose ports dotted the coastal area of northern Palestine. These remains, found in tombs at Achziv, date from the 8th to the 6th centuries BC

friendly Ammonites; in the south, Arabs of Edom (Idumea) whose province stretched from northern Arabia to southern Palestine; to the west, Phoenicians who had claimed the north Palestine coast.

Excavations in the 1920s and 1930s unearthed significant numbers of handles from pottery jars inscribed before firing with several types of circular stamp seals; the jars were most probably used for the collection of taxes in the form of oil or grain. The fragments date from the fifth and fourth centuries BC. Coins, too, began appearing in the same strata for the first time in Palestinian history. Coinage was an invention of the Greeks. It vastly simplified cumbersome transactions in gold and silver, which had to be weighed. At a time of accelerating international trade, currency with its fixed weights and values did away with the need for scales. The prominent symbol on early coins was the owl of Athena. When both the Persians and the Phoenicians adopted the idea of currency they also borrowed the owl for their coins, which became

One of the earliest coins used by the Jews of Judaea. It bears the design of a hunting falcon with spread wings, a bird venerated in ancient times, and the name of the Persian province 'Yehud' in archaic Hebrew

right An archaic Athenian tetrahedron dating from the end of the 6th century BC. The owl is the symbol of Athens

A papyrus deed written in Aramaic from the 5th century BC shown closed and sealed, and on the left, opened out

a generic symbol of money, as have the £ and $ signs in modern times.

Incidentally, Ya'akov Meshorer, Israel's leading specialist in ancient coins, made an important contribution to knowledge in his field. While walking to the Institute of Archaeology at the Hebrew University one day in 1960, he noticed on a hill nearby called Givat Ram a small round object in the dust at his feet, stopped to pick it up, and discovered that it was an archaic Attic coin dating from the sixth century BC. It is the oldest coin ever found in Israel— a one-in-a-million find for a coin expert!

The story of dispersion is one of the central themes of Jewish history, both haunting and tragic. Archaeology has located one of the earliest Jewish colonies outside the Holy Land at Elephantine, an island lying at the first cataract of the Nile opposite Aswan in Egypt. Elephantine means 'Elephant Town', and it was probably so named by the Greeks because of its importance in the ancient ivory trade. It was this settlement, originally called Yeb, which produced a vast hoard of ancient documents, the first major discovery of Aramaic papyri ever made. The Elephantine papyri were brought to light piecemeal by Arab peasants, and ended up in Britain, Germany and in the trunk of an American scholar named Charles Edwin Wilbur. The contents of the trunk were bequeathed to the Egyptian Department of the Brooklyn Museum.

The papyri represent the personal archives of a leader of the Jewish colony at Yeb in the fifth century BC, a man named Ananiah

Bar Azariah, and much of the correspondence they contain concerns a temple which the Jews had built at Yeb before the conquest of Egypt by Cambyses, the son of Cyrus, in 525 BC. The Jews of Yeb had apparently found little opportunity in Judaea after their journey from Babylon and had proceeded to Egypt. One of the documents is a record of contributions 'to the God Yaho' and to deities named Ishumbethel and Anathbethel, to whom (according to another letter) burnt offerings, incense offerings and sacrifices of grain and wine were made at the temple. Clearly there was heterodoxy among the Jewish cult at Yeb. Not only did they worship sub-deities, they also disregarded the religious reforms of King Josiah in the late seventh century BC, which had expressly forbidden animal sacrifice anywhere except in the Temple at Jerusalem. Heresy most probably lay at the root of Yeb's troubles, for in a petition to Bagoas, the governor of Judaea, the settlers seek official assistance in the rebuilding of their temple, which has been smashed and burned in a conspiracy between a local Egyptian priest and the commander-in-chief of the Yeb garrison, Vidaranag. '. . .When this happened, we and our wives and our children wore sackcloth, and fasted, and prayed to Yaho the Lord of Heaven', who permitted the Jews to take violent revenge on Vidaranag and his confederates. But, the petition complains, they have sent letters both to 'the high priest Johanan' in Jerusalem and 'to Delaiah and Shelemiah, the sons of Sanballat the governor of Samaria', who were most probably empowered to act for their father, and who have failed to heed the plea of the Jews of Yeb for help in reconstructing the temple of Yaho. It is interesting to note that the Book of Nehemiah mentions Johanan as one of the high priests of Jerusalem, and 'Sanballat the Horonite' of Samaria as an arch-opponent of Nehemiah's ambitious project to rebuild Jerusalem and its walls.

We learn from a memorandum in the Wilbur Collection that Bagoas heeds the petition of the Jews of Yeb and directs that the temple be rebuilt 'on its site as it was before, and the meal offering and incense to be made on that altar as it used to be'. But Bagoas omits any mention of animal sacrifices. In another communication to a local Persian official the congregation of Yaho pledges that none will take place in the new temple. Is this to be seen as a gesture of courtesy by the Jews to the sensibility of the Persians, who as Zoroastrians viewed the burning of bodies as the profanation of holy fire? Or was it a concession to Ezra and the priests of Jerusalem, who were then leading a new reformist campaign to restore strict observance of the religious codes and

opposite, above A pottery storehouse found by Israeli archaeologist Magen Broshi at the Phoenician port of Tell Megadim, south of Haifa

opposite, below A large amphora for shipping oil or grain. It was imported from Rhodes during the Persian period and bears a stamp in Greek on one of the handles: 'Made in the term of Vieron, Rhodes, Chief Magistrate'. It was exported or manufactured by a certain Socrates

precepts of Israel? The Elephantine papyri shed no light on the matter, but their discovery does provide an intimate glimpse of a segment of the Jewish Diaspora at a very early date as well as the temper of the times in which Judaism sought to re-establish itself in its original home.

It is at this point that a fundamental shift in the balance of power in the ancient world begins. The Greek city-states have come of age and are engaged in a test of strength with Persia. The winds of change now begin to blow from the west for the first time in history, posing a new challenge to Israel—a crisis as profound as the struggle for survival against exile and near annihilation at the hands of Babylon. The archaeological record foreshadows the conflict by several hundred years. It is not written in the ugly black cinders of destruction layers, but in fragments of painted foreign pottery, among the most beautiful ever imported into the Holy Land. From the last half of the sixth centry BC several sherds of a new type turn up, traceable to a Greek city of ancient Ionia called Clazomenae, about twenty miles west of the modern Turkish city of Izmir. By the end of the century a small amount of the pottery of Attica begins appearing in the ruins of sites like Gibeah, Mizpah and Athlit on the coast. In the next century the trickle becomes a torrent, then a flood, with specimens of the red-and-black-figured Attic ware at Mizpah, Tell Qasile, Shiqmona, Tell Megadim. Powerful Athens has broken the back of the ambitious Persians

at the battles of Marathon, Salamis and Plataea, and Greek trade
with the Near East has begun in earnest.

In war, politics, philosophy, literature and art this was the golden
age of Athens, and the eastern Mediterranean coastline became the
preserve of the Greek trader and mercenary. Even long before the
fateful showdown with Persia and the coming of the indomi-
table hordes of Alexander the Great in 333-331 BC, Greek ideas
had begun to establish a beach-head on the shores of Palestine.

There is grim evidence which attests to the coming of the legions
of Greece under Alexander the Great in 333 BC. We owe its discovery to the same enterprising tribe of Ta'amireh Arabs who uncovered much of the Dead Sea Scroll material from 1947 onwards. In
the spring of 1962, while combing the Judaean Hills in search of
more scrolls, they began a thorough investigation of a cave called
Mugharet Abu Sinjeh in a high ravine of the Wadi Daliyeh north of
Jericho.

The archaeological community in Jerusalem was alerted to another Bedouin windfall in April, when a middle-man brought a
sample selection of papyrus fragments to the Palestine Archaeological Museum in the hope of selling them all. One fragment,
which was studied by the late Professor Paul Lapp, then Director
of the American Schools of Oriental Research, contained the
words: 'This document was written in Samaria.' From its script
Lapp judged that it dated from the first quarter of the fourth century BC. By November the money had been raised, the negotiations
completed and the cache acquired by the American Schools of
Oriental Research for presentation to the museum. In addition,
the Bedouin supplied details of the location of the cave, which
Lapp was to excavate. The task of studying and translating the documents was given to Frank Moore Cross, Professor of Hebrew and
Oriental Languages at Harvard University. Altogether there are
twenty documents, many worm-eaten, and hundreds of fragments
of what have come to be called the Daliyeh Papyri. They are a collection of legal and official papers—mostly contracts dealing with
marriages, property sales, loans, slave acquistions—dating from
375 to 335 BC. A large number of identifiable coins in the cave span
this period, which significantly terminates on the very eve of invasion by Alexander the Great.

Lapp also found the owners of the archives. In two arduous
seasons of excavation into heaps of guano deposited by bats over
thousands of years, a jumble of skeletons representing perhaps
two hundred men, women and children was uncovered—clearly,
in view of the documents and personal valuables found with them,

opposite A collection of
imported red and black
glazed Greek pottery found
at various sites in Israel. The
pottery attests to the
growth of Greek trade with
the Near East in the 6th and
5th centuries BC

the remains of the leading families of Samaria. On a sealing, or *bulla*, on one of the documents was the partly decipherable name of a man who identified himself as the 'son of Sanballat, governor of Samaria'. This same appellation appears in the papyri themselves. The descendants of the original Sanballat, the foe and rival of Nehemiah of Jerusalem a century earlier, had obviously retained the office. For some reason desperation had overcome the Samaritan establishment, precipitating a panic flight for refuge to a desolate cave on the edge of the wilderness. Discovery and massacre followed. Is there a key that might explain this strange find in the wild heights of the Judaean Desert? Cross has reconstructed the events with the help of two ancient historians, the Jew Josephus and the Greek Curtius. The Samaritans saw themselves as the true masters of Jerusalem; hence the determined plotting of the original Sanballat to obstruct Nehemiah's plan to rebuild the city. Thwarted in their intentions, they erected their own temple on top of Mount Gerizim to rival the Second Temple of Jerusalem. From this schism emerged the Samaritans who would ultimately figure in the New Testament. Their temple was completed in 332 BC, the same date as the conquest of Alexander the Great. According to Josephus the Samaritans first won Alexander's favour in order to gain his support against their Judaean rivals in Jerusalem. But, Curtius relates, while Alexander was in Egypt the Samaritans burned alive his prefect in eastern Syria and northern Palestine, Andromachus. The reasons are not explained, but the results were predictable. Fearing widespread revolt, Alexander hurried back to Palestine, destroyed Samaria and dispatched the murderers.

A drawing of a Roman coin showing the temple on Mt. Gerizim above Shechem. It was built by the Samaritans, who broke away from normative Judaism to rival the Temple in Jerusalem

Cross believes that the leaders of Samaria were involved in the rebellion that led to the prefect's death. As Alexander marched upon Samaria they rushed from the city with their wives and children, grabbing what valuables they could. They hastened along the road which led into the wilderness through the Wadi Far'ah and hid in the Daliyeh cave. There the Macedonians found them, either through determined search or treachery, and they were 'mercilessly slaughtered to a man'.

After decimating Samaria Alexander repopulated it with Macedonian army veterans. Eventually the remnants of the Samaritans found refuge in the shadow of Mount Gerizim at Shechem, beside modern Nablus, where a small Samaritan sect survives to this day. Evidence of the Greek presence in Samaria is still visible—a line of solidly built round towers added to the casemate walls from the days of the Israelite kings. With the death of Alexander the Great in 323 BC, his generals, the Diadochi,

A 4th century AD
inscription in stone of the
Ten Commandments
executed by Samaritans

carved kingdoms from the conquered territory for themselves. The line of Ptolemy ruled Egypt, and at first, Judaea. The
kingdom of Seleucus extended over Syria, Mesopotamia, parts of
Asia Minor, India and Macedonia itself. Judaism met Hellenism,
and the encounter, turbulent though it would prove to be, helped
set a world alight. Under the tolerant rule of the Ptolemies Judaea
at first retained Persian autonomy. Jews adopted Greek customs
and manners, spoke a popular variant of Greek called *Koine*,
absorbed large numbers of Greek words into Aramaic and Hebrew,
studied Greek literature and history, called their sons Jason and
Menelaus and Alexander. The Bible was translated to produce a
Greek version, called the Septuagint, so that the Greek-speaking
Jews of Alexandria might continue to confess their faith although
they had lost command of their original tongue. The Greek Septuagint was the vehicle by which the Old Testament was transmitted to the early Christian Church.

The Greek appeal to the senses, to curiosity in the natural order,
to a balanced existence and wordly pleasures, offered an escape
from the stern, demanding and abstract character of the old desert
faith. The spirit of Hellenism in Palestine is implicit in a number
of archaeological discoveries. In 1902, archaeologists working at
Mareshah (Marissa) in south-western Judaea uncovered a set of
magnificently painted tombs (now unhappily fading) cut into
soft limestone rock, the work of a well-to-do family from Sidon

which came to settle in this Idumean (Edomite) town under the leadership of a man named Apollophanes. Dated to the second half of the third century BC, the tomb walls were decorated with bright frescoes and decorative motifs—birds, urns, a procession of wild animals whose inspiration may have been the great zoo at Alexandria—revealing the wonder the Hellenists felt in the natural sciences. The town itself was laid out in the quadrilinear fashion, with a large rectangular market or *agora*.

At Tell Anafa (Mound of the Heron) under the Golan Heights

above The interior of one of the painted tombs of Mareshah in south-western Judaea

beside the upper Jordan, Professor Saul S. Weinberg of the University of Missouri has been excavating what he jokingly calls a 'Hellenistic country club'. A great building of ashlars stood here, and its opulence can easily be imagined from the evidence that remains. Floors of white marble with borders of black stone and glass, walls of dark stucco with panels painted in whites, reds and yellows or patterns of green and black diamonds, bordered by egg-and-dart mouldings decorated in gold leaf. Fluted columns of the Doric, Ionic and Corinthian orders formed galleries or lined windows and doors. Weinberg's diggers have found semi-precious stones—garnets and amethysts; pieces from over five hundred moulded and cut glass vessels; magnificent ceramic ware of all descriptions; relief bowls from Ionia, glazed 'fish plates' from the Aegean stamped handles of wine jars from Rhodes; coins of Sidon and Tyre. The site, astride the ancient trade route from South Arabia and the Mediterranean coast to Damascus, still imparts a sense of the wealth and grandeur of the Hellenistic world in which tiny Judaea now found herself.

Standing as it did on the border of the kingdoms of the Ptolemies and Seleucids, Judaea was bound to feel the buffetings of the power struggles between them. In 198 BC it fell under the sway of Seleucid conquerors. They were zealous proselytizers of a barbaric pseudo-Hellenism stripped of any tolerance for the customs and practices of alien peoples which failed to conform with Seleucid 'truth'. Among such peoples, in the eyes of Antiochus IV (175–163 BC), were un-Hellenized Jews, who insisted on clinging to their laws, rituals and monotheistic faith. He called himself Epiphanes, 'God-manifest', sought to unify his kingdom round the worship of Olympian Zeus and his own person against the rising power of Rome and appointed his own Hellenistic proselytes among the Jews as High Priests. For the Jews, religious persecution was now to complement centuries of political persecution. Antiochus defiled the Temple in Jerusalem, sacrificed pigs there, sequestered its treasures and demanded compliance with his pagan edicts.

The result was an uprising under the militant leadership of a priest of Modein called Mattathias the Hasmonean and his five sons. The protracted war which followed was to last for several bloody decades, culminating in the rise of a new Jewish kingdom which extended far beyond the borders of tiny Judaea. Perhaps the greatest of the Hasmonean generals was Mattathias' third son, Judas Maccabeus, who defeated the Seleucid forces at Beth-zur in the hill country on the border between Judaea and Idumea and marched seventeen miles north to Jerusalem, where he recon-

A bronze ladle with a handle shaped in the form of a duck's head. It was found at the newly excavated Hellenistic settlement of Tell Anafa

secrated the Temple. Excavations by O.R. Sellers and Professor William Albright in 1931 uncovered extensive ruins at Beth-zur, including a large hill-top citadel which had undergone three periods of construction and then been levelled to the foundations. The excavators found some three hundred coins·in the ruins of the site, nearly half of them bearing the names of Antiochus Epiphanes and his son Antiochus Eupator. The bottom level was ascribed to the Persians, while the second fortress was a much more elaborate affair dated to between 165 and 163 BC and attributed to Judas Maccabeus, who rebuilt it to guard the vital north-south road to Jerusalem from further depredations by the Syrian Seleucids. Most probably the fortress was reduced and rebuilt for the final time by Bacchides, the crack Syrian commander who nearly succeeded in stifling the Hasmonean Revolt. However, internal troubles weakened the Seleucid kingdom. Though none of the sons of Mattathias survived, a grandson, John Hyrcanus I, led the Jews to final victory over the Greeks, and he and his Hasmonean successors even managed to rival the conquests of David—from the headwaters of the Jordan to the borderlands of Sinai, from the Carmel coast to the mountains of Transjordan.

It is a historic truism that in the fruits of victory lie the seeds of ultimate downfall. Once before the schismatic tendencies of the Jews, the split between north and south, had marked them out for disaster. Now again a deadly factionalism poisoned the bloodstream of the Jewish state. This time the dispute was not regional but ideological.

Two coins of the time, common enough finds in Israel, underline one of the precipitating causes. The first Hasmonean ruler to establish a mint is Alexander Janneus (Jonathan), a son of John Hyrcanus I. Some authorities believe that the first mint was actually established by John Hyrcanus. Alexander Janneus' earliest coins are of lead; they bear a lily on one side and an anchor on the other, and carry inscriptions in Greek and Hebrew: 'Of Alexander the King' and 'Yehonatan the King'. Shortly after, this same coin was restruck, to read: 'Yonatan (sic) the high priest and the *hever* (Senate or Community) of the Jews.' In either case the powerful faction of religious purists called the Pharisees, descendants of those who rose with Mattathias and his sons to take arms against the Greeks, could not have approved. To them, the Hasmonean House had no legitimate claim to the title of monarch, which could be accorded only to a descendant of David. As if that were not enough, the Maccabees had usurped the spiritual role of high priest, an office which could rightfully be held only by the line of the House of Zadok, high priest in David's reign. Not even the great Solomon had dared to combine the powers of temporal and spiritual authority. Besides, how could the religious elements of Judaea accept a leadership which had come to stand for the very Hellenizing tendencies against which the original Hasmoneans had rebelled in the first place? Thus the mere alteration of a coin to play down regal pretensions while emphasizing the sacred role of head of the Lord's House would never have mollified the zealots. The more worldly Sadducees, on the other hand, ardent nationalists, adherents of the more balanced and pragmatic world view of Hellenism, believed that the vital needs of the new state could not be served by the outdated tenets of doctrinaire pietists. If effective administration of the expanding state by central authority meant the union of the functions of Temple and Throne, so be it. It was in the midst of such turmoil that a potent third force was born; the Essenes, who saw the resolution of the debate not in terms of engagement but in retreat.

The tragedy of the pre-exilic days was to be played out again— in internal power struggles, cruel vendettas and external intrigues which sucked a helpless Judaea into subservience to the new imperial master, Rome. Archaeological accident has made a number of discoveries which bring us close to this colourful, violent and important age of change. One lies in a most unlikely place, tucked into a pocket of a small tree-lined quarter called Alfassi Street in Jerusalem's fashionable Rehavia district. It was found in a manner that is typically Israeli.

Uri Fritz Levisohn is an ubiquitous Jerusalemite whose interests, not necessarily in order of priority, are his hardware business, classical music, Rembrandt and archaeology. In February 1956, next door to Levisohn's home in Alfassi Street, workers were blasting in a vacant plot of ground to prepare the foundations of a new house. On investigation Levisohn discovered that they were about to destroy what appeared to be an ancient tomb site, remnants of which had been unearthed in the blasting. Levisohn hastily telephoned the Israeli Department of Antiquities. Late that night, armed with flashlights and candles, Dr Moshe Dothan and L.Y. Rahmani climbed over the barrier and crawled through the debris to look inside the cave. Dothan is the deputy director of the Department of Antiquities, in charge of excavations and surveys; Rahmani was the chief archaeological inspector for Jerusalem (he is now Curator of Israel's museums). The cave consisted of several hewn rooms, with inscriptions and drawings on some of the walls. From the stones, Dothan reminisced, they

The tomb of Jason in residential Jerusalem as restored by Israeli archaeologists. This magnificent example of a Hellenistic tomb, used by a well-to-do Jewish family in the late 2nd and 1st centuries BC, was accidently discovered and reprieved from destruction in 1956

A stone mould in which coin blanks were cast. Also shown is a fragment of one of the bronze blanks which were later stamped. They date from the period of the Hasmonean kings and were found in the Citadel in Jerusalem

'could tell that the place was quite complicated architecturally, and very promising. The next morning the Department got an order, the building was stopped, and the excavation started. We ultimately paid the would-be owner generous compensation to buy another plot of land.'

Today, impeccably reconstructed and standing as it did from the reign of Alexander Janneus at the beginning of the first century BC to the days of the Roman procurators, can be seen the magnificent tomb of Jason. Thanks to a mourner of Hasmonean days we know the name of the Sadducee dynast who built it: on the plastered wall to the left of the entrance is a partly-decipherable Aramaic funeral lament, derived from a formula well-known in Greek tombs. A fine, flowing hand has written these words in charcoal: 'My brother, raise a mighty lament for Jason the son of P. . . Shalom! . . .Who hast built thyself a tomb, Elder, rest in peace! Such a mighty lament will thy friends make for thee, who hast been. . .Shalom! Honiah. . .great. . .lament like these. Shalom!' That Jason was a revered and important citizen of Jerusalem (and Honiah his scribe) is evident. Jason may even have sat on the King's Council of Elders. That he was a cultured and very Hellenized Sadducee is obvious from the tomb he built.

Cut into the sloping rock of the hillside is a long open corridor of about sixty-six feet. It is divided into three sections. The visitor sees before him a forecourt of smoothly plastered rock; a smaller outer court separated from it by an arched facade of ashlars; and behind a stone partition originally sealed by a heavy stone door, an inner court. Beyond it stands the facade of the rock-cut tomb itself, flanked by two pilasters. A single Doric column supports a raised plinth bordered by a simple projecting frieze and entablature without decoration. Topping the roof of the entire structure is a pyramid of ashlar stones. It is a consummate example of eastern Hellenistic architecture, the perfect fusing of east and west. Branching off the plastered main chamber, or porch, are two rooms: to the left, a square-cut chamber with ten hollowed cavities or *loculi* bored in its walls like extended fingers, where the bodies were interred; and, directly behind the main chamber, a roughly hewn charnel room where bones were piled up as space was cleared in the *loculi* for new burials. The ten skeletons in the *loculi* room had been scattered, probably by tomb robbers. The unarticulated bones of 25 members of Jason's family lay in the charnel room.

The tomb was rich in objects of the Maccabean period— lamps with flares or nozzles for the wick, jugs, piriform bottles, flasks, shattered bronze mirrors, fifty bowls, eighty cooking vessels, a few fragments of glass bracelets. Somehow a fragment of a hairnet had survived—its cotton fibres probably imported from India. The Sadducees had buried some of their dead with coins, most probably in emulation of the Greek tradition of providing the deceased's fare across the River Styx. Seven coins from the reigns of the later Hasmonean kings, spanning the years from 103 to 40 BC indicated the period when the tomb was chiefly used. Two coins of Herod the Great lay in the porch and outer court. The largest number, however, forty-two coins of the Roman procurators, mostly dated from AD 30–31, were grouped round a single burial which had evidently been made in the tomb long after it had gone out of use.

The tomb's greatest 'treasure', however, lies in the sketches and inscriptions on the walls of the main chamber. In fading charcoal on the western wall is a unique drawing of a naval encounter. A sleek Hellenistic warship, a monoreme with mainsail full-blown, is pursuing two smaller merchantmen. At the prow just above the tridented ram or ombolon stand two warriors with bow and spear. Other warriors are crouching behind shields along the gunnels. There is a graceful line drawing of a red deer, and scratched into the plaster on the eastern wall is one of the earliest known representations of the *menorah*, the holy seven-branched candlestick—the most familiar symbol of the Jewish ritual. It has been etched into the plaster with a thin, sharp instrument. The caption of the entire tableau lies in the short charcoal inscription in Greek, written quickly in an elegant hand. It says simply: 'Rejoice, oh thou, the living!' This hedonistic note of worldly yearning epitomizes the drama of this rich Sadducean tomb, which speaks so eloquently of the meeting of the Jew and the Greek. It is far from the note struck by traditional Judaism.

The tomb went out of use shortly before the stormy arrival of King Herod the Great in Jerusalem. Rahmani, its excavator, has tried to visualize the end of the line of Jason:

We know of the widespread slaughter carried out by Herod among the Sadducees, who were fervent supporters of the Hasmoneans, upon his entry into Jerusalem in 37 BC. He even commanded his troops to loot their bodies of all gold and silver ornaments and all other treasures, all this in definite contrast to his behaviour towards the Pharisee leaders. This slaughter and plundering may have included tomb-looting as well... Looting of this sort would have been possible only if the tomb was abandoned—as, for instance, when its owners had been killed.

12 The Mark of Herod

The last days of Judaea were days of torment, which engulfed the Jews in a crisis of belief and a yearning for release from the endless storms which lashed the land. Rome sought supremacy in western Asia, and the discord it sowed was compounded internally by conflicts between the Hasmonean House and its enemies, between Pharisees and the ruling Sadducees. One act of brutality followed swiftly on another. Josephus describes the frightful vengeance of Alexander Janneus upon a group of Jewish rebels: 'Eight hundred of the prisoners he impaled in the middle of the City, then butchered their wives and children before their eyes; meanwhile cup in hand as he reclined amidst his concubines he enjoyed the spectacle.' It was very like the Apocalypse, whose advent many were now predicting. Thousands died when Pompey claimed Jerusalem for Rome in 63 BC. Catastrophe succeeded catastrophe. Hard on the heels of a disastrous earthquake in 31 BC came famine and plague. Herod's death in 4 BC was followed by a series of revolts which were brutally quelled by the Roman governor of Syria, Varus, who crucified two thousand of the ringleaders. Herod's son Archelaus marked his inheritance of Judaea by engaging in a frightful massacre of three thousand Passover pilgrims in the Temple court. There were risings against Roman persecution, taxes, unjust procurators. Each was followed by a brutal wave of repression, and new victims for the gibbets or crosses which awaited those who chose to flaunt established authority. Little wonder that in these barbarous times the Messianic movement which produced John the Baptist and Jesus, and swelled the ranks of the Essenes, began to spread among distraught and disillusioned Jews.

The bones of Yohanan Ben Ha'galgol and those with whom he was buried speak grimly of that early age of chaos. A bulldozer brought the remains of thirty-five Jews to light in the summer of

opposite An aerial view of Herod's northern palace at Masada during the first season's excavations

1968. The machine had been cutting swaths into the side of a hill called Givat Hamivtar to prepare for approach roads to a new state housing project on the outskirts of East Jerusalem. The archaeologist Vassilios Tzaferis of the Israel Department of Antiquities was quickly called to the site and found the orifices of three burial caves hollowed in the rock of the hill. It was clear that the bodies had been interred in Herodian times—that is, from the period which began with the reign of Herod the Great in 37 BC until the destruction of the Second Temple in AD 70, for it was only in this period that bodies were given secondary burial in ossuaries. These are limestone chests of varying sizes, but usually cut to a height of about sixteen inches; they are perhaps twenty-two inches long and fourteen inches wide. After a year, in which the flesh had mouldered, the bones were collected and given secondary burial in the chests. The custom drifted to Jerusalem from the Jewish community in Alexandria but, strangely, four thousand years earlier in the prehistoric period of Palestinian history, a people which had settled along the central coast had also buried their dead in ossuaries of baked clay shaped like houses (see Chapter 4). Scholars have argued for years about the possibility of cultural links with the prehistoric ossuary people. At any rate, Herodian ossuaries were covered with gabled, flat or rounded lids. The sides were frequently decorated with simple rosettes. The workmanship was usually poor, but now and then archaeologists encounter highly elaborate designs, and some are quite beautiful.

Ossuaries are often crudely inscribed with the name of the deceased, as is the case with Yohanan Ben Ha'galgol, in whose ossuary the bones of a child of three of four were also placed. We should single out a second ossuary found with Yohanan's in Cave 1; it is well-designed and inscribed simply in Aramaic: 'Simon, builder of the Temple.' In 20 BC Herod the Great undertook to enhance his popularity with and mollify his rebellious Jewish subjects by lavishly reconstructing and enlarging the Second Temple (see Chapter 13). It was to be the supreme act of a career given over to a feverish passion for building. In the ossuary of Simon lay the bones of one of the men entrusted with this work: a great engineer, perhaps, an architect, or a supreme administrator of Herod's grand design. We can infer, therefore, that he belonged to a family of some rank and substance, and that Yohanan was related to him, since both were found in the same family cave. However, Simon died a far less ignoble death: Yohanan had been crucified. A rusting nail seven inches long was found driven through both ankle bones, right above left. Between the bones and the

opposite, above A Herodian sarcophagus from a burial cave on Mt. Scopus. The ornamentation is of outstanding beauty and craftsmanship. The motifs, characteristic of the period, are known from similar sarcophagi found in Jewish graves and from facades of tombs in Jerusalem
opposite, below A typical Jewish tomb chamber with niches for ossuaries. In the foreground is the simple ossuary of 'Simon, builder of the Temple'

nail head were the remains of a wooden wedge. The point of the spike had been bent almost upon itself when it was pounded into a hard knot in the upright beam of the cross. An analysis of minute wooden slivers still clinging to the nail showed the cross to have been of olive wood. The wedge was made of acacia. When his agony ended after two or three days, Yohanan's executioners administered the customary *coup de grace*, the *crurifragium*, by shattering both legs with a blunt instrument, perhaps a mallet. It had also been necessary to cut off both feet, for in no other way could the body be taken down and the bent nail extricated from the cross. This deformed nail, is virtually the only material evidence for the practice of crucifixion that we have. Josephus called it 'the most pitiable of all forms of death'.

We know all this—and more—about Yohanan because of the work of a brilliant Israeli pathologist Dr Nicu Haas, to whom Tzaferis handed over many of the bones for examination.

Artists have lingered with reverence and passion on the theme of the crucifixion of Jesus since the early Christian centuries. The discovery of Yohanan's skeleton corrects some of their misconceptions about this grotesque form of execution. The arms were nailed to the crossbeam between the two bones of the lower forearm just above the wrist rather than through the palms of the hands. Haas found that these bones had been worn and abraded by the constant friction of Yohanan's agonized movements against the nails. As we have seen, a single iron spike was driven through both heel bones rather than one in each foot. This permitted the victim to flex his legs and bear his weight on a wooden crosspiece or seat, called a *sedile*, to ease the agonizing strain on his arms from time to time. But the *sedile*, too, had been conceived with a diabolical purpose, because it only prolonged the victim's suffering. Yohanan died within a period bounded by the death of Herod the Great in 4 BC (for in spite of all his cruelties he had banned crucifixion) and the destruction of Jerusalem in AD 70. He was most probably a contemporary of Jesus, who was crucified between AD 28 and AD 33. Yohanan's crime can only be guessed at. That it was construed by the authorities as political is virtually certain. Haas and Tzaferis could only conclude: 'This man was either a prophet of wrath, a soul of mildness, or an innocent. We shall never know.'

These were the convulsive times which produced a leader of Judaea who was perhaps the most flamboyant and controversial figure in Jewish history—Herod the Great. He is one of those complex legends which defy simple definition, for Herod was really larger

above The heel bones of
the crucified Yohanan
clearly showing the nail
hammered through them
below Dr. Nicu Haas
reconstructed the method of
crucifixion from evidence
from Yohanan's bones. His
findings cast doubt on the
form of execution
traditionally rendered by
artists through the centuries

than life. His father was made Commissioner for all Judaea by Julius Caesar. His patrons were Mark Antony and Octavian (Augustus Caesar), who elevated him to the rank of King of the Jews. Even though Antony and Augustus became mortal enemies, Herod could command the support of both. He was an indefatigable warrior and a feverish builder, whose grand conceptions rivalled those of Solomon. An Idumean, upon whose Arab ancestors Judaism had been forcibly imposed by Alexander Janneus, he tried to bridge the two conflicting forces of his world by appearing more Roman than his patrons and more Jewish than his subjects. As such, the Romans could accept him, but the unyielding Jews never did —though he lavished unlimited energies and resources upon a Temple whose like had never been known in Israel. He raised whole cities at home and bestowed great gifts abroad, becoming president of the Olympic Games. But he could never purchase the one thing he most desired—the love of his subjects and his family. Distrust, the sickness of the powerful, caused him to murder his wife Mariamne and three of his sons. He died in Jericho wracked by disease and consumed by paranoia.

In Herod's colossal programme of public works Hellenistic architecture in Palestine found its fullest expression. Meticulous descriptions of Herod's achievements occupy large portions of the narrative of his biographer Josephus. Archaeology has borne out the reliability of Josephus's testimony. At Caesarea, which Herod founded and built into one of the majestic port cities of the eastern Mediterranean, excavators have uncovered the podium of the great temple which he raised and dedicated to Augustus, as well as the foundations of the amphitheatre. The remains of the great harbour mole are still visible, as well as several pillars which Josephus says Herod erected on the seafront for 'three colossal statues'. At Samaria, which he rebuilt and called Sebaste, is the immense podium of yet another Herodian temple of Augustus, and a stadium 638 feet long and 190 feet wide. While earning the gratitude of his Roman overlords by erecting pagan shrines in their honour or to their gods he sought at the same time to pacify the devout Jewish Pharisees by lavishing attention on the holy sites. He erected two great buildings at Hebron—one at the traditional Cave of Machpelah, where the Patriarchs were buried, and another marking the supposed location of the Oak of Abraham at Mamre. Herodian masonry is still visible in these buildings, as well as in the retaining wall of the great Temple Compound in Jerusalem, of which the Wailing or Western Wall is a part.

The complex personality of the man is chiefly manifest in his three great fortresses: Herodium, built on top of a majestic hill on the border of the Judaean Desert two and a half miles south-east of Bethlehem; Machaerus, thirteen miles to the south-east across the Dead Sea; and the high plateau of Masada in the desolate yellow-white wilderness on the Sea's western shore. The fortresses formed a triangle, with Herodium at its apex. Each could see the signals of the others, and Herodium could see Jerusalem. These were far from ordinary citadels. They were royal redoubts, fitted to serve the needs and tastes of the royal family as they were served in Jerusalem, and conveniently sited within immediate reach in moments of sudden danger—either from rebellious subjects or from external enemies. Herod lived in mortal dread of both.

Masada looks like a great ark hanging motionless in a bleak sun-baked sea of rock, a mammoth hulk of dolomite rearing up 1,300 feet from the mottled wilderness on its northern and eastern flanks. Great precipitous tears in the crust separate it from the upthrust mass of the Judaean uplands on the south, and only on the west does it merge shallowly with the surrounding hills.

Explorers courted Masada for years, but it was a *kibbutznik* called Schmaryahu Gutman who introduced Masada and its historic meaning to the Israelis. In the early 1940s he began leading study groups of young people on arduous cross-country hikes there. Soon Masada became not only an object of pilgrimage but one of national reverence. Gutman cleared and restored the Snake Path, reconstructed one of the eight Roman camps whose remains still girdle the base, guided two brief expeditions of professional archaeologists to its top in 1955 and 1956, which undertook some preliminary excavation, and conducted an intensive lobbying campaign to persuade Professor Yadin to excavate the high plateau.

Yadin conceded that he needed much persuasion. He was officially invited by the Israeli Government and the Israel Exploration Society to tackle the project, but was determined to excavate Hazor first. Masada, as he put it, 'was a sitting duck and would wait.' With the completion of the Hazor expedition in 1958 it was the turn of the 'sitting duck'.

The Yadin expedition of October 1963 to April 1965 has been extensively reported in books, newspapers, magazines and television documentaries. It was after all one of the most exciting events in contemporary archaeology. The expedition required massive and complex preparation. Herod had selected his retreat all too well. Excavators faced impossible terrain, supply headaches, a harsh desert climate, prohibitive costs and the problems of attracting manpower to hardship duty. Yadin's superb organizational skills

A graphic example of the value of aerial photography to archaeology. From the

ground these Roman siege camps surrounding Masada are barely distinguishable

and salesmanship produced the answers: private funds from Britain, plus the backing and publicity resources of the Sunday newspaper the *Observer*; the use of energetic teams of youthful volunteers from Israel and all round the world; the Israeli army for logistical support, including the transfer of heavy machinery to the top of Masada and the airlifting of supplies in torrential winter weather. The logistics of the Israeli assault were worthy of Flavius Silva, the Roman procurator who was assigned the task of reducing the Zealot resistance at Masada after the destruction of Jerusalem in AD 70. In fact the expedition camp was sited beside the remains of Silva's main siege camp, and the earthen ramp built for the Roman siege engines by Jewish slaves at the western approach to Masada was used by Yadin's workers to reach the excavation site. The worldly Josephus would have appreciated the historical ironies.

The drama of Masada started in AD 66 with the great Jewish Revolt against Rome. Herod's sumptuous retreat was by that time a Roman outpost. But the enemy garrison was surprised and easily overwhelmed by Jewish warriors led by a certain Menahem. Thus it was that in the year 70, following the fall of Jerusalem and the Roman destruction of the Second Temple, Zealot survivors and their families fell back on the redoubt at Masada as a base for guerilla strikes against the enemy and, if need be, the site of their last stand. With rebellion in the air throughout the Roman Empire, news of a successful resistance by a mere handful of Jewish rabble would have been disastrous to Rome. Silva was assigned to reduce Masada at all costs. In 72 he marched on the great rock with the 10th Roman Legion, auxiliary troops, a colony of Nabatean Arab tradesmen and merchants to assist in supplying the vast needs of the campaign, and thousands of expendable Jewish slaves for the hard labour. Silva first hemmed in the defenders with a circumvallation or siege wall over two miles in circumference and eight military camps at strategic points round the base of Masada. The blockade was complete. Then Silva built his earthen ramp to the top of the redoubt and proceeded to breach the western wall. Each day the defenders could look over the edge of the casemate fortification ringing Masada's rim and measure the advance of their approaching doom.

In 73 Masada fell, but only after all but two women and five small children among the 960 defenders had fulfilled a desperate compact and taken their own lives. Exhorting them to it, Eleazar ben Ya'ir, their leader, had said: 'Life is the calamity for man, not death.' For the Romans, as their apologist Josephus conceded, it was a hollow victory. For Yadin the challenge was not only to discover the nature of Herod's redoubt, but to collect evidence of the Zealots, who chose death over 'a life of physical and moral serfdom'.

On three great descending tiers at the narrow northern tip of the escarpment Herod's builders constructed a small but magnificent personal palace, sheltered from the wind and blazing sun. It was a brilliant piece of engineering On the upper terrace, separated from the rest of the plateau compound by a great wall, were the royal living quarters. They were bounded by a great semicircular porch from which the king could look north to the lush green oasis of En-gedi, east across the blue of the Dead Sea to the pink palisades of the mountains of Moab, west across the serrated hills of Judaea. Fully sixty feet below hung a second terrace. It once held a magnificent semicircular structure of rounded double walls from which paired rows of columns rose to support the roof. Like the lower terrace another forty-five feet below, it was used for leisure and relaxation. The plastered walls of the lower terrace had been lined with pillars topped by Corinthian capitals decorated in gold paint. On the plaster were painted frescoes, still amazingly well preserved, simulating mosaics and veined marble. Also preserved was a grim but moving scene in a small bath-house installed on the lower terrace for Herod's pleasure. 'Even the veterans and the more cynical among us stood frozen, gazing in awe', writes Yadin in his book *Masada*. Three skeletons lay on the steps of what had been the cold water pool—that of a man of about twenty, a young woman and a child. Still adorning the woman's skull was the long dark plaited hair which had framed her face in life. Next to her was a pair of sandals. The plaster on which she lay still bore the stains of her blood—against the contrasting Herodian splendour, a cameo of the last agonies of Masada composed nearly two thousand years ago. There would be other such scenes.

This northern 'hanging villa' was not the official palace of Herod, however. That lay on the western edge of the plateau near the ramp where the Roman battering ram made its fatal breach in the defences. It was a huge complex 36,000 feet square made up of service and store rooms, administrative quarters and dwelling units. The benches on which official visitors awaited their royal audience, handsome geometrical mosaic pavements and the kitchen have all survived, together with the chamber in which Herod's throne stood. Among the other installations in the compound were a bath-house much larger than the one found on the lower terrace; two huge groups of store houses rich in pottery vessels, some with the names of Jewish defenders who had appropriated

Hundreds of silvered scales of armour were discovered adjacent to the skeleton of a Zealot on Masada

them for their personal use; a block of dwellings where officials of Herod's garrison once lived. And, in all the major buildings, a blanket of burning—thick layers of ash, charred beams, blackened walls and rubble.

Josephus writes that ten Zealot leaders were chosen by lot to serve as executioners for the rest; then one was chosen by lot to kill the remaining nine, set fire to the palace and then kill himself. There had certainly been a fierce blaze in the western palace. Whether the other buildings had been set alight by accident or design will never be known.

Yadin's diggers also found a Herodian swimming pool or public bath which the defenders had also used. But there is less than one inch of rainfall a year here. How could Roman baths and pools and the drinking, cooking and washing needs of a large community have been served? In solving the problem of the water supply Herod's engineers excelled themselves. Deep into the dolomitic rock of the western cliff they hollowed two rows of huge cisterns, with a total capacity of nearly a million and a half cubic feet of water. They also dammed up two small wadis passing north and south of Masada. Aqueducts were built from the wadis to the cisterns. All the rain that ever falls at Masada is the result of just a few annual storms—literally violent cloudbursts—that arrive with

Two cooking pots on top of an open oven as found in Zealot living quarters on Masada

terrifying suddenness in the winter months. The excavators endured the great discomfort of experiencing them. But what they also witnessed were the tremendous torrents of run-off which churned through the two wadis after each storm, more than enough to have filled the ancient cisterns when the aqueducts were in repair. Water carriers with donkeys or mules then hauled it in pottery jars to the top of the plateau where another set of storage cisterns had been gouged into the living rock. We have direct testimony, of course, to the effectiveness of the Masada water system: it sustained nearly a thousand Zealots for three years.

It was these defenders who provided Yadin's expedition with the most dramatic and important discoveries of the dig. When it began Yadin had hoped that treasured Scroll documents might emerge. Ever since 1947 these same Judaean Hills had proved to be a treasure trove of ancient documents, and Qumran lay only a short distance to the north. The Masada excavators were not to be disappointed. In all, portions of fourteen scrolls—biblical, apocryphal and sectarian—were recovered from the ruins of Masada. Most were found in one of the western chambers of the casemate wall, Room 1039 on the excavation charts. Among the scrolls were parts of the Books of Psalms, Leviticus, Ezekiel, Deuteronomy, the Wisdom of Ben-Sira or Ecclesiasticus, and the pseudepigraphal Book of Jubilees. Together with the Qumran finds these discoveries represented a turning-point in biblical research. They established beyond a shadow of a doubt the relative accuracy of the scribal transmission of the biblical texts from ancient times, particularly those which originally reached the West not in the Hebrew in which they were first written but via a Greek translation.

Another scroll fragment produced a surprise. It was part of a sectarian religious work called *Songs of the Sabbath Sacrifice*, which was first discovered in Cave IV at Qumran thirty miles to the north. The question it raised is obvious. What was a copy of a document from the library of the Essenes doing at Masada? Yadin believes that when the Romans destroyed Qumran, Essene survivors joined the Zealots at Masada, bringing copies of their holy writings with them.

Part of the drama of the Zealot remains is the striking contrast between their austerity and starkness and the Herodian grandeur in which they were found. Yadin found the floors littered with the essential objects of everyday life—a woven basket of palm fronds, a gaming die, a wooden spoon, a woman's comb, an oil lamp, a stone measuring cup. He wrote in his book *Masada:*

We would find in a corner a heap of spent embers containing the

above Schmaryahu Guttman, who served as field supervisor with the Masada expedition, painstakingly cleans silver coins in the excavations

below A woman's comb made of bone found on Masada

remains of clothing, sandals, domestic utensils and cosmetic items, which told the poignant story of how, perhaps only minutes before the end, each family had collected together its humble belongings and set them on fire. . .These small heaps of embers were perhaps the sights that moved us most during our excavations.

There was a large number of bronze and silver coins, many in mint condition, struck in Jerusalem during the great Revolt and dated according to the year of the war—Year 1 down to Year 5, the latter corresponding to AD 70 when the Temple was destroyed and resistance all but ended. These coins were variously inscribed: 'Shekel Israel', 'Jerusalem the Holy', 'For the Freedom of Zion'. Year 5 coins are extremely rare. Only six of them were known before the excavation of Masada, which produced three more. Yadin imagines that since the coins had lost all practical value they were most probably used by the besieged defenders as a means of rationing supplies.

Their faith figured heavily in the lives of the Zealots: in the preserved remnant of a prayer shawl, a vessel marked 'Mas'aser Kohen' ('priestly tithe'), the religious documents, two mikveh or pools for ritual purification baths, and a synagogue, the oldest ever found. The house of prayer, with its rude benches and pillars, was oriented towards Jerusalem, and stood like a challenge on the western rim in full view of Silva's camp below.

Two finds in particular document the Zealots' defiant end. In one of a network of caves just below the casemate wall in the southern cliff were found the scattered bones of twenty-six skeletons—fifteen men, six women, four children and an embryo; the bodies were probably flung here during the Roman mopping-up.

But there is no doubt in Yadin's mind as to the most haunting discovery of all. Two volunteers sorting through a pile of debris in the northern sector of the plateau came upon eleven small inscribed potsherds, all written in the same hand and each containing a different name, in many cases a nickname. 'Could it be', Yadin wondered, 'that we had discovered evidence associated with the death of the very last group of Masada's defenders?' You will recall Josephus's tale of the dramatic choice by lot of the executioners who would slay first their brethren and then each other. Could these sherds have been the very lots by which the final choice was made? 'I can recall Yadin's face', one volunteer told me. 'In two years I never saw him so visibly shaken.' For one of the inscribed sherds bore the name of the Zealot leader: 'Ben Ya'ir'.

It seems probable that this ostracon and ten others found with it are the very lots used by Eleazer Ben Ya'ir and his fellow Zealots in selecting the executioners of their brethren and themselves

13 Jerusalem the Golden

Jerusalem is one of man's oldest living communities, the magnet of Judaism and Christianity, the third holiest site of Islam. Ancient maps place it at the centre of the earth. Rarely has a historic age passed in which men and nations have not sought it as a focus of worship or an object of conquest. Its roots lie in deep rubble which speaks of the Apocalypse. But its honey-pale stone is tinted by an ageless serenity. In the name of no other place has more evil been committed in the name of piety, or more idealism inspired in the search for spiritual identity and concord. The enigma of Jerusalem is the paradox of man himself.

Traditionally Jerusalem is identified with 'the land of Moriah' where Abraham prepared to sacrifice Isaac to the Lord. It lies on a spur of the hilly central spine which divides the Mediterranean zone from the fiery Dead Sea rift. From east or west a visitor ascends to Jerusalem, looking up to the buildings, towers and battlements which cling to its slopes and crown its heights. The quest to know Jerusalem has drawn pilgrims and scholars to its holy and learned precincts for over two thousand years. For the past century archaeologists of varying shades and degrees of competence have been drawn to this movement. Their mission has largely been to rediscover the nature of the biblical city. Their essential reference tools have been the Bible itself, the graphically detailed annals of Josephus and Talmudic sources.

Jerusalem does not give up its secrets easily. An endless cycle of demolition and reconstruction has obliterated its earlier features or buried them in debris up to sixty feet deep in places. The modern building boom, and the concentration of the holy sites in the most ancient quarters, means that many focal points of archaeological interest are out of bounds to the excavator's pick and spade. Britain's Palestine Exploration Fund launched the first extensive expe-

opposite An aerial view showing the excavations of Prof. Benjamin Mazar at the southern and western walls of the Temple Mount

A sketch made from measurements taken by Lt. Charles Warren of an elevation of the south-west corner of the Temple walls. Robinson's Arch protrudes just below the larger of the four windows at the top. The lower part of the drawing shows the rock-cut aqueduct

ditions into the heart of old Jerusalem (see Chapter 1). One of the pressing questions that they were asked to solve was the location of the original City of David, whose conquest of the Jebusite stronghold in about 996 BC united the northern and southern tribes of Israel both physically and politically.

Between 1867 and 1870 the British military engineer Lieutenant Charles Warren and his Bedouin workmen sank shafts and subterranean galleries round the outskirts of the vast Temple Mount, the site since the seventh century AD of the Moslem Dome of the Rock. Two decades later, archaeologists working for the Palestine Exploration Fund excavated south of the same area. The result of these and other researches was to pinpoint the earliest city to a small rocky spur called Ophel; it is no larger than eight acres in area and lies south of the Temple. Ophel is bounded on the east by the precipitous Kidron Valley, and on the west by a long-vanished depression called by Josephus the Tyropoeon (or Cheesemakers') Valley.

Archaeologists sank shafts up to sixty feet deep through the fill and rubble to rediscover the Tyropoeon. Between it and Hinnom (or Gehenna) Valley lies a second stony spur. It is on this western ridge that Christian tradition has placed the biblical Mount Zion. The Jews identify Zion with the Temple Mount. In fact the 'stronghold of Zion', the site of David's conquest and seat of his capital, was Ophel. Precipitous valleys defended it on the east and west, and artificial fortifications protected its narrow northern neck below the Temple. Most important, a dependable supply of water gushed from a stony recess in Ophel's eastern flank; this is the spring of Gihon, which is called the Virgin's Fountain by Christians. It was through a 'water shaft', according to the Bible, that Joab and the

men of David's army penetrated and overthrew the Jebusite redoubt. A deep shaft to the Gihon spring was in fact found by
Warren in 1867. Over forty years later, a flamboyant British
treasure-hunter called Captain Montague Parker sent a member of
his expedition on a hair-raising ascent up the eighty-five-foot
shaft together with a Welsh miner to prove that Joab could have
made the climb.

An oil lamp decorated with
the traditional Jewish
symbol of the candelabrum
or *menorah*, from Prof.
Mazar's excavations

A few details must be given here of the Parker expedition,
most hare-brained ever to embark for the Holy Land. Its inspiration was a Finnish eccentric named Walter Juvelius, who claimed
that he had found a coded message in the Book of Ezekiel containing the secret burial place of the treasure and relics of Solomon's
Temple, which had been hidden when Nebuchadnezzar marched
on Jerusalem. Montague Parker, banking on the Finn's 'revelation',
raised enough capital on the strength of it—some £25,000—to
launch his expedition in 1909. Parker probed the ancient tunnels of
Jerusalem, directed by a reputed clairvoyant who cabled his instructions from Denmark. When the treasure failed to turn up
Parker decided to assault the Temple area itself, which is not only
sacred to Jews, but the third most holy shrine in Islam! He bribed
the Turkish governor of Jerusalem, a powerful sheikh, and officials
of the Dome of the Rock to give him the keys to the Temple
Compound, which the Arabs call the Haram esh-Sharif. Near
disaster followed. An unhappy Arab workman leaked word of the
plot, and soon the Arabs of Jerusalem were in an uproar, threatening to launch a holy war against any Christians they could lay their
hands on. Parker and his staff fled for their lives to Jaffa, and managed to escape aboard his private yacht. The officials whom he had
bribed were sent to jail

The only saving grace of the escapade was that a French Domini-
can, Père Louis Hugues Vincent, founder of Jerusalem's Ecole
Biblique et Archéologique, had received Parker's permission to
follow the exploits of the expedition, recording anything of archaeological value which might emerge. As Parker cleared the complex
of tunnels leading from the Gihon spring and some caves in Ophel's
eastern slope Père Vincent identified a unique piece of pottery,
twin bottles decorated in yellow and brown, dating from about
3,000 BC. It is the earliest piece of ceramic ware found in Jerusalem.
Vincent also measured, mapped and studied the tunnels, producing
one of the most valuable pieces of research ever done on the ancient
city, 'Jerusalem Underground'.

In 1923, fourteen years after his exhausting labours at Gezer,
R.A.S. Macalister returned briefly to Palestine, and undertook

excavations on Ophel, tracing the line of an ancient stone wall which Warren had first uncovered half a century earlier. It began at the south-east corner of the Temple Compound, or Haram, and followed the crest of the ridge to the southern tip of Ophel. Macalister also discovered a massive tower associated with it, ascribing both the tower and the wall to the Jebusites and King David. This created a major archaeological problem. The head of the deep water shaft leading from the Gihon spring lay about eighty-nine feet outside Macalister's 'Davidic' city wall. The Jebusites would certainly have wanted to protect their vital water source by placing it within the precincts of the fortification wall.

The inference of the biblical story of David's conquest is that his forces penetrated the city by means of the water shaft without having to breach the walls. If Macalister's findings were correct, Joab and his men would have made their heroic trip up the water shaft only to find themselves still outside the city.

Kathleen M. Kenyon was determined to sort out this riddle when she launched six seasons of excavation in Jerusalem in 1961. She made a huge cutting into the sharply sloping eastern flank of Ophel, exposing the foundations of the tower Macalister had credited to David. Below it she found the ruins of Israelite houses which had been destroyed by the forces of Nebuchadnezzar in 587 BC. How could a 'Davidic' tower lie on top of ruins dating from more than four centuries later? Basing her conclusions on pottery and other evidence, Miss Kenyon has been able to make sense of Macalister's wall. She has dated it to Nehemiah, who rebuilt Jerusalem when the Jews returned from the Babylonian Exile. The tower was added to the wall in the last half of the second century BC, perhaps by Simon Maccabeus or John Hyrcanus.

Towards the end of the 1961 season, Miss Kenyon set the final piece of the puzzle into place. At the very foot of the deep cutting, about forty-nine feet below the crest, her labourers struck the line of another wall—built of large, rough boulders. She was able to date pottery associated with its construction to 1,800 BC. This was the impregnable barrier of the Jebusite city which David and his warriors so artfully avoided breaching eight hundred years later by climbing the water shaft. The Israelite king incorporated the wall into his own defences and it remained in use for several hundred years.

Miss Kenyon's trench may have solved another mystery. In the Bible David and his successors are repeatedly concerned with the rebuilding and repair of the 'Millo'. The word derives from a Hebrew word meaning 'filling', but scholars have debated its exact

opposite An aerial view of Herod's three-tiered northern palace at Masada after completion of the excavations. Compare this with the partially excavated site shown on page 204

meaning for years. Miss Kenyon discovered that the ruins of Israelite houses on the eastern slope had stood on a series of artificial terraces of stone fill and retaining walls, some of which dated to as
far back as the fourteenth or thirteenth century BC. She maintains
that these terraces were first built by the Jebusites to create addition-
al building space within the constricted perimeter of tiny Ophel.
They would have been highly vulnerable to collapse due to earth-
quakes, landslides, erosion and the ravages of an enemy. The
ruins of a terrace house would cascade onto the one below, creating
a chain reaction of havoc. Miss Kenyon believes that these terraces
constituted the Millo. Their continual maintenance and repair
would understandably have figured heavily in the public works of
the Judaean kings. And their destruction would have accounted
for the havoc wrought in Jerusalem by the army of Babylon when
Nebuchadnezzar overwhelmed and destroyed all Judah in the sixth
century BC—the devastation so vividly described in the Book of
Lamentations and Jeremiah.

One of the last acts of David was to purchase the threshing floor
of Araunah the Jebusite for fifty shekels of silver on which to build
an altar to the Lord. This was the great flat shelf of rock which
reared above Ophel to the north—Mount Moriah or Zion. Here,
in about 950 BC, Solomon erected the crowning achievement
of his reign, the First Temple of Israel. Between it and Ophel
stood his palace, the House of the Forest of Lebanon. The Temple
became the focus of Israel's political and religious life and, in periods
of exile, her fervent aspirations. So well did conquering armies do
their work, and so deeply did future builders anchor their foundations, that barely a trace of Solomon's grandiose project survives.
Miss Kenyon sank a deep sounding pit just north of Ophel and
found a single proto-aeolic capital and a few finely drafted building
stones typical of Israelite royal construction which had tumbled
from the ridge above. There were also traces of a casemate wall,
a Solomonic trademark, which may have served as a portion of
the city's fortifications or screened off the royal enclosure. Apart
from this the Solomonic archaeological record in Jerusalem remains blank.

Our only hope of reconstructing the great Temple lies in the
detailed descriptions in the Books of I Kings and II Chronicles, and
the Vision of the Prophet Ezekiel. It is also a safe assumption that
the courtly officials charged by Solomon with building the Temple
were heavily influenced by the architectural styles of the cultures
round them, not the least of which were the Canaanite and the
Phoenician cultures. From the ranks of the latter came the craftsmen

opposite Another view of
the excavations conducted
by Prof. Benjamin Mazar
at the walls of the Temple
Mount. The enormous
Herodian masonry is
clearly visible

Proto-Aeolic capital discovered by Kathleen Kenyon during the excavations at Ophel. It may have been part of a Solomonic building

and artisans supplied by King Hiram to help Solomon erect his ambitious architectural wonders.

The 'House of Israel' was a rectangle ninety feet long, thirty feet wide and forty-five feet high, facing east to a vast courtyard and the rising sun. It was flanked by 'side chambers' three storeys high. The building itself was divided into three parts: a vestibule, or *Ulam;* the main room, or *Hekal;* and the dimly lit Holy of Holies, or *Debir*, which housed beneath the wings of two olive-wood cherubim the Ark of the Covenant and the sacred Tablets brought from Sinai by Moses. On either side of the vestibule entrance stood two great free-standing bronze columns, called Jachin and Boaz. In the courtyard rose a horned altar for burnt sacrifice fifteen feet high, and an immense basin of cast bronze called the Molten Sea, most probably used by the priests for lustrations. Scholars calculate that it held ten thousand gallons of water and weighed up to thirty tons.

The plan of the Temple is similar to a number of ancient sanctuaries, among them the orthostat shrine to the Canaanite god Hadad found by Yadin in the Lower City of Hazor. It, too, consisted of three chambers, their entrances all on the long central axis, as in Jerusalem. Flanking the vestibule entrance, their expertly sculptured bases still in place, there once stood two free-standing pillars of basalt. This last of four temple phases was dated to the fourteenth century BC. In 1963 Aharoni, excavating a small desert citadel at Tell Arad in the south-eastern Negev which dated from the reign of Solomon, found the first known Israelite sanctuary outside Jerusalem. It consisted of a Hekal and a raised Debir. On either side of the entrance of the Hekal were two stone slabs, most probably pillar bases reminiscent of Jachin and Boaz. Near the centre of the courtyard stood a massive altar five cubits square and

opposite The earliest settlement of Jerusalem was at the small rocky spur of Ophel which is today outside the walls of the Old City. This, the City of David, is shown during the course of Kathleen Kenyon's excavations

The first Israelite sanctuary outside Jerusalem was excavated in 1963 by Israeli archaeologist Yohanan Aharoni at Arad, a frontier city of the Judaean monarchy. The runnels on the altar for draining off sacrificial blood are clearly visible

three cubits high, the exact measurements stipulated in Exodus for the desert tabernacle of Moses. The slab was bordered by two plastered runnels for draining off the blood of animal sacrifices. The main features of the Hazor and Arad shrines are vividly reflected in the biblical portraits of the Holy House raised by Solomon.

The first great archaeological discovery in Jerusalem was the combined result of enterprise and chance spanning a period of forty-two years. When Edward Robinson, the pioneer explorer of biblical Palestine, arrived in Jerusalem in 1838, he was told of an ancient rock-cut tunnel connecting the Gihon spring with a reservoir called the Pool of Siloam at the southern foot of Ophel. Long after the boring of the Jebusite shaft the system had clearly been improved by diverting the waters of Gihon so that they flowed through the tunnel and directly into Jerusalem. The Bible tells us who was responsible: Hezekiah (716–687 BC) was King of Judah during the siege of the Assyrian Sennacherib; I Kings says that among his feverish preparations for the siege Hezekiah 'made the pool and the conduit and brought water into the city...'
II Chronicles is even more specific. Hezekiah, it says, 'closed the upper outlet of the waters of Gihon and directed them down to the west side of the city of David.' Armed with candles and 'a pair of wide Arab drawers', Robinson half-waded and half-crawled through the narrow tunnel. He measured its length as 1,750 feet.

But above ground the distance between the spring and reservoir is only 1,200 feet as the crow flies. The Parker expedition determined that the tunnel had been bored in a curious S-shape by Hezekiah's labourers. The reason for this remains a mystery.

At any rate, forty-two years after Robinson, on a blazing hot day in the summer of 1880, a young Arab student of Herr Conrad Schick, a German architect who devoted considerable time to the study of ancient Jerusalem, waded into the cool waters of the Siloam Pool and entered the tunnel. About twenty feet inside the young Arab slipped and fell. Recovering his balance, he noticed what appeared to be an inscription chiselled in the rock. He told Herr Schick, who examined the six-line text and excitedly telegraphed the news to the scholarly world: it was written in archaic Hebrew; part is missing, but it tells how Hezekiah's workmen dug the tunnel:

> ...While there were still three cubits to be cut through, [there was heard] the voice of a man calling to his fellow, for there was an overlap in the rock on the right [and on the left]. And when the tunnel was driven through, the quarrymen hewed (the rock), each man toward his fellow, axe against axe; and the water flowed from the spring toward the reservoir for 1,200 cubits, and the height of the rock above the head(s) of the quarrymen was 100 cubits.

This is a most graphic description of the proud achievement of humble workmen who carried out the ambitious project of the king. But in the large fragment that remains there is no reference to the monarch at all. Even the great Israelite kings must have courted popular and prophetic wrath if they indulged in splendid vanities on inscribed monuments of stone.

above The ancient rock-hewn tunnel connecting the spring of Gihon with the Pool of Siloam which formed part of the water system of ancient Jerusalem. It was probably dug during the reign of King Hezekiah.

below The inscription on the wall of the tunnel made by King Hezekiah's workmen

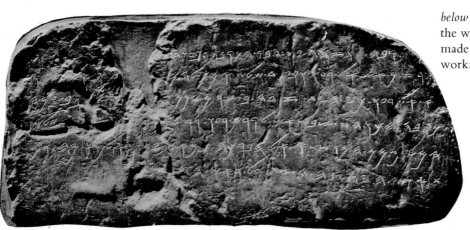

Solomon's Temple stood until 587 BC, when it was levelled by the legions of Nebuchadnezzar. Its reconstruction was the dream of those who began returning from Babylonian exile half a century later. The Second Temple, as well as Jerusalem itself, reached the zenith of its magnificence in the era preceding the Roman destruction of AD 70. Pliny the Elder, writing at that time, eulogized the city as the 'most famous in the Orient'. It boasted a great gymnasium, an amphitheatre, a hippodrome, and a splendid palace built by Herod, whose 'magnificence and equipment were unsurpassable', according to Josephus. Jerusalem consisted of three major parts. Ophel was now the Lower City, a mass of workers' dwellings, workshops and factories. On the hill to the west of the Temple rose the Upper City (the present Jewish Quarter of the Old City), established by the Greeks and expanded by the Hasmoneans into a model of Hellenistic planning and architecture. It contained the spacious homes of the well-to-do, the Hasmonean palace, and the Acra fortress. Two great bridges connected the Upper City to the Temple Mount.

Jerusalem was defended by three walls. One enclosed the Lower and Upper Cities. A second girdled the area to the north-west of the Temple. A third was begun by Agrippa I to contain the sprawling northern suburb of Bezetha. Remains of the first and third walls have been found. At the Citadel, where the three walls met in the west, Herod the Great raised three majestic towers which he magnanimously named Phasael after his martyred brother, Hippicus after a friend, and Mariamne in memory of his murdered wife.

Excavating in the Citadel between 1934 and 1940 C.N. Johns uncovered the Herodian foundation which supports the present 'Tower of David'. It was fashioned from perfectly cut stone blocks weighing between five and ten tons. Most scholars believe that this was the foundation which originally supported 'Phasael'. Where the second wall joined the north-west corner of the Temple Compound Herod raised another fortress, Antonia, named after Mark Antony. Père Vincent recovered the plan of Antonia and part of the pavement which covered its courtyard. Here it is believed that Pilate scourged Jesus and presented him to the mob; here Paul was imprisoned; and here the Roman soldiers made their fatal breach into the beleaguered Temple Compound in AD 70.

The pulse and pinnacle of Jerusalem, the crown of Zion, was the Second Temple. In place of the spartan edifice rebuilt by Zerubbabel and improvised upon by the Hasmoneans, Herod trained a thousand priests as stonemasons and recruited ten thousand workmen to build a temple that would outshine even Solomon's and earn him the popular loyalty he could not himself command. The temple was his most spectacular single undertaking. Herod raised it on a great trapezoidal platform or podium founded on bedrock. Its perimeter was 1,509 yards, an artificial bluff of stone 525 yards long on the western side and 328 on the northern side. Eight gates gave access to its vast colonnaded Outer Court. The Inner Court was separated from it by a barrier and divided into separate areas for women, men and priests. There stood the Holy Temple itself. 'To strangers as they approached', wrote Josephus, 'it seemed in the distance like a mountain covered with snow; for any part not covered with gold was dazzling white.'

Of all this splendour, toppled in rage and pillaged by the Romans, only the most meagre traces remain. There is the great platform itself with its massive foundation walls, including the Western or Wailing Wall. Some of the original Herodian stone courses are still visible. There is the single unfinished column, probably intended for the colonnade of the Outer Court, which had been flawed in quarrying. It still lies where it was found some years ago in the compound of the Russian Cathedral. The pillar's measurements correspond to those given by Josephus for the columns of the Temple portico and the royal basilica. There are also two inscriptions. They were found in 1872 and 1935—the former by the French archaeologist Clermont-Ganneau in a cemetery on Ophel, the latter outside the Lion's Gate leading to the Old City. They had once been set in the barrier which cordoned off the Inner Court, for they bear this prohibition in Greek: 'No Gentile shall enter the fence and barrier around the Holy Place. Whosoever is caught (therein) will be (himself) responsible for (his subsequent

A fragment from a tablet bearing a Greek inscription barring the entrance of Gentiles to the Inner Court of the Temple

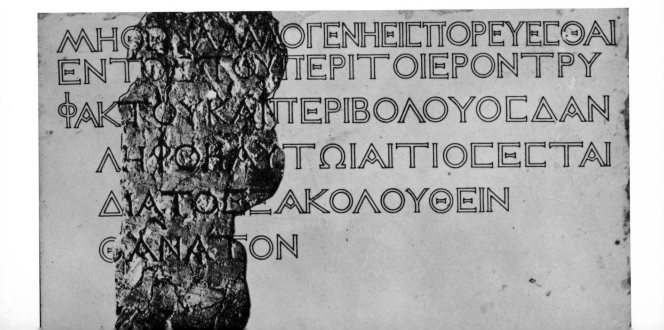

death.' The inscription confirms the statement made by Josephus that 'no foreigner was to enter the Sacred Precincts'—the name given to the Inner Court. He even refers to these very engraved proscriptions, in Hebrew, Greek and Latin.

The Israeli reunification of Jerusalem in June 1967 paved the way for two of the most extensive and exciting digs in the city's history: since February 1968 one of Israel's most eminent historians and archaeologists, Professor Benjamin Mazar, has been supervising excavations into the untenanted areas immediately to the south and west of the Temple Compound, or Haram esh-Sharif; and an energetic campaign of rebuilding in the old Jewish Quarter 220 yards to the west of the Temple site, an area badly damaged in the 1948 War, opened up areas of ground into which digging teams directed by Professor Nachman Avigad prospected in 1969 and 1970 to determine the nature of the ancient Upper City.

The Mazar and Avigad excavations have begun to add a welter of detail to the all but empty material record of the closing days of the Jewish Temple. As established by Solomon, the Temple had functioned as a royal chapel. In the life of the early nation it served more as the dominant symbol of God's all-pervading presence than as a centre of popular religious observance. But in the time of the Herods and the Roman procurators it had become the hub of the city—an object of pilgrimage, a public gathering place, its Outer Court the teeming crossroads of a large and bustling city. On high holy days thousands of Jews flocked there, not only from Judaea, but from the neighbouring lands where a proliferating segment

The remains of an elegant stone table on a single pedestal found by Prof. Nachman Avigad in the house of Bar-Kathros, which was destroyed in the Roman devastation

of the Diaspora had settled. At these times Roman troops were particularly vigilant, for the Temple grounds also served as the rallying-point for potential sedition and revolt.

Mazar's expedition has provided us with a host of fresh details. Pilgrims converged on the Holy House on two roadways, one running east from the Upper City, another running north from Ophel. They intersected under the overhanging north-western corner of the high Temple platform in the shadow of the royal bridge erected by Herod to link his splendid palace south of the Citadel with the Temple Court. The springing of the bridge's first arch, called Robinson's Arch, is still visible high on the western wall near the south-west angle of the podium. The excavators uncovered the monolithic stone base of the pier. Its measurements reveal that the royal bridge, or stoa, was fifty feet wide—easily one of the most massive in the Roman Empire. The rest of the bridge's span was supported by the walls of a monumental building which may have served as a reception centre for arriving pilgrims. In its basement Mazar's assistant Meir Ben-Dov showed me four ritual pools in which pilgrims may have bathed to purify themselves before ascending to the Temple.

Built into the bridge pier facing the north-south roadway near the thronged intersection were four chambers. Mazar believes that they were shops in which pilgrims could purchase vessels for Temple offerings, perhaps incense, grain, pigeons and other sacrificial items. At the crossroads the pilgrims turned east where the road from the Upper City began its ascent along the high southern wall toward the double 'Huldah Gates' leading into the Outer Court of the Temple. Adjacent to the crossroads was a large Herodian plaza of large squared flagstones where the pilgrims could congregate before climbing to the Temple.

Residents of the fashionable Upper City on the western hill looked down upon this panoramic spectacle. On the ridge there once stood a formidable building whose remains Avigad discovered and dated to the Hasmonean and Herodian period. Its walls were massive, and it boasted a huge defensive tower. Avigad is tempted to wonder whether it may have been the palace of the Hasmonean kings themselves. Its decoration would have been worthy of an edifice of monarchs. In the rubble Avigad found painted plaster remnants which once lined its frescoed walls—panels of imitation marble like those at Masada, well-wrought designs of fruit and flowers. There were fragments of finely fashioned Ionic capitals, and a relief of cornucopiae and pomegranates. Most evocative of all was a graceful and elaborate engraving on plaster of the most

Prof. Benjamin Mazar explains some features of his excavations at the southern wall of the Temple to the doyen of Palestinian archaeologists, Prof. William Foxwell Albright, of Johns Hopkins University in Baltimore, Maryland

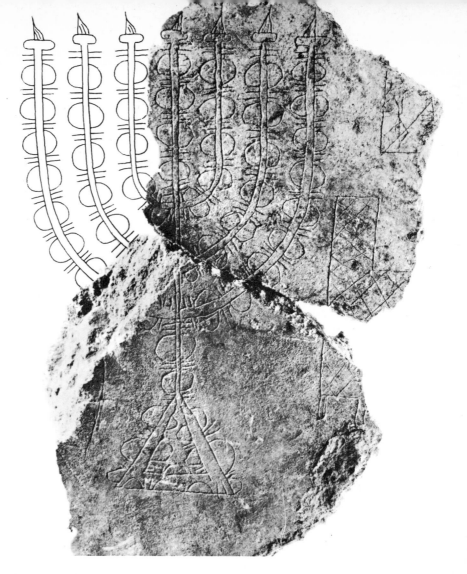

The famous seven-branched *menorah* or candelabrum engraved in plaster, discovered by Prof. Avigad in the ancient Upper City of Jerusalem in 1969

universal emblem of Judaism, the seven-branched *menorah*, from the late Hasmonean or early Herodian period. Only a handful of such early representations survive and this is without doubt the finest. The delicate 'leaf-and-button' design of its branches is somewhat like that of the Temple *menorah* carried away as spoil by the Romans in AD 70 and graphically sculptured on the triumphal arch of Titus in Rome. The workman who incised the representation found by Avigad could easily have been inspired by the original, which was housed in the Temple so close at hand.

Residents of the once-stately home of a man named Bar-Kathros could also look across to the great Temple and the activity that swirled about it. Avigad learned the name of the owner from an inscription on a stone weight found within the ruins of the house —the residence of a Temple priest, no doubt, because the Talmud lists Bar-Kathros as one of the priestly families of Jerusalem. At

any rate the owner seems to have enjoyed certain priestly conces-
sions attached to the Temple. Avigad found a large number of
vessels used in essential chemical or pharmaceutical processes—
large cooking pots, flasks, basalt mortars and pestles in every room,
weights, stone bowls, stone measuring cups. A mould for casting
coin blanks was also found. The workshop-like character of some
of the rooms is obvious, but the exact nature of the industry must
remain a mystery—it may have been the processing of scented
balm or incense, material used in sacrificial offerings, fine oils for
the lights of the Temple, perhaps even the minting of coins.

The Upper City was the last stronghold of the Jews in Jerusalem
in the frightful devastation of AD 70. Its scars lie deeply on the house
of Bar-Kathros. The house had been seared in a tremendous fire.
A bank of red and black ash lay thickly on the floor. Scattered
among it was a litter of objects turned lobster pink, white and pitch
black by the intense heat. A litter of broken objects had been
thrown in a heap in a corner of the room, together with a shattered
stone slab and pedestal which had once been a handsome table.
Leaning grotesquely against a wall of the kitchen were the skeletal
remains of a human forearm—that of a young lady—its gnarled
hand clutching at the ground. In a corner of a room stood an iron
spear. A litter of coins from Year 4 of the Revolt fixes the date
of the fall of the House of Bar-Kathros. The same coins were also
found in the coating of debris which smothered the Herodian street
at the south-west corner of the Temple Mount—from charred
wood to the smashed remnants of mighty stones and architectural
fragments hurled by the Romans from the highest courses of the
Temple wall itself. One of these stones, six feet long and weighing
ten tons, had evidently served as a cornerstone of a tower in the
Temple complex. Still visible in it are the remains of a niche in
which, Mazar believes, a priest may have stood, announcing the
beginning and the end of the Sabbath with the blast of a trumpet,
or *shofar*. The great stone carries an inscription in Hebrew, only a
portion of which had been deciphered by Mazar at the time of
writing: '*l'beit hatekiya*' or 'belonging to the house of the blowing
of the trumpet.'

The period which follows is marked by the red tile stamped with
the emblem of the Tenth Roman Legion *Fretensis* and Roman coins
bearing the words *Judaea Capta*.

'Now many', wrote the eyewitness Josephus, 'who were wasted
with hunger and beyond speech, when they saw the Sanctuary in
flames, found strength to moan and wail. Back from Peraea and the
mountains round about came the echo in a thunderous bass.'

above Prof. Nachman
Avigad *below* A tile bearing
the emblem of the
conquerors of Jerusalem,
the Roman Tenth Legion
Fretensis

14   The Signals of Lachish

Ask archaeologists in Israel to describe the particular kinds of artifacts they most value: in virtually every case their lists begin with the identical item, ancient inscriptions—signals from the past. One of Israel's most respected senior archaeologists, Professor Nachman Avigad, has enthusiastically devoted much of his career to the study and translation of these ancient written signals. 'Every stone and sherd we uncover has something to tell us', he said to me, 'but writing is obviously most eloquent of all. Through it, our ancestors speak directly to us. The value of inscribed materials is even greater here because, compared with other cultures, we have been left with so relatively little.'

Monumental inscriptions on palaces and tombs like those extolling the deeds and virtues of the kings of Assyria and nobles of Egypt are virtually non-existent among the ruins of ancient Israel. Professor Avigad believes that self-commemoration was scorned as an anathema in Israelite culture. 'One does not erect monuments to (or for) writers', says the Jerusalem Talmud. 'Their words and deeds alone shall be their memory.' One is forcibly struck by the fact that in the entire corpus of known ancient Jewish inscriptions, only one example of monumental writing contains the name of a monarch.

Archaeologist E.L. Sukenik regularly prowled through the collections of Jerusalem antiquities dealers, museums and church institutions seeking unrecognized Israelite treasures. On 9 February 1931 he went to see the collection of ancient burial inscriptions gathering dust at the monastery of the Russian Orthodox Church on the Mount of Olives. His attention was drawn to a small marble slab with an Aramaic inscription which said: 'Hither were brought the bones of Uzziah, King of Judah – Do not open.' At first he considered it might be a fake, but the next day he recorded in his

opposite The small but highly important tombstone of King Uzziah, one of the greatest of the Kings of Judah, whose bones were transferred to another (unknown) burial place in the time of Herod, bearing the legend 'Hither were brought the bones of Uzziah, do not open'

diary that he had 'no doubt' about the inscription's authenticity. The textual formula 'Do not open' had been unknown in Jewish epigraphy up to then.

The unpretentious tombstone, only thirteen by fourteen inches, was a link to one of the greatest of Judah's kings, who died a leper. It once marked the unknown resting-place to which the bones of the king were for some reason moved for re-interment long after his death in 734 BC. The style of the script dates the plaque to the first century AD. The Russian churchmen who found it at the end of the last century failed to record the spot, and simply moved it to their monastery without realizing its importance. Some time between 1962 and 1967, it was quietly shipped to the United States, where it was sold back to the Israel Museum for over half a million Israeli pounds. The slab was flown back to Jerusalem in 1968 by Mayor Teddy Kollek, who cradled it protectively as hand-luggage.

Scholars can only speculate about the reasons for the scarcity of monumental epigraphic material in Palestine. Perhaps Professor Yohanan Aharoni's conclusion is the best. Being a relatively small and poor country, he points out, Israel boasted comparatively few examples of architectural grandeur. What there was was repeatedly destroyed and pillaged, with anything of ceremonial or historic value either robbed or discarded by an endless array of conquerors. Often the Israelites, particularly in Judah, would themselves embark on waves of religious reform, smashing and destroying anything which profaned their spartan religious codes—idols, high places, altars that threatened the pre-eminence of the Temple at Jerusalem. Could these zealots have classified monumental inscriptions as graven images as well? Then, too, some of the material upon which scribes wrote were easily per- ishable: wood, leather and papyrus. The ravages of time and man could be far kinder to the durable baked clay tablets of the Mesopotamians than to the archives of Israel—unless they were stored in unique circumstances, for instance the dry, cool Judaean caves which preserved the Dead Sea Scrolls. Despite all this, enough written material from daily life has survived to let us be certain that writing was in common use in ancient Israel. Fortunately for the archaeologist and posterity, the writers of biblical times also made use of another far more indestructible medium on which to write. With reed pens and iron-carbon ink, they wrote on ceramic sherds, large broken pieces of pottery which were both cheap and readily available. As we have seen, students of antiquity call them ostraca (singular, ostracon). In addition to ostraca, there

Two 8th–7th century BC Hebrew seals from Lachish shaped in the form of Egyptian scarabs. The upper seal bears a Phoenician inscription 'Jezebel', and the lower seal, a Hebrew inscription: '(belonging) to Ahimelech (son of?) Samach'

are original seals, their imprints on clay bullae or on pottery jars, masons' marks inscribed on stone, symbols on merchants' weights and measures, and in later periods, coins.

The great epigraphic discoveries of the last hundred years, few though they are, have brought the life and times of ancient Israel uniquely alive. These finds began with the Mesha Stone, the Siloam Tunnel inscription which followed it and the Gezer Stone. The Irish archaeologist R.A.S. Macalister measured the sand limestone plaque only four inches high and two inches long. Its eight inscribed lines bore a slight resemblance to the script of the Mesha Stone and it has been dated a hundred years earlier to the reign of Solomon. It is through the Gezer text that we have a first-hand picture of the early biblical farmer, whose labour constituted the burden and mainstay of the country's economy.

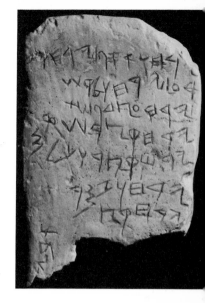

One of the most important epigraphic discoveries in Palestine is the so-called Gezer Calendar, discovered in 1902 by R. A. S. Macalister

> Two months of ingathering,
>   Two months of sowing,
>   Two months (of) late rains;
> Month (of) plucking (of) weeds,
>   Month (of) harvesting (of) barley,
>   Month of harvesting and measuring;
> Two months (of) harvesting produce;
>   Month (of collecting) summer fruit.
>   (Signed ?) Aby

The Gezer Calendar gives us the general setting of rural life on the rich broad plains, the gently sloping hillsides and the terraces of the ancient Israelites. The stage itself is dark. But, occasionally, the appearance of an ancient ostracon projects a sudden beam of light. Within it, people move, people so real that for a few moments we can often trace their actions and share their emotions.

One such person is the hapless and distraught peasant employed in reaping the fields adjacent to a large Judaean coastal fortress. Its original name was long ago lost to us, but since its rediscovery in 1958 it has been called Mezad Hashavyahu. About ten miles south of Tel Aviv, the Israelite citadel once straddled the international highway called the Via Maris, which linked Egypt with the markets of the north and east. One day, probably in the last third of the seventh century BC, during the reign of King Josiah (who in all probability built the fortress), we can imagine a lone peasant striding urgently from the fields to its main gate. He moves intently in that confused state of indignation and helpessness so characteristic of a humble man who has been wronged. At the guardhouse of the gate he pleads his case to an official, who gives him little satis-

A touching plea addressed to the governor of Mezad Hashavyehu by an unnamed peasant to restore his confiscated garment, recorded on a broken sherd, from a large jar

faction. As a last resort, the peasant then turns to the public scribe who sits beside the gate and hurriedly dictates a petition to the governor of the garrison. It conveys a tone of high emotion and, indignation but also a frantic quality.

Twenty-five hundred years later, in January 1960, Dr Joseph Naveh asked a volunteer to begin digging in what he presumed to be the ruins of the ancient guardroom. Working slowly amid the rubble of broken pottery and ashes, the volunteer came upon a potsherd with a few lines of writing. He found four more fragments. A sixth piece of the ostracon lay just outside the entrance. The shattered document was carefully washed and reassembled, but the original damage had defaced some of the script. Dr Naveh could make out fourteen lines of writing. 'Within some days', he relates, I was able to distinguish the letters of the opening phrase, and I could tell it was some sort of message or petition to the governor. It took several weeks, and the aid of infra-red photo-graphy along with pictures shot with red and green filters, to make the writing more distinct, before I could understand its gist.

Inked on a pinkish clay sherd with a pale green slip, which had been broken from a large jar, the surviving portion reads:

Let my Lord the Governor hear the words of his servant. Thy servant, [behold,] the servant was reaping in Ha-zar-asam, and thy servant reaped and finished; and I gathered in as usually before my rest.

When thy [se]rvant had fi[nished] his reaping, he gathered in as usually, and there came Hosha'ayahu the son of Shobai, and he took thy servant's garment. After I had finished my reaping as usually did he take thy servant's garment.

And all my brethren will witness on my behalf, they who reap with me in the heat [of the sun], my brethren will witness on my behalf, 'Verily (this is so)'. I am free of gu[ilt. Restore] my garment. And I will pay the Governor in full to re[store my garment]... (?)... thy [se]rvant, and be not helpless to save...'

From the repetitive phrases and ideas one can almost see the petitioner wringing his hands in agitation as he paces before the scribe in the gatehouse entrance, who dutifully takes down everything he says in simple but awkward biblical Hebrew.

Hosha'ayahu is evidently an official of the garrison. It seems that he has charged the peasant with failure to fulfill his quota of harvesting before taking his rest and shelter 'from the heat of the

opposite An incised ostracon with a brief message concerning a consignment of barley to be delivered, from Samaria, 8th century BC

sun'. As a penalty, Hosha'ayahu has confiscated his garment. The peasant argues that he has been falsely charged, and that his fellow workers will testify under oath that he performed his quota of labour before resting. He assures the Governor that if he is found guilty, he will work off his fine, but clearly he is a poor man and places the return of his garment above all else.

The peasant, as careful readers of the Bible will instantly recollect, has the ancient law on his side. In both the Book of the Covenant and in Deuteronomy, it is stated that a garment may be used by a poor man as a pledge or collateral against a debt. In the case of our peasant, his quota of work seems to have been his debt, a concept that smacks heavily of the obligations of serfdom, or forced labour. But the Bible adjures the creditor to restore the debtor his garment in pledge 'before the sun goes down; for that is his only covering, it is his mantle for his body; in what else shall he sleep?' On this the petitioner may be resting his case. Naveh has written that peasants like the one who sought the return of his cloak were possibly serfs on royal estates who helped supply the troops of the garrison with provisions. He sees our humble petitioner as 'just as much the king's property as the cattle'.

We get a vivid and dramatic impression of the tormented times of Judah from the correspondence files of the military commanders two important Judaean citadels, Lachish and Arad. The walled cities of Judah and Israel knew relatively little relief from the agonizing trials of invasion and siege. The first confirmation of such events from extra-biblical Palestinian sources came to light during the ambitious excavations at Lachish, the great mound city which once guarded the approaches to Hebron and Jerusalem from the lower-lying Shephelah and coastal plain.

Early in 1935, an excavation labourer probing slowly through the thick black destruction layer underlying a later Persian roadway at the city gate picked up a small blackened fragment of pottery. Unlike thousands of similar sherds, his sharp eyes had quickly discerned that this fragment was different. His excited supervisor quickly confirmed that the soot all but obscured what appeared to be archaic Hebrew writing. The news was swiftly relayed to chief excavator, James L. Starkey. He ordered that all potsherds from this stratum were to be washed carefully in filtered water. Of the total of twenty-one sherd 'documents' found, only seven were sufficiently legible to produce a coherent translation.

The task of deciphering them fell to the veteran epigraphist Professor Harry Torczyner (now Tur-Sinai) of the Hebrew University who spent long and patient hours on the coveted assignment.

opposite An aerial view of Qumran, site of the ancient Essene community and where one of the most significant and exciting archaeological discoveries ever, the Dead Sea Scrolls, was made

Scholars throughout the world anxiously awaited his publication. Not since the turn of the century had continuous old Hebrew texts of this kind come to light. The Lachish Letters, as they have come to be called, were obviously connected in some way with an event of catastrophic destruction. Starkey believed that it was the uncompromising campaign of Nebuchadnezzar, which ended the life of the Judaean kingdom in 587 BC.

That the Lachish Letters were associated with the Babylonian ordeal seems to be reflected in their texts. They represent a file of correspondence from Hoshaiah, the commander of a nearby military post, to his superior Yaosh, in all likelihood chief officer of Lachish. The death-knell of Judah is implicit in a grave report on the state of the fire signal system, which was evidently used in time of emergency for military communication from point to point. In Letter IV, Hoshaiah gloomily advises Yaosh: 'And let [my lord] know that we are watching for the signals of Lachish, according to all the indications which my lord hath given, for we cannot see Azekah.' One by one, the signal fires marking the cities and towns of Judah were being extinguished by the angry army of Nebuchadnezzar. Letter IV balefully confirms what we are told in the Bible: 'Then Jeremiah the prophet spoke all these words to Zedekiah, king of Judah, in Jerusalem, when the army of the king of Babylon was fighting against Jerusalem and against all the cities of Judah that were left, Lachish and Azekah; for these were the only fortified cities of Judah that remained'.

The Lachish Letters have a spartan grandeur. Through them we are eyewitnesses to the final contacts between two doomed men, written in the classical biblical Hebrew of the era of the prophets Jeremiah and Uriah. Not only do the letters project the troubled and chaotic mood of the time, but also the religio-political internal unrest. As we shall see, it may be, as some scholars contend, that both Hoshaiah and Yaosh are directly involved in the crisis between the prophetic school, which counsels that Judah's only hope is surrender, and King Zedekiah and his princes, who stubbornly choose to reject such seditious talk and defy Nebuchadnezzar.

Hoshaiah is forever defending himself against a serious charge of some sort by Yaosh: 'The heart of thy servant hath been sick since thou didst write to thy servant.' In Letter II, Hoshaiah invokes Yahweh to 'afflict those who re[port] an (evil) rumor about which thou art not informed!' In Letter V a humble Hoshaiah asks Yaosh: 'How can thy servant benefit or injure the king?' In Letter VIII: 'Truly I lie not – let my lord send thither!' Has Hoshaiah been charged with plotting rebellion or treason against Jerusalem?

One fascinating suggestion about the solution of this mystery came from Professor Tur-Sinai, the first translator of the Lachish Letters. He proposes to link them to the unpopular king Jehoiakim, a predecessor of Zedekiah by several years. Jehoiakim first inspired the wrath of Jeremiah and the prophetic school by invalidating religious reforms instituted by the late King Josiah, and then, as a vassal to Pharaoh Necho, by allowing himself to be used as a pawn in the power struggle between Egypt and Babylon. It is his rebellion against Babylon which first inspires the virulence of Nebuchadnezzar against Judah.

In the Bible, Jeremiah is not the only prophet who in the eyes of the Court preaches sedition by opposing resistance to Babylon. Another is Uriah, whom Jehoiakim is determined to put to death. Hearing of it, Uriah flees to Egypt. But the King dispatches a military detail there, under the command of 'Elnathan the son of Achbor', that captures Uriah and returns him to Jerusalem, where he is slain. In Lachish Letter III, curiously enough, it is 'Coniah son of Elnathan' who leads a detail into Egypt. Tur-Sinai proposes that the name Elnathan has been erroneously transposed in the biblical account; that Yaosh is a member of the prophetic party which opposes the militaristic policies of Jerusalem; that Hoshaiah has betrayed the prophet Uriah's whereabouts in Egypt by forwarding details to Jerusalem of letters entrusted to him by the prophet. This, argues Tur-Sinai, is the charge levelled against Hoshaiah by Yaosh, who then preserved the docket of correspondence in the heavily defended gatehouse as evidence in any future court-martial proceedings against his subordinate. The charges were never pursued. Nebuchadnezzar brought misfortune and disaster upon Judah, as the prophets had foreseen. Valid or not, it is a fascinating hypothesis.

The noted epigraphist David Diringer wrote of the Lachish Letters that their discovery established that 'there were many Early Hebrew inscriptions, but that the vast majority were destroyed through the agency of man or by the action of time and climate.' Two and a half decades later, exciting new finds lent confirmation to Diringer's statement. The Arad ostraca, the largest archive of ancient writings ever found in Israel, have helped to illuminate the times and trials of the Israelites.

Like Diringer, Professor Yohanan Aharoni was sensitive to the loss of priceless historical material. But he was also aware that much of the problem was due to earlier excavations having failed to sort out the ostraca from the chaff of excavation. From the start of his

The laborious process of hand washing over two hundred inscribed sherds discovered by Prof. Aharoni's team during the excavations at Arad; one of the richest finds of written material ever made in Israel

excavations at Arad in the summer of 1962 when the outlines of an ancient Israelite citadel began to emerge from the thin layer of desert loess, Aharoni instructed his field team and a force of a hundred volunteers that they were to watch particularly for ink-inscribed potsherds. He instituted a screening procedure that has no archaeological counterpart for sheer tedium, drudgery—and results! Every single sherd was dipped in water and examined on both sides. In five seasons, between 1962 and 1967, over two hundred inscribed sherds were spared from the rubbish dump, virtually doubling in a single dig the number of known ostraca from the days of the First Temple. Much is still being studied and translated.

Aharoni dates one inscription, containing perhaps ten preserved and readily identifiable characters, to the tenth century BC, when cursive Hebrew began to emerge from the parent Phoenician script. This would make it the oldest ostracon known, roughly contemporary with the Gezer Calendar. Another provides a precise example of Israelite military book-keeping. It reads: 'To Nahum and now: Come to the house of Eliashib son of Eshyahu, and take from him one (jar of) oil, and send (it) to me quickly, and seal it with your seal.' The requisition was found in the 'file room' of Eliashib, receipted with this business-like notation on the reverse side: 'On the 24th of the month gave Nahum oil by the hand of the Kitti, one (jar).'

An archive of seventeen sherd communications addressed to Eliashib was found in a series of small rooms against the southern wall of the citadel. Aharoni dates the missives to about 600 BC, the turbulent era of King Jehoiakim, just before Nebuchadnezzar's final campaign against Judah. Aharoni has produced evidence which portrays Eliashib as a loyal senior official of incredibly long standing on the dusty Negev frontier. In a room adjacent to the archives he found three seals, 'two still with remnants of the cord on which they had been strung', reading '(Belonging) to Eliashib son of Eshyahu.' 'Astonishing as it may seem', Aharoni writes, 'the Eliashib seals do not belong to the same stratum as the Eliashib ostraca, but are actually from the earlier stratum. . . This means that Eliashib served in his capacity at Arad through two strata, for a period of twenty or thirty years.'

This veteran official is clearly the senior military commander and/or governor of Arad, most probably chief officer of the entire south-east Negev frontier commanding the defence of the troubled road from Edom. His correspondence seems to bear this out. In addition to notes requesting provisions for travellers and troops moving through his fortress, and confirming receipt or delivery of vital foodstuffs, there is a pregnant military dispatch—clearly written on a yellowish-pink fragment of a storage jar which was sheared into a small tablet:

> From Arad 50 (?) and from Kin [ah. . .] and you shall send them (to) Ramath-nege [b by the han] d of Malkiyahu the son of Qerab'ur and he shall hand them over to Elisha' the son of Yirmiyahu in Ramath-negeb, lest anything should happen to the city. And the word of the king is incumbent upon you for your very life. Behold, I have sent to warn you today: [Get] the men to Elisha' ! Lest Edom should come there.

Military men through the ages have possessed the ability to project a mood of urgency and command in a mere handful of words. Thus it is with this missive to Eliashib, perhaps from southern headquarters in Beersheba. Sensitive to the slightest nuance after two decades of service within the Judaean bureaucracy, Eliashib would have hearkened quickly to the imperative tone of the order.

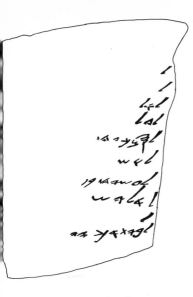

A tracing of another ostracon found by Prof. Aharoni in 1969 in Lachish

Two altars showing remains of a burnt offering from the Israelite sanctuary at Arad dating to the 9th century BC

These two pictures of Israelite pottery show domestic utensils, incense burners and other ritual objects found at Lachish

Throughout the history of Israel and Judah, the 'way of Edom' from the low-lying Arava to the Negev of Arad was the principal axis of attack by the Israelites on the east and the Edomites on the west. Aharoni has identified the city of Ramath-negeb, which was placed in danger by a new Edomite offensive, with a ruined fortress called Khirbet Ghazza, some six miles south-east of Tell Arad. At its foot begins the precipitous descent from the Negev to the Dead Sea. Thus, writes Aharoni, 'Ramath-negeb is the first point against which an Edomite attack would be expected...'

Is there any historical record of trouble with Edom about 600 BC, the date to which the Eliashib docket is ascribed? It was a turbulent time for King Jehoiakim, with the 'third world' of the Near East jockeying for advantage amid the great 'superpower' struggle between Egypt and Babylon. In several passages, the Bible makes this clear. II Kings tells us: 'In his days Nebuchadnezzar king of Babylon came up, and Jehoiakim became his servant three years; and he turned and rebelled against him. And the Lord sent against him bands of the Chaldeans, and bands of the Syrians, and bands of the Moabites, and bands of the Ammonites, and sent them against Judah to destroy it...' In such an unsettled climate, one could well expect bands of Edomites to take advantage of the parlous position of Judah as well. As Aharoni points out, it is clearly a time of war. With intelligence of the approach of an Edomite army, Malkiyahu is sent to Eliashib to collect reinforcements from Ramath-negeb—a unit of fifty men from Arad and others from Kinah, though the exact number is undecipherable because of damage to the ostracon. The writer of the order invokes the name of the king. Is it because Eliashib is unhappy about diminishing the strength of his sector during these threatening days? There is nothing obscure about the intent of the formulation:

'And the word of the king is incumbent upon you for your very life. . . I have sent to warn you. . . [Get] the men to Elisha'! Failure to obey the king's command will not be brooked.'

With Israel, the tradition of the word centred upon its spiritual life and beliefs. Through the transmission of the Bible and the archaeological discoveries of recent times we see this tradition preserved and magnified. Though preservation of its daily record was by no means as important to Israel, archaeology has begun to recover enough to offer rare insights into the character of Israelite life and to establish the accuracy of the biblical reporters. Thus the discoveries described in this chapter are among the most treasured finds of Palestinian archaeology.

The objects shown on the previous page after cleaning and restoration

15 Qumran: The Voice of the Essenes

'It has long been the dream of Biblical scholars that very early manuscripts of the books of the Bible might be recovered by archaeological research. What would we not give for a first edition, so to speak, of Isaiah. . . Unfortunately, no such treasure exists, so far as we know.' The American biblical scholar Millar Burrows voiced that apparently forlorn hope in 1941 in his excellent book *What Mean These Stones*. Ironically, the 'treasure' was to begin materializing just six years later; the American Schools of Oriental Research in Jerusalem, of which Burrows was the head at the time, was to play a pivotal role in its identification and transmission; and Burrows himself would serve as editor in the historic publication of three major finds, one of which would be a 'first edition, so to speak' of the Book of Isaiah!

The Dead Sea Scrolls have not only provided us with the earliest biblical documents known, affording scholars an insight into the accuracy of biblical transmission over the centuries (the oldest fragments have been dated to the third century BC). The Scrolls also illuminate that important era of chaotic change when normative Judaism was again struggling for its very life: against the Romans, divisive political and religious schisms, growing popular despair and a breakdown of the moral order—when Messianic yearnings were being answered by the first faint stirrings of Christianity.

Nowhere—either in the New Testament or in Jewish religious writings—is there a reference to the Essenes. Our principal sources are three historians writing at the dawn of the Christian era: the Jews, Josephus and Philo of Alexandria, and the Roman, Pliny the Elder. We are told of a rudimentary monastic order of those 'weary of life' who have largely abandoned the ways of the city and have withdrawn into 'colonies' of their own. Pliny calls them a 'solitary people', and identifies their major centre as the western

opposite The 'Copper Scroll' shown *in situ* during the first meticulous cleaning operation in Qumran Cave III where it was found. It is the only scroll written on material other than parchment. Behind it lies a fascinating riddle, for it purports to describe the hiding places of the great treasures of the Jewish Temple. But many of the clues are cryptic, and scholars cannot agree on the scroll's translation

One of the original clay jars with lids in which the Essenes stored their priceless scrolls. These distinctive jars, found both in the caves and the Qumran settlement, provided the major archaeological clue linking the two

shore of the Dead Sea north of En-gedi—precisely where the Scroll finds were made and the remains of the Qumran site excavated.

Philo refers to the Essenes as the 'Holy Ones'. Josephus mentions them together with the two major schools of Jewish thought known to have existed at the time, the Pharisees and Sadducees, but says that the Essenes 'profess a more severe discipline'. In fact, they have abandoned the Temple at Jerusalem for an austere desert existence of prayer, work and ritual cleanliness that goes well beyond the requirements of the Scriptural ordinances. They have sworn 'terrible oaths' to revere God and dedicate themselves to a life of charity, sobriety, temperance and honest dealings with other men. Offences are dealt with severely, and may lead to expulsion. Blasphemy is a capital offence. They 'champion good faith and serve the cause of peace.'

Josephus says they are 'communists to perfection', scorning wealth. Initiates surrender all their property to the order, everybody sharing in it freely. Their dress is of the simplest variety, and is not discarded until it is 'dropping to pieces or worn out with age'. A candidate must prove himself for a year before he is accepted as a novice, and must be tried and tested for a further two years until he is elected to full membership by the order. Then he may share in their secrets and communal meals. In their conversations, there is no swearing, no shouting or interruption. 'If ten sit down together,' says Josephus, 'one will not speak against the wishes of nine.' They are spoken of as farmers and students of ancient healing techniques. They are described as being clairvoyant. While they believe the body to be corruptible, the soul is immortal. They hold, too, to the existence of Heaven and Hell. Some practise celibacy, while a second order takes wives, but only indulges in intercourse to propagate their kind.

They value death with honour rather than an empty life, says Josephus. 'Their spirit was tested to the utmost by the war with the Romans, who wracked and twisted, burnt and broke them, subjecting them to every torture yet invented in order to make them blaspheme the Lawgiver or eat some forbidden food, but could not make them do either. . . . ' We should stress that one of their stern oaths is to 'preserve the books of the sect'. Because they discharged this duty so faithfully we now know that the Essenes represent the common inheritance of Judaism and Christianity through the scrolls which they faithfully preserved.

The rediscovery of the material legacy of the Dead Sea sect may be said to have begun a little more than a century after it had disappeared from view. Early in the third century AD, an Egyptian named Origen, an early Christian theologian, published a great work called the *Hexapla*, a critical synopsis of all the versions of the Old Testament known to exist at that time, including seven editions of the Book of Psalms, one of which Origen said he had found, along with other Hebrew and Greek documents, in a jar near Jericho! Five centuries later, there is a record of another curious discovery similar to the sensational events of 1947. In a letter which has been dated to the late eighth century, Timotheus I, the Patriarch of Seleucia, informs the Metropolitan of Elam that an Arab who had been hunting 'near Jericho' followed his dog into a cave and 'found a chamber, in which there were many books, in the rock'. The Arab sped to Jerusalem, where he told the story to a group of Jews, 'who came out in great numbers and found books of the Old Testament and others in the Hebrew script. . .'

The gaunt cliffs of the Judaean Wilderness a few hundred yards west of the Dead Sea. The gaping mouth of Qumran Cave IV is clearly visible. It held one of the richest caches of scroll material

One of them must have found its way to Cairo. In AD 882, the Jewish community of that city founded the Ezra Synagogue, a house of prayer and centre of study that was to become one of the most influential Jewish institutions of the mediaeval Diaspora. Over the centuries Cairo's Jewish scholars and scribes collected or copied a veritable treasure of cultural and religious materials. Their repository was the dark and musty *geniza*, a storehouse of worn and disused holy writings and documents in the attic of the synagogue. In 1896, a thousand years after the founding of the synagogue, two London ladies called on Solomon Z. Schechter, a Romanian-born Talmudic scholar who was lecturing in rabbinical studies at Cambridge University. While touring in Cairo, they had been sold several yellowed pages from the *geniza* cache, written in square Hebreo-Aramaic script. They had the good sense to appreciate the potential value of the documents, and wanted Schechter to value them.

He was thunderstruck. What they had brought him was a portion of the apocryphal Book of Ecclesiasticus, or the Wisdom of Ben-Sira, a late (second-century BC) scriptural work which had been incorporated into the biblical canon of the Jews of Alexandria, and was known to succeeding generations only in its Greek translation. Here suddenly was part of a copy of Ben-Sira in the original Hebrew! What other wonders might the Cairo *geniza* contain? Schechter wento to Cairo to find out. Within months, he was on his way back to Britain with a hundred thousand pages of ancient manuscript. To their study he would devote much of the rest of his life. In 1910 he touched off a heated scholarly controversy with the publication of two related documents from the *geniza* under the title 'Fragments of a Zadokite Work.' The larger fragments consisted of eight sheets of parchment written on both sides, which he called Text A. Text B, covering two sides of a single sheet, contained some variations from the longer A text, and also illuminated certain of its defaced and undecipherable portions. The 'Zadokite Work' related some of the history and statutes of an otherwise unidentified sectarian group composed of 'all those who know righteousness', a congregation of the 'New Covenant' which was formed '390 years after God gave Israel into the hands of Nebuchadnezzar'. 'God took heed of their doings', says the text, 'and raised for them a Teacher of Righteousness to lead them in the way of His heart.' Who was the Teacher of Righteousness? What was the name and nature of the group which he led? Scholars were divided not only over these questions, but also over the date of the documents' original source. They had been copied between the tenth and twelfth centuries, but when had the work itself been composed?

An illiterate Ta'amireh Arab shepherd named Mohammed ed-Dib (the Wolf) and his goat were destined by accident to help supply the answers in the spring of 1947. Through the telling and retelling, the tale has acquired a familiar folk ring, with the scurry along the angry upthrust dolomitic hills behind Khirbet Qumran in search of a lost goat; the playful lobbing of a stone into an opening in the cliff-face; the answering shatter of something breaking. Mohammed scrambled away in fear, as though confronted by a djinn. The next day, with reinforcements in the person of his cousin Achmad Mohammad, he entered the narrow cave chamber, treading on fragments of broken pots. The Bedouin found eight tall jars, some with the lids still on. Inside were blackened bundles of leather, some in coverings of linen. Outside the cave they unrolled the bundles and saw columns of writing on them. A total of seven Scrolls were found in Qumran Cave I, miraculously preserved in the cool, dark, dry surroundings.

Bethlehem is a major trading post for the Bedouin of the Judaean Desert. Here they buy their few supplies, trade their wares and market their acquisitions, legal and otherwise. One of the tradesmen frequented by the Ta'amireh was a Syrian Christian named Khalil Iskander Shahin, known as 'Kando', a cobbler and sometime Oriental middleman who has since amassed a fortune from the traffic in Scrolls. To him the Bedouin brought their strange leather bundles. At first Kando considered using the material for shoe repairs. Reflecting on the writing, which he believed to be Syriac, he thought better of it and took four of the Scrolls to Mar Athansius Yeshue Samuel, the Metropolitan in residence at the Monophysite

Syrian Convent of St Mark in the Old City of Jerusalem, as a sample.

Though he cannot be called a scholar, the Metropolitan recognized the four scrolls as ancient Hebrew documents. He bought them, asked the Bedouin for the location of the cave and began to seek expert opinion on their nature and worth. He also dispatched one of his priests, Father Bulos, to the cave to check on the Arab story. With only a few melons and no water, the father was not exactly equipped for the rigours of desert exploration, but he stayed in the cave long enough to notice the broken jar fragments, pieces of linen wrapping, and numerous scroll fragments that the Arabs had left behind. He also learned that they were using some of the scroll jars to carry water.

In February 1948 the Metropolitan had the scrolls taken to the American Schools of Oriental Research. The director, Professor Burrows, had just gone on a two-week trip to Iraq, leaving behind Dr John C. Trever as acting director. He and a colleague, Dr William Brownlee, began examining the scrolls. The largest one was carefully unrolled. Trever recalled that as he studied it he was 'not yet sure that what I was seeing was not a forgery, though the scrolls had every appearance of great antiquity'. On his desk was a series of boxed slides labelled '*What Lies Back of our English Bible*'. Thumbing to the section on early Hebrew manuscripts, he compared a fragment called the Nash Papyrus, dated to between the second century BC and the 1st century AD, with the Scroll. 'The similarity of the script was striking.'

The American scholars persuaded the Metropolitan to let them photograph and publish the scrolls, convincing him that 'the value of the manuscripts would be enhanced' should he decide to sell them. With the exception of one scroll, which he insisted be left unopened, the Metropolitan agreed. The three were identified as an ancient copy of the Book of Isaiah, a commentary on the Book of Habbakuk, and a non-biblical document which Burrows called the 'Manual of Discipline'. The unopened document was called the 'Genesis Apocryphon' when it was finally unrolled some years later. Trever made several prints from negatives of the Isaiah Scroll and sent them to Professor Albright at Johns Hopkins University in Baltimore. On 15 March his exuberant airmail reply arrived: 'My congratulations on the greatest manuscript discovery of modern times! There is no doubt in my mind that the script is more archaic than that of the Nash Papyrus. . . I should prefer a date around 100 BC. . . What an absolutely incredible find! And there can happily not be the slightest doubt in the world about the genuiness of the manuscript.'

Bethlehem cobbler and tradesman Khalil Iskander Shahin, nicknamed 'Kando', (left) a Syrian Christian who played a key role in the rediscovery of the Dead Sea Scrolls. He opened a souvenir and antiquities shop in Jerusalem on the proceeds

Three stages in the delicate process of unrolling a Dead Sea Scroll. The one shown is the Genesis Apocryphon, which was written in Aramaic. *top* The tightly-rolled scroll as found.*middle* The scroll partly unrolled.*bottom* The entire scroll has been unrolled. Much of the outer material was found destroyed

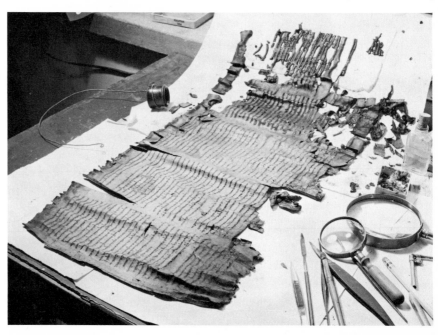

Seven Scrolls had been found in the cave at Qumran. What had become of the other three? We must look back several months in time.

On 23 November 1947, Eleazar Sukenik, Professor of Archaeology at Hebrew University, had returned to his office on Mount Scopus after a lecture tour. There was a message to telephone a friend named Ohun, an Armenian dealer in antiquities with whom he had done a good deal of business. The man wanted to show him 'some items of interest', which could not be discussed further on the telephone. They agreed to meet the following day at the gateway of Military Zone B.

Something must be said of the atmosphere of those days. It was a new testing time for Palestine. On 29 November the UN General Assembly would meet to vote on ending the British Mandate and partitioning the country between Jews and Arabs—a climax to months of terrorism by the Jewish underground against the British presence, which had been restricting the landing of Jewish refugees from Europe. In the background was the Arab community, tense and sullen in the knowledge that war with the Jews was inevitable when the British left. The British had zoned off Jerusalem with barbed wire barriers, and placed the Jewish sector under martial law. Through the strands of the netting at Zone B, Ohun showed Sukenik a scrap of inscribed leather, and on the next day showed him four more in his shop. Ohun told him the story of the Bedouin discovery. Three scrolls were now in the hands of a Bethlehem dealer in antiquities called Feidi Salahi. 'A *geniza*!?' Sukenik wondered in his diary. '. . . I saw a beautiful Biblical Hebrew, a text which I can't identify.' He decided that the scraps he had seen were both ancient and genuine, and he was empowered to buy them for Hebrew University. He risked a dangerous trip to Arab Bethlehem with Ohun for the involved oriental ritual of negotiation and purchase. 'I looked and I looked', he later recorded, 'and suddenly I had the feeling that I was privileged by destiny to gaze upon a Hebrew Scroll which had not been read for more than two thousand years.' Sukenik brought the three scrolls back to Jerusalem and began to study them in his home. That very night— 29 November—the General Assembly voted in favour of partition, recreating a Jewish territorial entity that had not existed since the Qumran sect had hidden their precious library away.

Two of the scrolls were documents central to the sect's creeds and customs. Sukenik labelled one, the 'Thanksgiving Hymns', and the second, 'The War of the Sons of Light against the Sons of Darkness'. The third scroll was biblical—another copy of the

One of the sheets of the Thanksgiving Scroll. The scroll is clearly marked with ruled guidelines for the scribe and the letters have been 'hung' from them, rather than written on the line. Parts of the manuscript were blackened by humidity but have been nearly all deciphered by the use of infra-red photography

Book of Isaiah. Sukenik was as yet unaware that there were four more held by the Syrian Metropolitan. But towards the end of January he was shown them as well. However, before negotiations could be completed, the American scholars convinced the Syrian prelate that their publication of the material would ensure him a higher price on the US market. Sukenik died in 1953, convinced that the Metropolitan's scrolls were lost to Israel for ever.

One interesting note in his diary deserves particular mention. Dated 6 February 1948, it reads: 'I am beginning to think that the *geniza* belonged to the Essenes.' The '*geniza*', as Sukenik liked to call it, was not yet exhausted. In January 1949 soldiers of Jordan's Arab Legion found the original cave at Qumran. It was excavated by Père Roland de Vaux of the Ecole Biblique and G. Lankester Harding, director of Jordan's Department of Antiquities, and more scroll fragments were found. Over the next seven years a seesaw race developed between the archaeologists and the Arabs, whose appetites were stimulated by the financial rewards of the scroll 'business'. The indefatigable Bedouin won the contest hands down. Literally thousands of fragments were turned up. Their richest hauls were made in Cave IV, carved into the very marl of the plateau on which the settlement stands, and Cave XI in the cliff face to the north-west.

In January 1949 the Syrian Metropolitan arrived in the United States to sell the four scrolls in his possession. He was unable to do so. The publication of the documents by the American Schools had satisfied rather than intensified the appetites of the scholarly world; and, as Edmund Wilson points out in his definitive book *The Dead Sea Scrolls*, collectors, institutional and private, with the means to buy them were more interested in literary first editions than in primary religious sources.

In 1954 destiny, coincidence, or human shrewdness, interceded. Professor Yigael Yadin, Sukenik's son, travelled to the United States on a lecture tour. Early in June his attention was drawn to a somewhat exceptional advertisement in the Wall Street Journal. It read:

THE FOUR DEAD SEA SCROLLS

Biblical Manuscripts dating to at least 200 BC are for sale. This would be an ideal gift to an educational or religious Institution by an individual or group.
Box F. 206 The Wall St. Journal

Yadin wrote in his *The Message of the Scrolls;* 'I read and re-read the advertisement. It was almost incredible. . .' Through an intermediary he entered into negotiations on behalf of the Israeli Government with a trust which had been set up by the Metropolitan Samuel to sell the scrolls, the proceeds to be devoted to the work of the Monophysite Syrian Church. A month after the advertisement appeared the four scrolls were on their way to Israel to join the other three. The selling price had been $250,000. Only a few years earlier the Bedouin and their middlemen in Bethlehem had been parting with scroll material at the going rate of £1 ($2.80) per square centimetre.

The original scrolls have all been published. Since 1948 teams of technicians and editors have worked to restore, photograph, sort, collate and translate the tens of thousands of fragments which were also salvaged. They represent portions of almost six hundred manuscripts and include texts covering the entire Hebrew Bible with the single exception of the Book of Esther. Deciphering and publishing the fragments alone represents a mammoth task, the final stages of which are proceeding far too slowly to suit voracious armies of scholars who have been digesting, interpreting and contesting the meaning of the scrolls for two decades. Apart from the biblical documents, the Qumran library contains two other types of material: non-biblical religious writings on the rules, creeds and customs of the sect; and 'commentaries' or works of interpretation (in Hebrew, *pesherim*). The *pesherim* quote and interpret the Bible to prove that the teachings of the order were in agreement with the ancient sacred writings; in other words, that they were confirmed by divine revelation; and that the events of the day could be explained within the same context. As Dr Geza Vermes

This photograph taken by the eminent French archaeologist Père Roland de Vaux of the Jerusalem Ecole Biblique shows a Bedouin carrying a large Essene jar marked with the Hebrew name 'Yohanan'

explains: 'In the mind of the sectaries, the law was a sealed book whose true meaning escaped all but the initiates of the order.' It is from these two types of documents that we learn most about the nature and message of the Dead Sea sect.

As we have noted, the Damascus Document says that God raised a Teacher of Righteousness 'to guide them in the way of His heart'. This is the time when 'The Scoffer' arose, who caused Israel to 'wander in a pathless wilderness' as he abolished 'the ways of righteousness'. The disciples of the Teacher of Righteousness were tormented and persecuted. Among their enemies were the seekers of 'smooth things', who 'justified the wicked and condemned the just'. The leader of the sect abandoned the Temple in Jerusalem and established their community in the wilderness. It was most probably there that the Wicked Priest 'plotted to destroy the Poor' and 'pursued the Teacher of Righteousness to the house of his exile' during the sect's observance of the Day of Atonement. He 'appeared unto them to destroy them and to cause them to stumble on the day of the fast. . .' One document infers that the Wicked Priest tried to kill the Teacher of Righteousness.

Scholars doubt whether even the sect's priestly adversary would have violated a high holy day in the pursuit of violence. Instead they suggest that he took advantage of the separatist community's special calendar, which differed from the lunar system observed by other Jews. The sect based its year on the sun. It was divided into 364 days, thirty in each month. An extra day was added to every third month. The sect's festivals therefore fell on different days from those in the official Temple calendar. This was evidently exploited by the Wicked Priest, who would not have been violating standard Jewish observance by surprising the Qumran community on its Day of Atonement.

After the death of the Teacher of Righteousness from causes unknown, 'the land was ravaged' by an unspecified disaster, and the community for a time 'went out of the land of Judah to sojourn in the land of Damascus'. Scholars disagree on whether 'the land of Damascus' should be taken literally or is merely used metaphorically. As we will see, the sect returned to Qumran, where it girded itself up for the 'last days' foreordained by God, the 'end of the world', when a priestly Messiah and a royal Messiah would arise within the community—the true heirs of a new Israel. But first the disciples of the community, the Sons of Light, would wage a great eschatalogical war lasting forty years against the Sons of Darkness—the Romans and other Gentiles without, and the wicked within. Victorious, the Sons of Light would create the

The staircase descending to one of the main water reservoirs of Qumran. The crack in the stairs is thought to be the result of the devastating earthquake of 31 BC after which the settlement was abandoned for a time

'New Jerusalem', restore proper worship in the Temple, and the new Messiahs would ascend to the spiritual and temporal thrones of Israel. Like Moses, Joshua and the Israelites of old, they were the 'Elect of God'. They too would sweep out of the desert like avenging spirits, cleansing Israel of wickedness for all time and establishing a 'New Covenant' with the Lord.

What can archaeology do to clarify what we know of this vanished community? The ruins at Qumran had long been known, but had never been deeply investigated until four years after the discovery of the scrolls. They lie on a high shelf of marl in the silent and sunbaked desert wilderness. Immediately to the west are the Judaean cliffs; to the south and east the sweet water springs of Ain Feshka and the Dead Sea. Qumran lies immediately south of Jericho, and north of En-gedi and Masada, the exact location of the Essene Community specified by Pliny. Père de Vaux and Harding directed four campaigns of excavation there between 1951 and 1956. Most of the activities of the order had centred about one large rectangular building measuring about 98 by 120 feet and made of roughly dressed stones. On the north stands the stump of a defensive tower which once rose three storeys high. Two rooms command the visitor's attention. One is a narrow hall seventy-two feet long which lies against the south wall of the complex. In one corner de Vaux found a pile of ceramic dishes, perhaps mute evidence of the last meal of the sectarians before the Romans advanced upon the settlement. This was the refectory, which was used both for religious gatherings and as a dining hall. Over a thousand ceramic bowls in shattered stacks were found littered in an adjoining

pantry. North of the refectory lay another narrow room thirteen feet wide and about forty-six feet long. Here de Vaux found a series of long tables, benches of plastered clay and several cylindrical inkwells. It was in this scriptorium that scribes of the order worked. With pens of reed cut from the marshes nearby they copied and corrected their sacred books—the scrolls hidden from the Romans and found two thousand years later. The compound round the main building included a dyer's shop, a laundry, pottery, stables, workshops and a complex of aqueducts, pools and cisterns. South-east of the building, toward the Dead Sea, lies the cemetery, containing about a thousand graves. The bones include those of women and children, confirming Josephus' report of the sect's marriage customs.

Much of the settlement's history can be read in the distribution of coins which de Vaux found in the ruins. They confirm that it was most probably constructed in the reign of the Hasmonean king John Hyrcanus (135–104 BC). The coin sequence continues until 37 BC, when the Hasmonean dynasty was supplanted by Herod the Great. Then there is a lapse of three decades, during which the settlement stood empty and silent as the desert around it. Was this the span of time noted in the scrolls when 'the land was ravaged' and the sect sojourned in 'the land of Damascus'? Most scholars believe so. The settlement contains an archaeological clue as to what may have happened. Qumran was wracked by an earthquake which cracked walls, split cisterns and rendered the upper storeys of the main buildings and tower unsafe. The fissures can still be traced. Josephus tells us of such an earthquake, 'which destroyed 30,000

Three stages in opening one of the graves in the cemetery of Qumran. The right hand picture shows the skeleton found in the grave after the stones laid over the body during its burial were removed

An ink well found in the *scriptorium* or writing room of Qumran

people and numberless cattle' in 31 BC. Whether or not natural disaster alone was to blame, Qumran lay abandoned until the advent of Archelaus, a son of Herod who reigned over Judaea from 4 BC until AD 6. The sect returned, repaired and strenghthened the buildings, and prepared for the apocalyptic war to come. It arrived at Qumran in AD 68, the third year of the Jewish War with Rome, borne by the legions of Vespasian and Titus; but it ended in a manner which the sages of Qumran had not envisaged; fire raced through the settlement; stone walls and beams fell. The next phase of datable artifacts includes the coins and arrows of Imperial Rome.

How can we be sure that the scrolls from the caves belonged to the sect of Qumran? They could, after all, have been secreted by other religious groups fleeing the Roman tide, refugees from Jerusalem, say. This possibility has been firmly disproved by the archaeologists: the site was strewn with thousands of pottery fragments from the same unique vessels in which the scrolls were found. Can we be sure that the colonists of Qumran and the Essene sect described by Josephus, Philo and Pliny were one and the same? A few scholars will not accept the connection in the absence of explicit documentary evidence but the overwhelming majority are satisfied that the evidence in the documents and the location of the communal settlement agree in sufficient detail with the historical accounts to leave no doubt that the Essenes and the Qumran sect were one and the same.

The movement was one of the symptomatic offshoots of the deterioration which afflicted the Jewish body politic from the time of the Seleucid kings and the confrontation between pious

Enormous quantities of pots and jars, many shattered, suggested that this was either a storehouse for finished domestic utensils or a pantry

Jewry and Hellenism. The cryptic—in fact, deliberately coded—Essenic references to contemporary figures and events have forced many a scholar to look for historical clues. Most agree that the seed of both the Essenes and the Pharisees lay in the Hasidim, the body of devout orthodox Jews who rose to oppose the Hellenizing campaigns and religious profanations of Antiochus Epiphanes. They joined forces with the Hasmonean rebels (Maccabees) to drive the Greeks from Jerusalem. Most now agree, too, that the Essene schism began during the reign of the Hasmoneans. In all probability the Teacher of Righteousness and his disciples abandoned Jerusalem some time between 160 and 134 BC, in the reign of either Jonathan or Simon Maccabee, because these Hasmoneans usurped the hereditary priestly line of Zadok and assumed the High Priesthood of the Temple in its stead. Jonathan or Simon could well have been the Wicked Priest, and the Pharisees, who remained in Jerusalem, were the 'seekers of smooth things'. Except that he was most probably a rightful member of the priestly house itself, we will probably never know the identity of the Teacher of Righteousness.

The scholar David Flusser calls the Essenes 'one of the most influential communities in human history'. The scrolls have enabled us to see that the Jewish world which emerged from the wreckage of the Roman disaster felt the impact of their moral theology, which helped to rejuvenate the prophetic sense of social justice abandoned by the leaders of late Judaean days. The Essene techniques of biblical commentary and interpretation deeply influenced the great works of talmudic literature which formed the new cement of Judaism after the destruction of Jerusalem.

Beyond that, as Flusser was one of the first to see, Jesus and the disciples who converted his teachings into the historic mission to the Gentiles were among the earliest heirs of Essene thought. The Essenes are an essential link between Judaism and early Christianity, and some Essenes may well have been numbered in the ranks of the Judaeo-Christians who first accepted Jesus as the Messiah. Some scholars believe that John the Baptist, who is known from the New Testament to have conducted his ministry in the area of Qumran and the Judaean Desert, was another link between the Essenes and the earliest Christians. Baptism was a fundamental feature of the Essene rite. Monasticism, sexual continence, election to grace, apocalypse and judgment at the 'end of days' were concepts forged in the crucible of Essenism and adopted by Christianity. In fact the New Testament is heavily laced with images and ideas which it shares with the scrolls.

Flusser, with his intimidating genius and sheer enthusiasm, dominates the field of comparative religion in Israel. He compares Jesus' Sermon on the Mount with the deeply moving Scroll of Thanksgiving, a personal testament of faith which may have been written by the Teacher of Righteousness himself.

The contest between Light and Darkness, an image which is an insistent theme in Essene writings, is evoked again and again in the New Testament; in I John ('God is light and in him is no darkness at all'), or in Paul's Letter to the Ephesians ('Take no part in the unfruitful works of darkness. . . Christ shall give you light'). Similarly, the martial spirit of the Essenes' War Scroll is echoed by Paul: '. . . Take the whole armour of God. . . having girded your loins with truth, and having put on the breastplate of righteousness. . . ' In Jesus' parable of the dishonest steward, as recorded in the Gospel of St Luke, Flusser sees not only an actual reference to the Essenes, but a direct reproof, reflecting the central issue on which Christianity and Essenism diverged. Jesus preaches that one must befriend the servants of Mammon in order to convert them: '. . . For the sons of this world are wiser in their own generation than the sons of light.' Flusser believes that Jesus was gently berating the Essenes, the Sons of Light, for abandoning the world and withdrawing their ministry to the desert. In their bitterness and alienation lay the Essene tragedy; in its mission to the market-place lay the success of Christianily. Flusser says:

> Jesus combined the social message of Qumran with the Pharisaic teaching of love. But the Essene philosophy was compounded with egoism, self-righteousness, apartness and exclusivity which blinded them to their own rigidity. Their revolutionary social philosophy was influential, yes, but in the hands of others. In the end, they proved to be as majestically pathetic as Lear.

There was a sequel to the Odyssey of the Scrolls—one that was in every way as bizarre as the events of the first acquisitions. Yadin was in London on a long sabbatical when he was approached in 1961 by an American who revealed the existence of yet another scroll—intact, complete, the largest of all. He told Yadin that he was prepared to negotiate its sale on behalf of a Jordanian dealer in antiquities. The asking price was a million dollars. The American showed Yadin an enticing 'sample'—a fragment torn from the leather roll. It was enough to convince Yadin that the scroll was extremely important. Negotiations dragged on for over a year, but collapsed when the American accepted a $10,000 advance and

An important find from Qumran was a set of ritual head phylacteries (*tefillin*). The upper picture shows the closed capsule and the lower opened with the small niches each containing a tied slip of skin with a portion of the law written upon it

disappeared. Six years later—only hours after Israeli troops had captured Jordanian Jerusalem and reunited both halves of the city— an exhausted Yadin, who had been serving as special military adviser to the prime minister during the May–June crisis, awoke from a deep sleep with the scroll on his mind. He had long suspected that the Jordanian dealer who had it was Kando, the one-time Bethlehem cobbler to whom the Bedouin had brought the first scrolls. Both Kando and the new scroll were now in Israeli-occupied territory. Within hours the dealer was in jail and Israeli soldiers were combing every inch of his house. The scroll lay in a shoebox hidden beneath the flooring. Over the years humidity had eaten away perhaps a third of it—'melted it to dark pitch, like a gob of chocolate', says Yadin. 'I was appalled.'

Still much was intact. It was, indeed, the largest of the Scrolls— 28 feet long and over 8 inches wide, and copied in a beautiful Herodian hand at the beginning of the Christian era. Kando was released, and was then paid $100,000 for the document 'so as not to jeopardize the acquisition of future material'.

Yadin calls it the Temple Scroll because thirty of its sixty-six sections deal with the Temple. 'It is a strange document', Yadin says, 'one of the strangest.' The Essene author has attempted nothing less than major amendments to biblical law. In the text, God speaks to Moses in the first person, as in Exodus, promulgating divine decrees on three major subjects: ritual cleanliness; architectural specifications for the Temple in Jerusalem; and statutes affecting Israel's king. The Bible fails to define the duties and responsibilities of the monarch, an omission which the Essenes apparently took it upon themselves to correct. In much the same vein, the Bible contains descriptions of the Temple as it was built, not as the Lord wished it to be built. This lapse, too, the Temple Scroll attempts to put right. It even goes so far as to specify God's choice of a location for Jerusalem's public privies—out of sight of the Temple to the north-west.

The statutes of the king contain regulations covering the mobilization of Israel's fighting men in case of attack. (Yadin points out that they are strangely similar to the call-up system which was actually employed during the 1967 crisis.)

Characteristic Essene severity dominates the Scroll's dictates on cleanliness and purification. They are far more extreme than anything envisaged by normative Judaism. The Essene document also depicts a temple in splendid isolation, separated from the city by three courts and a moat—a dramatic reflection of the self-imposed policy of exclusivity which doomed the sect to extinction.

As for the scroll itself, Yadin believes that it was found by the Ta'amireh in Cave XI in 1956, and secreted by Kando shortly afterwards against the higher price which future years might—and did—bring.

The hopes and expectations of the scholarly world are that still more of the priceless legacy of the Essenes is yet to come. In 1969, for example, the archaeologist Pesach Bar-Adon excavated and identified the remains of another Essene settlement and cemetery on the shores of the Dead Sea nine miles south of Qumran. Although no new documents were found, Bar-Adon's discovery strengthens the possibility that the Judaean Desert has not yet yielded all that the sect left behind.

In providing posterity with a window through which to view the Judaea-Christian era, the sect realized its aspirations. Through the knowledge they preserved, the Essenes truly became the Sons of Light.

An aerial view of the ruins of the Essene community's agricultural 'station' at at Ein Feshkha near Qumran. It is a verdant oasis with lush vegetation surrounding natural springs and sweet water pools on the shore of the Dead Sea

Epilogue

On 2 May 1960, Professor Yigael Yadin rose before a hushed audience in the official residence of President Yitzhak Ben-Zvi and announced with ill-concealed excitement: 'Mr President, I have the great and unusual honour of informing you that we have discovered the dispatches of the last President of the former State of Israel, Simon Bar-Kokhba.'

With those words, and the reading of a military order inscribed on papyrus early in the second century AD, Yadin confirmed the news which had first come from Jordan. Now it had been dramatically corroborated and enlarged upon in Israel itself. From the haze of legend, archaeology had given substance to one of the great chimerical figures of Jewish history.

Only a century earlier, Palestine had been a *terra incognita;* its map incomplete, its early record a patchwork of guesses, gaps and unproved theories. Legend and fact were indistinguishable.

After a gap of two millennia, a people in search of itself now began to study the land avidly.

Historic accident (some would say destiny) elevated the campaign of discovery to a grand passion—the discovery of the Dead Sea Scrolls from the last days of Judaea on the very eve of the United Nations vote recreating Israel in 1948; the excavations at Masada as the Zealots' descendants were confronting a new siege evocative of the days of Rome; and the re-emergence after nearly 2,000 years of ancient Israel's last hero.

Talmudic sources spoke of how Bar-Kokhba, the 'son of a star', had led an army of four hundred thousand men in a last bid for Jewish independence against Rome. Throughout the centuries of Jewish dispersion, fathers told their sons these tales—of how the venerable Rabbi Akiva had followed Bar-Kokhba and had proclaimed of him: 'This is the king Messiah'; of how Hadrian totally eradicated the Jewish nation, even the name Jerusalem, when the Second Revolt collapsed in AD 135 after three years of bitter fighting.

In 1951, bedouin prowling a set of caves in Wadi Muraba'at inside Jordan, produced for scholars dramatic testimony to the tale of Bar-Kokhba, a military order on parchment reading: 'Simon, son of Koseba, to Joshua, son of Galgula. . . greetings. I take Heaven as witness against me (that) if any one of the Galileans who are among you should be ill-treated, I will put fetters on your feet as I did to Ben-Aphlul. (Signed) Simon, son of Koseba . . .'

Later the bedouin conducted clandestine searches inside Israeli territory, and more finds from the Bar-Kokhba period appeared in Arab Jerusalem. The result was a decision by Israeli authorities in 1959 to launch their own massive sweep of all the caves in the Dead Sea area for any of the priceless material which might have been overlooked by the Arabs.

On the rim of a steep cliff, the remains of an extensive Roman military camp, evidently built to bottle the Jewish fugitives within the cave, were found. Yadin concludes his book on the Bar-Kokhba expedition with these words:

> Here we were, walking every day through the ruins of a Roman camp which caused the death of our forefathers. Nothing remains here today of the Romans save a heap of stones on the face of the desert. But here the descendants of the besieged were returning to salvage their ancestors' precious belongings.

Military technology comes to the aid of archaeological research. A mine detector is used to locate metal objects under the debris of centuries during the Bar-Kokhba excavations directed by Prof. Yigael Yadin at Nahal Hever

The spades of scholars and missions representing virtually every sect, creed and nation in the West have contributed to the knowledge mined from the ancient debris. Catholic missions have, for example, made invaluable contributions in the field of pre-history and to knowledge of Herodian times. Protestant institutions pioneered an archaeological understanding of the Old Testament. Israeli excavators long ago expanded their interest in 'Jewish' archaeology to encompass the entire spectrum of pre-history and history buried in their soil, from *Homo Erectus* to the Crusaders. Some of the definitive scientific publications on the archaeology of Palestine and Western Asia have been issued by Buddhist scholars at the University of Tokyo, who have led two expeditions to Israel in the past decade.

After one hundred years, archaeologists have only barely sampled the treasures awaiting excavation. There is enough digging here for many lifetimes. The rescue of these cultural treasures from oblivion and the neglect of centuries has only just begun.

Acknowledgements

The author wishes to convey his deep gratitude to the following for permission to reproduce passages from their works: to the Princeton University Press, and its invaluable reference volume *Ancient Near Eastern Texts Relating to the Old Testament*, edited by James Pritchard; Thames and Hudson and McGraw-Hill, publishers of *Early Mesopotamia and Iran*, by M.E.L. Mallowan; the Clarendon Press for passages from *Archaeology and Old Testament Study*, edited by D. Winton Thomas; Ernest Benn and Praeger Publishers for passages from *Digging Up Jericho*, by Kathleen M. Kenyon; Penguin Books for quotations from *The Archaeology of Palestine*, by William Albright; S.C.M. Press and The Westminster Press for passages from *A History of Israel*, by John Bright; Harper and Row for a passage from *The Ladder of Progress in Palestine* by Chester Charles McCown; and Weidenfeld and Nicolson for permission to quote from *Rivers in the Desert* by the late Nelson Glueck, and *Bar-Kokhba* by Yigael Yadin.

Appreciation is also due to the American Schools of Oriental Research, publishers of the *Biblical Archaeologist* and the *Bulletin* of the ASOR, and to the Israel Exploration Society, publishers of the *Israel Exploration Journal*, and the *festschrift* series *Eretz Israel*, for permission to quote from their periodicals.

Extracts from Josephus have been taken from the modern translation of G.A. Williamson, published by Penguin. For the most part, biblical quotations are from the English Revised Standard Version, though in certain cases other versions have been drawn upon.

The author and publishers wish to express their thanks to the following institutions and individuals, who were kind enough to grant permission to reproduce photographs and objects from their excavations or collections in this book:
Department of Antiquities, Jerusalem 35–37, 40, 42, 44 below, 45, 48, 49, 51, 53, 63, 64, 68–71, 74 below, 75, 76, 87, 93, 99, 102, 104, 106, 113, 117–120, 124–127, 130, 131, 133, 136, 138, 139, 142, 143, 147–151, 153, 155 top, 157, 159, 160, 163, 167–169, 171, 179, 180, 185, 186–189, 190, 193, 194, 198, 202, 206, 208, 224, 229, 230, 236, 239, 243; Israel Museum, Jerusalem 11, 35, 36, 38, 40, 42, 44 top, 49 top, 51 below, 63, 71, 74 below, 75, 91 top, 98–100, 102, 104, 106, 119, 125, 126, 128, 130, 134, 136, 138, 142, 143, 147–149, 150, 151, 153, 155 top, 159, 166, 167, 176, 179, 183, 186, 189, 190, 197, 206 top, 213, 214 below, 224, 227 below, 234, 236–239; British Museum 78–81, 85, 103, 172, 173, 178; Ecole Biblique et Archaeologique, Jerusalem 109, 248, 258, 259–261, 265; Hebrew University of Jerusalem 32, 34, 77, 162, 206; Jerusalem Archaeological Excavations *endpapers*, 202, 219, 230; Palestine Exploration Fund, London 10, 13, 15, 21–24; Masada Expedition 212, 213, 214 top, 215; Louvre 72, 80, 128, 155 below; Shrine of the Book, Jerusalem 254, 256, 264; Prof. Yigael Yadin 114, 154, 162; Archaeological Institute, Tel Aviv University 244–247; Israel Academy of Sciences and Humanities 38, 39, 41; Dr Benno Rothenberg 88, 165; Isotopes, Inc. 56, 57; Moshe Dayan *frontispiece*, 99; Pontifical Institute for Biblical Studies, Jerusalem 65, 66; Arad Expeditions 96, 100, 226; Miss Kathleen Kenyon 60, 225; James A. Rothschild Expedition to Hazor 114, 118, 120, 123, 127; Tel Megadim Expedition 193; Oriental Institute, University of Chicago 158; University of Pennsylvania 134; Archaeological Museum, Istanbul 177; Beersheba Museum 76; Musée Biblique de l'Association Bible et Terre Sainte 250; Brooklyn Museum 191; University of Missouri 200; Iraqi Museum, Baghdad 82; Leyden Museum 101; Government Press office, Tel Aviv 92; courtesy of Dr Eliezer Oren © University Museum, Philadelphia 149; Arava Expedition 88

The photographs are by the following:
David Harris *frontispiece*, 17, 29, 30, 36, 37, 48, 49 top, 51 top, 59, 64, 65, 66–70, 84, 87, 94, 98, 99, 106, 124, 130, 133, 135, 139, 142, 143, 148, 149, 152, 155 top, 159, 160, 163, 166, 170, 171 top, 181, 183, 187–190, 193, 194, 197, 200–202, 206, 212, 213 top, 227 below, 229, 234, 236, 238, 239, 251, 267; Hillel Burger 35, 40, 51 below, 63, 71, 74 below, 75, 100, 102, 104, 125, 126, 128, 131, 136, 150, 151, 153, 159 top, 167, 214 below, 227 top, 237; Ze'ev Radovan 27, 38, 91 top, 112, 119, 138, 147, 176, 186, 217, 230–233; Hirmer 80, 82, 83, 90, 105, 146, 172, 173, 177; David Rubinger 31, 52, 55, 165, 175, 208 top, 210–211; Werner Braun 26, 28, 74, 107, 174, 222, 240; Rolf Kneller 73, 140, 204, 216, 221; A. Strajmayster 62, 164; Giraudon 103, 155 below; M. Schweig 77, 96; Micha Bar-Am 18; Keren Or 39; Menachem Azouri 41; Nir Bareket 76; John Moeller 121; Reuven Milon 179
The drawings on pp. 46–47 are by Judith Ogden, that on p. 208 by Alex Berlyne after an original sketch by Dr Nicu Haas, and the maps on pp. 2 and 108 by Carta, Jerusalem.

Index

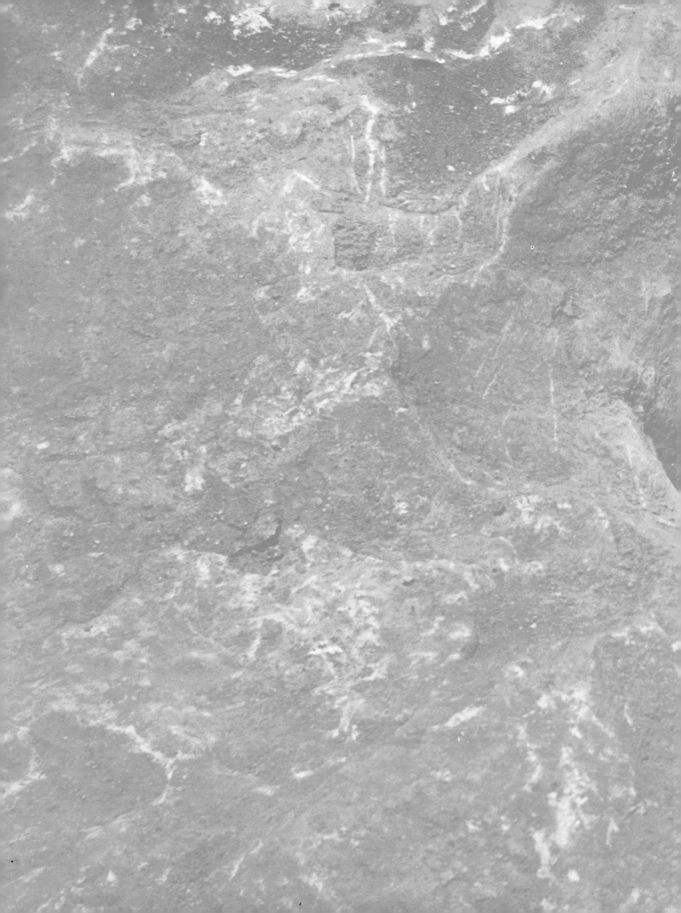